# The Angry American

# Dilemmas in American Politics

Series Editor   **L. Sandy Maisel,** *Colby College*

Dilemmas in American Politics offers teachers and students a series of quality books on timely topics and key institutions in American government. Each text will examine a "real world" dilemma and will be structured to cover the historical, theoretical, policy relevant, and future dimensions of its subject.

---

## BOOKS IN THIS SERIES

*The Angry American: How Voter Rage Is Changing the Nation, Second Edition,*
Susan J. Tolchin

*Checks and Balances? How a Parliamentary System Could Change American Politics,*
Paul Christopher Manuel and Anne Marie Cammisa

*"Can We All Get Along?" Racial and Ethnic Minorities in
American Politics, Second Edition,* Paula D. McClain and Joseph Stewart Jr.

*Remote and Controlled: Media Politics in a Cynical Age, Second Edition,*
Matthew Robert Kerbel

*Two Parties—Or More? The American Party System,*
John F. Bibby and L. Sandy Maisel

*Making Americans, Remaking America: Immigration and Immigrant Policy,*
Louis DeSipio and Rodolfo O. de la Garza

*From Rhetoric to Reform? Welfare Policy in American Politics,*
Anne Marie Cammisa

*The New Citizenship: Unconventional Politics, Activism, and Service,*
Craig A. Rimmerman

*No Neutral Ground? Abortion Politics in an Age of Absolutes,* Karen O'Connor

*Onward Christian Soldiers? The Religious Right in American Politics,* Clyde Wilcox

*Payment Due: A Nation in Debt, a Generation in Trouble,*
Timothy J. Penny and Steven E. Schier

*Bucking the Deficit: Economic Policymaking in the United States,*
G. Calvin Mackenzie and Saranna Thornton

# The Angry American

········································································

*How Voter Rage Is
Changing the Nation*

SECOND EDITION

**Susan J. Tolchin**
*George Mason University*

Westview Press
A Member of the Perseus Books Group

*Dilemmas in American Politics*

Copyright © 1999 by Westview Press, A Member of the Perseus Books Group

Published in 1999 in the United States of America by Westview Press, 5500 Central Avenue, Boulder, Colorado 80301-2877, and in the United Kingdom by Westview Press, 12 Hid's Copse Road, Cumnor Hill, Oxford OX2 9JJ

Library of Congress Cataloging-in-Publication Data
Tolchin, Susan J.
    The angry American : how voter rage is changing the nation / Susan
J. Tolchin.—2nd ed.
        p.   cm.—(Dilemmas in American politics)
    Includes bibliographical references and index.
    ISBN 0-8133-6754-9 (pbk.)
    1. Voting—United States.    2. United States—Politics and
government—1989–    3. United States—Economic conditions—1981–
4. United States—Social conditions—1980–    I. Title.    II. Series.
JK1967.T65    1999
3—dc21                                                                                          98-42303
                                                                                                        CIP

The paper used in this publication meets the requirements of the American National Standard for Permanence of Paper for Printed Library Materials Z39.48-1984.

10      9      8      7      6      5      4      3      2      1

*To Martin with love*

# Contents

# 4 The Cultural Divide: Zones of Intolerance on the Battlefield of Values                                     79

# 5 Raging Pol: Governing Angry Americans                                      109

# 6 The Vision Thing: Competing Angers and Political Change                    143

# Tables and Illustrations

## Tables

## Figures

## Cartoons

## Photos

# Preface and Acknowledgments

A month after the famous Republican electoral sweep in 1994 my husband and I traveled to London for a week of theater-going with our playwright friend Irene Wurtzel and her husband, Alan. To my surprise, London newspapers were bursting with stories about public anger leveled at the ruling Conservative Party. Voters in Great Britain had grown so angry, declared the articles, that if an election were held that very week Prime Minister John Major would have been ousted from office and replaced by the Labour Party. What a switch, given the conventional wisdom about the U.S. election symbolizing the rejection of "liberalism."

With the benefit of this transoceanic perspective, I started thinking seriously about political anger as a phenomenon of the 1990s. In fact, by the time Americans were agonizing over the impact of the angry white male, political anger had achieved a new universality. No matter what culture or nation was involved, they all shared one target in common: government. No wonder the Tories looked nervously across the Atlantic at Canada, where their counterparts in the Conservative Party had been recently swept out of office by a flash of voter anger. In Morocco, 100,000 university graduates faced the future without jobs, no longer blaming "Allah for their poverty and misfortune," as one political leader told me. "Instead, they now blame government."

This book has many mentors, intellectual and personal, and I am deeply indebted to them all. When I returned from London, Pranay Gupte, my editor at the *Earth Times* (where I write a column from Washington), asked me to pursue the anger theme in relation to President Clinton's first year in office. Pranay is a wellspring of ideas, and I am grateful for all his advice, for forcing me to write fast, and for dispatching me all over the world. I would also like to thank Arthur Gelb of the *New York Times* for coming up with the idea for the column and for putting Pranay in touch with me.

After writing the Clinton piece, I knew there was a book out there somewhere; indeed, this was a book I felt in my bones from the beginning. With me from the "creation" were a great many people who also shared my belief in the book and who helped and encouraged me to further develop the ideas and publishing possibilities. Among them were Nick Veliotes, Roz and Dick

Kleeman, Barbara Bergmann, Sandee Brawarsky, Richard E. Cohen, Judith Rosener, and Cathy Rudder.

My relationship with Westview Press began one balmy evening when I was waiting for a taxi at the American Political Science Association convention in Chicago. As I described the book project to my friend, Beryl Radin, sotto voce, I thought, Sandy Maisel overheard our conversation. "Do you have a publisher yet?" he asked. Sandy and I had worked on several projects together over the years, and before I knew it, he and the editors had signed me on as an author for his series Dilemmas in American Politics. My experience with Westview has been all an author could ask. Specifically, I would like to thank Sandy as well as Matt Kerbel for their intellectual input and for editing chapters almost as quickly as I finished them. I would also like to thank Jennifer Knerr, the original editor of the book, for her incisive, meticulous editing and for sticking with the project even after she had left the company. I owe Leo Wiegman, the editor of Westview Press, a deep debt of gratitude for taking over the book and skillfully guiding it through its first and second editions. I would especially like to thank Linda Simpson for helping with the editing of the second edition. Thanks also to the talented and dedicated members of the Westview family, including Brenda Hadenfeldt, who guided the book to publication; Shena L. Redmond, project editor; Diane Hess, copy editor; Michelle Schayes, assistant college marketing manager; and Lisa Paradise and Ellen Williams, directors of publicity.

The book is based on data collected from a variety of sources, including discussions and formal interviews with members of Congress, political scientists, officials from the executive branch, historians, trade-association representatives, and journalists. All direct quotes in the text that are not cited in the notes are drawn from these interviews. Many thanks to the following respondents for sharing their insights, knowledge, and experience with me: Gary Ackerman, Nan Aron, Dwayne Austin, Susan Bauman, William Becker, Lloyd Bentsen, Ira Berlin, Barry Bluestone, Sid Blumenthal, Daniel J. Boorstin, Leroy Bridges, Pat Choate, David L. Clay, Mary Cleveland, Matthew Dallas, Janet L. Douglass, Roger Durbin, Lillian Darrington, Barbara Dixon, Harriet Eckel, Eva Eronakowski, Amitai Etzioni, Bill Frymoyer, Lynn Gerber, Ralph Goldman, Stan Greenberg, Roy C. Grosswiler, Charles Guggenheim, Linda Gustitus, Phyllis Hanfling, Ron Harris, Marvin Kalb, Marcy Kaptur, Kitty Kelley, Lou Kerr, David Kusnet, Ann Lewis, Betty Lewis, Michael Lieberman, Robert Jay Lifton, Frank Luntz, Sandra McElwaine, Rick McGahey, Chris McLean, Cynthia McSwain, Marianne Means, Mark Melman, Abner Mikva, Tim Miles, Scott Murray, Gladys Ottman, John Owad, Bruce Perry, Margy Perz, James Pfiffner, Irene Pollin, Tarso Ramos, Leo Ribuffo, David Rosenbloom, Barbara

Rosenfeld, Jim Sasser, Karen Schlossberg, Chuck Schumer, Barbara Shailor, Cynthia Stachelberger, Richard Stott, Jim Thurber, Alan Tonelson, Sherrie Voyles, Stephen J. Wayne, Mike Wessel, and Betsey Wright.

The staffers in Marcy Kaptur's office, both in Washington and Toledo, helped maximize my short time in Toledo, making it an especially rich and fruitful experience. In addition to Marcy Kaptur, I would especially like to thank Susan Lowe, George Wilson, Sarah O'Neil, and Steve Katich.

When the book was just a gleam in my eye, Charles Goodsell invited me to give a lecture on political anger to his graduate students at Virginia Polytechnic Institute in Blacksburg. The author of many well-known works, including the groundbreaking *The Case for Bureaucracy*, Goodsell has contributed to my own thinking, and I thank him for providing me with an early opportunity to test my theories.

My former professional home at George Washington University has been supportive of my research over the past twenty years with grants of time and resources. A Dilthey research grant, matched by Deans F. David Fowler and James Edwin Kee of the School of Business and Public Management, enabled me to begin working on this project. Special thanks also to my friend and colleague William C. Adams for his ideas on the political role of values.

Three graduate research assistants from the Public Administration Department contributed their enthusiasm, time, and editorial advice to this project. For the skill with which they tracked down leads, checked facts, read successive drafts of the manuscript, and overcame enormous obstacles, I thank Jill Moses, Stephen Burns, and especially Scott Haggard, who bore the brunt of this book, working tirelessly to help me meet the tight deadlines. The second edition of the book benefited from the effort of my graduate research assistant, Andrew Sisk, who worked cheerfully and quickly to meet a tight deadline.

Former academic vice president and provost Roderick French's early vision and concrete support of interdisciplinary scholarship came to fruition with this book, which draws on more disciplines than I have ever tackled on one project, namely, psychology, English literature, biology, sociology, political science (of course), and history.

I am especially thankful also to Judith Plotz, chair of the English Department at George Washington University, for inviting me to keynote a conference on postcolonialism. Preparing the paper, as well as discussions with Professor Plotz, introduced me to a range of ideas and literature on anger that substantially enhanced my own thinking.

Actually, my daughter, Karen, a graduate student in English at Brandeis University, first introduced me to the concepts of postcolonialism and to the relevance of English literature to political science. Karen has been wonderfully supportive, as well as a great editor. My son, Charles, a writer and advertising executive, has also provided me with penetrating criticism, very helpful editing, and constant encouragement. Both Charles and Karen have turned into very talented fiction writers, and I am very proud of them both.

For her friendship through thick and thin, I thank Nancy K. Schlossberg, who also helped educate me about the psychological elements of anger. I also feel especially lucky to be part of a few groups that have provided me with literary advice, steadfast support, and intellectual fodder. I thank Irene Wurtzel, Patricia O'Brien, and Linda Cashdan in my Shakespeare group; Irene and Patricia read drafts of my original outline and provided useful suggestions, and Linda read and critiqued my work and contributed many new ideas to my thinking. The manuscript has also benefited greatly from the comments of my friends from the New Synthesis group and its leader, Ruy Teixeira. I would also like to thank Pat Choate, who also read the manuscript, for his contributions and his friendship.

Sadly, my dear mother died in the winter of 1996, while I was writing the first edition of this book. One of my best friends, as well as a superb proofreader and critic, she was way ahead of her time in believing in women's achievement. She had a profound influence on my own life, and I'm grateful that she lived to see the third generation of teachers emerge in our family as Karen began her stint as a teaching assistant in a freshman writing class.

Most of all, I would like to thank my husband, Martin, for his love, devotion, support, steady flow of ideas, and close attention to this manuscript. We have collaborated on five books and numerous other ventures, including two children. I missed him on this project, but on the bright side at least I could finally dedicate a book to him.

*Susan J. Tolchin*

*The Angry American*

# 1

...................................................................................................

# Political Anger

## *The Dilemma of Voter Rage for Democratic Government*

Politics, as a practice . . . had always been the
systematic organization of hatreds.

—Henry Adams[1]

T HE SIGNS WERE ALL THERE for those who cared to look. Leaders of the House Democratic Congressional Campaign Committee ignored videotapes of focus meetings held in early fall 1994 that revealed scenes of voter rage unfolding in the heart of Middle America. In Idaho, "people were so frustrated, they were talking of armed revolt. These were not the gun folks. They were normal voters," said Monica Maples, director of the committee. "There is voter anger at both political parties, but the Republicans addressed it, and the Democrats didn't."[2]

The Democrats held on to the tapes until well after the 1994 congressional election, when they held a meeting on political anger for fellow members of Congress. "Fazio [Vic Fazio, D–Calif. and chair of the committee] talked about the anger tapes," recalled Representative Marcy Kaptur, a Democrat from Toledo, Ohio. "I asked him, 'Why didn't you share them with us before the election?' Fazio answered: 'Because I didn't want more members to lose.' I said, 'Is that what you call leadership?' The Democrats were into massive denial. They are supposed to be for us."

"Anger" has become the political watchword of the 1990s: Leaders from both parties worry about the absence of civility, the decline of intelligent dialogue, and the rising decibels of hate in political discourse. Polls reveal that Americans are angrier at government than at any time in recent memory. Disputes that traditionally gravitate toward centrist compromises instead move to opposite extremes, where they divide into intransigent stances. A political form of bipolar disorder has emerged that is a symptom as well as a cause of anger. At peace for the first time in almost a century, Americans question the legitimacy of their own democracy. They are "mad as hell," and political leaders constantly ask why.

## Anger in the Mainstream

Two watershed elections, in 1992 and 1994, revealed increasing waves of anger among the voters, which eventually led to political changes of historic proportions. Democrats blamed angry voters for their debacle of 1994, when the Republicans took power in Congress for the first time in forty years and not a single Republican incumbent was defeated for reelection. Republicans attributed their own disastrous loss of the White House in 1992 to angry and disaffected Republican voters who switched from the GOP to Ross Perot. They claimed their congressional victory in 1994 was a mandate to unravel the programs developed by the New Deal of the 1930s and the Great Society of the 1960s. To them, both periods symbolized big government, which meant larger expenditures, greater benefits, and higher taxes.

The 1996 election reflected new forms of anger: apathy and divided government. Under divided—or separated government—voters reelected a Democratic president but made sure that the Congress remained firmly in the hands of the Republican Party. This meant that many voters split their tickets, perhaps reasoning that each party would keep the other honest, the quintessential checks and balances. What this also conveyed was a deepening sense of mistrust of government, expressed as anger at political corruption and poll-driven leadership. Ironically, divided government probably exacerbates corruption and encourages timidity, as each party tries to outdo the other in exposing their rivals' weaknesses.

After the 1996 election, polls also exposed a new form of anger from the American public: apathy. In 1960 nearly 63 percent of the voters turned out for the presidential election. The choosing of the leader of the world's only superpower in 1996 with less than 50 percent of the vote marked the lowest turnout since 1924; another percentage point would have pushed us back to 1824. The American public was clearly turned off from politics. (An interesting historical tidbit: The electorate peaked in 1876 with 83.3 percent of the electorate—at that time only about 10 million people—who turned out to vote for that hotly contested match between Samuel J. Tilden and Rutherford B. Hayes.)

Public apathy grows even worse at lower levels of politics. The election that transported the Republicans of the 104th Congress to power drew only 38 percent of the eligible voters. Presidential primaries, which make or break the candidates for the nation's highest office, attract the lowest numbers of all, some hovering around the 5 percent mark.

Public disaffection from politics and anger at the ineffectiveness of political leaders took another form in 1996: the explosion of referenda. The elections of 1996 recorded the highest number of referenda in history, with a record of ninety-three citizen-initiated ballot questions contested in twenty states, compared with seventy-three initiatives in 1994. To some extent these growing numbers signaled a steep decline in representative democracy, an indication that Americans no longer trusted their elected officials to represent them on the issues about which they cared most deeply. Propositions ranged all over the political map, involving term limits (in fourteen states), affirmative action, victims' rights, bear trapping and other hunting issues (six states), the use of marijuana for medicinal purposes, and gambling. The state of Oregon led the pack with seventeen ballot initiatives. The large number of referenda, whose advocates spent upwards of $200 million, also robbed candidates of good stump issues. Take presidential candidate Bob Dole's efforts to champion himself as the enemy of affirmative action. One of the reasons Dole lost California, with its rich lode of electoral votes, was that Proposition 209, which opposed affirmative action in hiring, contracting, and university admissions, was on the state's ballot. Proposition 209 effectively eliminated affirmative action from Dole's issue portfolio in California; after all, if voters can express their preferences on this issue with more immediacy at the ballot box, why should they bother voting for a candidate who can only deliver promises?[3]

In Congress, public anger prompted the resignations of key members, a pattern that continues to this day. Senator James Exon of Nebraska, attributed his decision not to seek another term to the "ever increasing vicious polarization of the electorate," openly denouncing "the us-against-them mentality . . . that has all but swept aside the former preponderance of reasonable discussion . . . the traditional art of workable compromises for the ultimate good of all." Exon said that old friends in the supermarket would ask him if he was going to protect them from the federal government. "The essence of democracy," he charged, "has demonstrably been eroded. The 'hate level' fed by attack ads has . . . become the measurement of a successful campaign."[4]

Political appointees also found themselves under siege. After being grilled at the House of Representatives hearings on Waco in July 1995, former Secretary of the Treasury Lloyd Bentsen confided, "I've seen more anger than I've ever seen in my life. There's no civility up here. Sure, business can be tough and mean, but this is worse."

Narrowly reelected in 1990 by voters angry at tax increases, Senator Bill Bradley (D–N.J.) complained that by 1995 the anger was even broader and more intense than during his previous campaign. Attributing the anger to a general sense of "unease . . . about people's circumstances," as well as specific worries about everything from "transit fare to taxes and health care costs," he worried aloud that voters were rapidly losing confidence in government's ability to solve their problems.[5] Bradley also declined to run again in 1996; as a former professional basketball player, he must have found it especially hard to be sidelined, the fate of Democrats suddenly thrust into minority status.

Clearly more of a problem for Democrats, anger also assaults Republicans, who confront as well as exploit political fury. "Our negative campaigning and mudslinging have made anger the national recreation," declared Illinois Repre-

Has the white male become a symbol of anger at the ballot box? Mark Cullum and
Copley News Service. Reprinted with permission.

sentative Henry Hyde when he opposed term limits in a passionate speech on
the House floor. "The 12 Apostles had their Judas Iscariot, and I refuse to con-
cede to the angry, pessimistic populism that drives this movement, because it is
dead wrong."[6]

The 1992 efforts of Ross Perot showed how anger has fueled the rise of
third-party movements. By garnering 19 percent of the popular vote, Perot not
only cost George Bush his reelection but robbed the Clinton presidency of the
mandate to govern that comes only with a majority vote. What was astounding
about the 1992 election was that it catapulted Perot, a Texas billionaire who
had never before entered mainstream electoral politics, into the national lime-
light. He was included in the presidential debates, he forced the issues of a balanced budget and international trade onto the campaign agenda, and he rose
from ground zero to form a national organization—United We Stand America—that still plays a pivotal role in national politics as the Reform Party. The
*Gallup Poll Monthly* designated 1992 "The Year of the Angry Voter," citing the
Perot factor as one of the major causes of the "high level of voter ire."[7]

The two-party system has always worked in tandem against the emergence
of competition, and it is no coincidence that throughout history third parties—their ideas, leaders, political capital—have typically been absorbed into

the mainstream parties. At times, they have changed their character; at others, their names and platforms. In 1996 the Republican and Democratic parties capitalized on history and their own experience, and spent a great deal of time and money on the effort to prevent Ross Perot from appearing in any of the presidential debates. Even though Perot qualified for federal funds, his opponents were successful. The Commission on Presidential Debates, the nonpartisan, nonprofit group that determined whether a candidate would have the chance to debate, unanimously decided that since only the candidates who had a realistic chance of winning would merit an invitation, Perot would not qualify. As a result the debates were bland, boring, and devoid of any discussion of trade—one of Perot's key issues.

Other groups disaffected from centrist politics have also inserted themselves into the political mainstream, garnering surprising shares of power and votes. The best example of this new spurt of power, the 1.5 million–member Christian Coalition, claimed credit for electing dozens of new members to Congress in 1994.[8] Impressed by its clout, Republican candidates from all over the political spectrum scurried to redefine their views to conform with those of the coalition's, particularly on issues such as abortion and "family values." As they face the next presidential election in 2000, Republicans struggle with the dilemma that cost them the election in 1996: the Christian Coalition influenced 40 percent of the party, but only 10 percent of the general public. By attempting to conform to the coalition's political positions, Bob Dole found himself unable to attract centrist voters, who ultimately determine the direction of national elections.

Two election cycles later, in 1998, Frank Luntz, the Republican pollster credited with designing the 1994 congressional Republicans' Contract with America, declared that "there is no angry voter out there," although many analysts agreed that a slowdown in the economy, or more partisan showdowns between Congress and the president, could quickly alter the public's mood.[9] One of the most interesting developments of the 1990s has been an attempt on the part of both parties to focus their troubles on the desertion of the white male. "If you want to see anger, just look at the white male struggling to make ends meet with three jobs, and see how he feels about welfare mothers," said Luntz. He advised fellow Republicans to stick to one theme: "Talk about denying cash benefits to people who have more kids while on welfare."[10]

As African Americans viewed with alarm the political mainstream's frantic obsession with the white male vote, their leaders doubled their efforts to organize outside their traditional home in the Democratic Party. The Million Man March on Washington, organized by the Nation of Islam on October 16, 1995, reflected the mounting aspiration of black males to develop and present a unified agenda. A similar march two years later sponsored by the Promise Keepers, a Christian men's movement, drew 600,000 men to the Mall in Washington at a total cost of about $9 million. One of the largest religious groups in the nation, the Promise Keepers encourages men to become better husbands and fathers. The National Organization for Women and other feminist groups have criticized the movement for preaching a subservient role for women.

## Anger at Government

The unifying theme behind the otherwise free-floating anger of the 1990s is the target: government. Government has suddenly become the scapegoat for all that has gone wrong with society. Anger is routinely expressed at congressional hearings and city council meetings and on billboards, talk radio, shortwave radio, and the Internet. In 1992, 43 percent of the public said the federal government "interfered with their lives"; in 1994, the figure rose to 70 percent.[11] The anger is real even though it often seems misguided, as Senator Nancy Kassebaum (R–Kans.) found when constituents informed her they "didn't want government in their Medicare." In effect, government has virtually become the victim of its own success. On the one hand, people's expectations have risen so high that they presume the public sector will address their problems. On the other, they resist the taxes, the intrusiveness, and all the other quid pro quos of the social contract that accompany all the benefits.

Anger has made government such a high-profile target for all that has gone wrong with society that even the term itself has become anathema. On the grounds that the word "government" was "arrogant" and "off-putting," Democratic County Executive Douglas Duncan of Montgomery County, Maryland, banished it by official edict from official letterheads, cars, and business cards. Ironically, many federal bureaucrats live in Montgomery County, a region immediately north of the nation's capital.[12]

The public anger at government exploded in a nationwide campaign for term limits, viewed by many politicians as "capital punishment for politicians." Term limits were approved by seventeen states before being narrowly defeated by Congress—one of the first planks in the GOP's Contract with America to fail. And although the Supreme Court by a 5–4 vote declared term limits for congressional seats unconstitutional, they remain legal for state and local races. Many believe it is only a question of time before members of Congress are forced by the electorate to approve a constitutional amendment that will override the Court.[13]

Of course, politicians have always suffered public opprobrium in this country, well before Mark Twain referred to Congress as America's only "native criminal class." Leaders of the decade-old term-limits movement share the view that "politicians are beyond rehabilitation, beyond redemption . . . and are driven by anger," explained Ann Lewis, deputy director of the 1996 Clinton-Gore campaign, former vice president for policy at Planned Parenthood, and currently White House Director of Communications. "There is no other good explanation, except for the desire to punish. The movement for term limits is wholly punitive and irrational, and rooted in anger. Why did it explode recently? It matches the public mood of anger at a political class [politicians] and is the best symbol of a politics transformed by anger."

Supporters of term limits believe that lawmakers are out of touch with their constituents and that term limits are needed to counter the insularity of Washington and the cozy relationships that often develop between lawmakers and interest groups. Influenced by the extent to which the issue of term limits has resonated among the voters, many new members of Congress elected in successive elections after 1994 have committed themselves to a limited number of terms—most of them say they will retire after three terms—and proceed to legislate on that basis. This means that they must find a way to move faster than the glacial pace that was characteristic of past Congresses, particularly when it comes to getting their pet bills on track. Some constituents seem to trust the new breed more than they trust the more traditional "career politicians." Others fear that with such quick turnovers of Congress, lobbyists will soon become a permanent government, accruing for themselves even more power than they currently hold.

The term limits issue has also shifted the burden of proof so that many political leaders feel they must establish that they have *not* engaged in scurrilous behavior. In the past, politicians have habitually played groups against each other to great effect: William Jennings Bryan, the eloquent Populist and presidential candidate, railed against eastern bankers with his "cross of gold" speech; Harry S. Truman attacked the plutocrats; and Andrew Jackson earned his political capital as a backwoodsman maligning aristocrats.

But today many politicians still think they can manipulate anger in their own interest, only to find that anger coming back at them. Like deer caught in the headlights, they are astonished, surprised, and occasionally angry themselves:

- "Don't forget about us, the politicians," cautioned Gary Ackerman (D–N.Y.). "We're angry, too. The voters tell us they want the truth. We give them the truth; then they turn fickle on us."
- "And how about the virtues of experience?" asked Representative Henry Hyde. "When the neurosurgeon has shaved your head and made the pencil line across your skull and he approaches with the electric saw—ask him, won't you, one question: 'Are you a careerist?'"
- "They say, 'Vote for me, I have no experience,'" argued Senator Byron Dorgan (D–N.D.) referring to neophyte candidates. "A year or so later, the public discovers they were telling the truth."
- "It takes twenty years to get a road built," Marcy Kaptur told a gathering at the South Toledo Senior Citizens Center. "That is why [the issue of] term limits is so silly."
- Even Senate Majority Leader Robert Dole complained to a conference of corporate executives hosted by *The Hill* newspaper in February 1995 about the atmosphere of distrust manifested by the term-limits movement: "We want the American people not to trust us. . . . It's almost ridiculous."

Together with other salient issues, term limits crosses party lines and—like other issues propelled by anger—exhibits a striking bipolarity in the poll numbers. The polls reflect the deep conflicts plaguing Americans, and the most striking poll data appear in the 1990s. Most significant are the indicators of antigovernment sentiment that stand out dramatically in every poll that measures these attitudes, particularly those that have asked similar questions testing attitudes toward government in the 1960s, 1970s, and 1980s.

A few findings from the data:

- The Gallup polls show that in answer to the question "Are you satisfied or dissatisfied with the way things are going in the United States at this time?" 30 percent said they were "dissatisfied" in 1986; the number rose to 66 percent in 1995.[14]
- In 1992, the Gallup poll reported that 90 percent of all adults (including "young adults, baby boomers, the silent generation, and the G.I. generation") were "dissatisfied" with the "state of the national economy"; 76 percent were "dissatisfied" with the "way the political process is working in this country"; and—a hopeful sign in this era of social Darwinism—81 percent were "dissatisfied with the success of the na-

tion in taking care of its poor and needy." To find a "comparable level of dissatisfaction," wrote the pollsters, "one must go back to the early 1980s, when the national unemployment rate reached 10.8 percent and a record number of Americans received unemployment benefits."[15]

- A Times Mirror poll revealed that "nearly 70 percent of the public now believes that something run by the government is usually inefficient and wasteful, that the federal government controls too much of our daily lives, and that dealing with a government agency is often not worth the trouble." Interestingly, despite these negative feelings about government, the public generally felt empowered, "better about itself and better about the campaign process than it had four years earlier." Another fascinating question exposed the punitive cast to the welfare issue: To the statement "It is the responsibility of the government to take care of people who can't take care of themselves," 57 percent expressed agreement in 1994 compared with 71 percent in 1987. Divisions among Republicans and Democrats on this issue produced an eleven-point spread between them with more Democrats favoring aid to the needy than Republicans.[16]

- A Harris poll concentrated on voter frustration, showing that feelings of futility toward government rose dramatically in the 1990s. Some of the sources of anger revealed in the polls: corruption, the power of interest groups, and government being out of touch. "Nearly 2 out of 3 [voters] feel government is corrupt," 75 percent that "special interest groups have too much control," 66 percent that "government is corrupt," and "a remarkable 83 percent feel some degree of frustration" as indicated by their response to the statement "The political situation in the country often makes me feel frustrated." "I often get angry about actions government takes" generated 76.1 percent agreement from the sample. Those seeking to mine the numbers for future political manipulation can take heart from the polls supporting the view that government cannot solve problems: A whopping 59.5 percent agreed that "government won't do anything about problems." The Harris pollsters call this "an excellent indicator of frustration."[17]

- Equally troubling results emerged from studies conducted in 1998 showing very little progress in citizen confidence in government. Seventy-six percent of the voters polled felt that wasteful government spending was a major problem, along with government's inability to solve the problems of crime, drugs, and poverty. Public confidence in leaders was similarly low, particularly on ethical issues.[18]

## Anger and the Bipolarity of Issues

Polls reveal that people have expressed specific anger about taxes, job loss, injustice, globalization, inequities, worsening schools, overregulation, corruption, and the breakdown of families. Poll data on these issues, combined with figures testing dissatisfaction with government, show that massive changes in public wrath first appeared in the early 1990s; the increases in dissatisfaction were especially dramatic in comparison with the 1960s. Under the rubric of the populist-sounding Contract with America, the very legitimacy of all federal programs has come under scrutiny, including such icons as Social Security, Medicare, Medicaid, veterans' benefits, wheat subsidies, and environmental protection. What stood out during the first two years of the contract was the absence of a real counterforce: Groups that traditionally defended the poor, children, the elderly, and the disenfranchised reeled under the effects of the 1994 election and its mandate to reduce government programs and expenditures. Shell-shocked by the unraveling of government that followed in its wake, public interest groups found themselves forced to spend most of their time and resources simply stanching the flood of antigovernment activity.

Even the hardiest souls find survival difficult in this harsh environment. Issues are cast in stark bipolar terms, the middle ground erodes with each election cycle, and the enviable consensus on which American political culture prides itself keeps receding into history. Few talk shows are immune to the ratings wars, and candidates for public office find it increasingly harder to resist the pressures to present their views in extremist terms.

Not surprisingly, in this environment the truth—and civility—often emerge as the first casualties. One particularly egregious example was Republican Senate candidate James Inhofe, who rode to victory on campaign rhetoric that rarely failed to mention the voter "in southeastern Oklahoma who predicted Dave McCurdy [his opponent, a Democratic member of Congress] would lose because of the 'three G's: God, gays and guns.'"[19]

Inhofe's campaign encapsulated themes that played with great success throughout the 1994 campaign and showed how effectively extremes played on the hustings. Such extremes are now so significant because public policies are also forged at the extremes, molded by political leaders fearful of the wrath of the voters. In this climate no wonder it has been relatively easy to hasten the dismantling of Presidents Franklin Delano Roosevelt's New Deal and Lyndon Baines Johnson's Great Society programs, following the inexorable rule of public policy: Whoever controls the formulation of an issue eventually determines its outcome. Who would ever have believed, for example, that the debate over Medicare—initially scheduled by the 104th Congress for only one day—or over Social Security would even have been discussed in terms that challenged their very existence or that an antiregulatory bill bears the deceptive title Job Creation and Wage Enhancement Act? The take-no-prisoners bipolar approach to issues has also rendered them easier to manipulate, and nuances become harder and harder to convey in an age given to sound bites and easy answers. Many issues forged at the extremes remained in a bipolar mode as the new century approached: Social Security was still at risk, as many debated whether that venerable program would bring higher returns if turned over to the private sector; antiregulatory fervor competed vigorously with the now-formidable environmental movement; and benefits dwindled even as the federal budget neared balance and states began reporting huge surpluses in their budgets.

The dilemma posited by political scientist Theodore Lowi in 1969 in *The End of Liberalism*—the corruption of "democratic liberalism"—has finally come to roost in the swirl of political anger affecting the polity in the 1990s.[20] In the nation's zeal to accommodate the needs and pressures of its growing interest groups, government expenditures grew exponentially with federal government the major benefactor. At the same time government bounty expanded, government became increasingly "gridlocked," a word used to great effect in 1992 by Ross Perot and in 1994 by the congressional Republicans, led by Representative Newt Gingrich of Georgia, who rode to the speakership of the House of Representatives on the issue of shrinking the government. In his reelection campaign in 1996, Bill Clinton turned "gridlock" against the Republicans, charging the GOP with closing down the government and blaming them for the two government shutdowns.

Have the Founders, who envisioned a society where multiple groups negotiated their way to societal harmony, finally been proven wrong about pluralism? And what are the alternatives? The view of pluralism envisioned by James Madison and his compatriots emerged from a more restricted circle of groups, many of them representing overlapping constituencies—gentlemen farmers, military heroes, and slaveholders. Their vision also assumed that each group would relinquish some of its wishes for the good of the greater society. The new pattern of bipolarism obstructs the spirit of mutual sacrifice necessary for Madisonian democracy and the pluralism on which it rests to work.

The dilemma posed by political anger is also a dilemma of the very pluralism that has constituted the cornerstone of American democracy. Has pluralism finally reached its most pessimistic finale, producing the kind of ubiquitous political anger that now influences every corner of the polity and strangles government? And where will this anger-soaked politics, with its historic changes in the direction of government, really lead? "When interests are so strong but so polarized, how can we talk to each other?" asked Representative Kaptur.

And what of the future dilemma, produced by the changing mechanics of federalism? In this new era of decentralized power, will the states be able to deliver medical care to the indigent, low-interest loans to students, secure retirement for the elderly, and the benefits that all classes of American society now take for granted? And if not, will these fundamental changes result in fresh waves of anger from newly disaffected groups of voters whose loftier expectations of government confront the inevitable realities of decline?

## Anger and the Open Challenge to Government Legitimacy

Government "legitimacy" has become a big factor in provoking the growing repository of antigovernment feeling, particularly out West, where the Wise Use movement boldly confronts the federal government's right to regulate public land. This organization includes armed groups that favor the "use" of military tactics to prove their point, such as burning the property of wetlands advocates and others who disagree with them. Again, it is the mainstream nature of this organization that is striking, especially given its extremist tactics. Funded by individuals and corporations associated with timber, mining, and ranching interests, the movement is "closely connected to the gun lobby, . . . growing rapidly, and [directing] people's economic insecurity into anger at an identifiable, if contrived, enemy—the environmental movement—setting them at war with themselves and with government," according to Tarso Ramos of the Western States Center, which monitors the movement's activities. "Property rights" passions run so high that federal park rangers, who have been subject to accelerating physical attacks and threats, must now travel in pairs.[21]

The political anger that has been building for most of this century crested in the horrific bombing of a federal building in Oklahoma City on April 19, 1995, the worst antigovernment incident in the nation's history. The senseless loss of life, particularly the deaths of babies and young children in the on-site day care center, left the country mystified by the political passions that spawned this terrorist act. The grisly event and its aftermath awakened the nation to significant changes marking the political landscape—most notably, the development of a network of militias across the country—that until that time had gone unnoticed.

After Oklahoma, it became clear that these groups were more than frivolous mobs of fanatics playing war games in the woods; on the contrary, thanks to the advances of the communications revolution, they were highly organized, well funded, growing rapidly, and most significant, regarded themselves as part of the political mainstream in selected states such as Colorado, Michigan, and Montana. Many of their members were hardened and trained for combat in Vietnam and Iraq before coming back to the United States with nothing to do and no enemy to fight. The convicted perpetrator of the Oklahoma bombing, Timothy McVeigh, also returned from the 1991 Gulf War a changed man, unable to reconcile his glory days in the desert—where he drove a Bradley tank that killed and buried hundreds of Iraqi soldiers—with his humdrum life back home. By joining a militia group linked to a nationwide network of paramilitary organizations determined to prevent the government from taking away their [constitutional] right to bear arms, McVeigh found ample validation for his delusional views.

Timothy McVeigh and his ally, Terry Nichols, were both later convicted in separate trials for their roles in the bombing of the federal building in Oklahoma. McVeigh was sentenced to death. Neither man, as the trials revealed, had formal ties to militia or patriot groups, but both shared the fundamental beliefs of these groups, namely, their hatred of federal law enforcement agencies, particularly the Bureau of Alcohol, Tobacco, and Firearms (ATF).[22]

A similar group claimed credit for derailing an Amtrak train in Arizona in October 1995, which led to the death of one passenger and the injury of many others. The group claimed a linkage to the incident at Waco, which recurs as a unifying antigovernment theme among groups such as the militia that regard government law enforcement agencies as out of control. At Waco, both the ATF (in the Treasury Department) and the Federal Bureau of Investigation (in the Justice Department) conducted raids on a compound owned by the Branch Davidian sect. The FBI-led raid in April 1993 resulted in a conflagration that led to the deaths of over seventy Davidians, including women and children. Driven by constituent mail in districts all over the country, Congress held two weeks of hearings in July 1995 on the incident at Waco, followed by similarly highly charged hearings on the incident at Ruby Ridge, Idaho, where the wife and fourteen-year-old son of white separatist Randy Weaver were killed by FBI

Rescue personnel walk out of the blast area after
a 1,200-pound car bomb blew the north side of
the federal building off in downtown Oklahoma
City (April 1995). Photo by Jeff Mitchell; courtesy
Reuters/Bettmann.

agents. A hearing on the militia movement that followed the Oklahoma bombing, chaired by Senator Arlen Specter (R–Pa.), was widely criticized for its respectful approach toward the militia, the upshot of which was that militia
leaders were allowed to portray themselves as reasonable men with legitimate
grievances.

The militia movement showed that anger that seems innocuous at first can
grow into violent forms, some of them even legitimized by the political culture. The gun lobby, in particular, has sent out literature from the National Rifle Association calling federal agents "jack-booted thugs," which has hardened
many Americans' feelings about gun ownership. "I would never register my
guns. How could I ask you to register yours?" said a local sheriff in a video en-

couraging the formation of a branch of the deceptively apple-pie-sounding MOM (Militia of Montana) in his hometown of Eureka.[23]

Surprisingly, antigovernment rhetoric continues to grow even after the Oklahoma bombing linked the violence to the decline in respect for government. Recognizing how antigovernment rhetoric contributed to the Oklahoma disaster, retiring Senator David Pryor (D–Ark.) vowed never again to use the word "bureaucrat" for fear of demonizing federal employees. What is also striking is the political legitimacy these groups have managed to achieve at the highest levels of government and in the media. Militia members have been identified working in the campaigns of Representatives Helen Chenoweth of Idaho, Linda Smith of Washington State, and Steve Stockman of Texas—all conservative Republicans. Stockman, the number-one recipient of PAC funds from the Gun Owners of America, drew fire after the Oklahoma bombing for forwarding a fax with information warning about the bombing to the National Rifle Association instead of straight to the FBI, where it belonged.[24]

"Our sense is that this is a growing movement," said Michael Lieberman of the Washington office of the Anti-Defamation League (ADL), one of the leading groups that tracked militia organizations well before the crisis in Oklahoma City. "They denigrate government and they are totally interconnected. The bombing will mean a setback to these activities."

"It was not inappropriate for a reporter to ask [Speaker of the House Newt] Gingrich about whether his [antigovernment] rhetoric has exacerbated the climate surrounding the Oklahoma bombing," added Lieberman. "It is not inappropriate to link him. The political rhetoric does in a way contribute to the decline in the respect for government, the decline in civility; it all feeds in." Gingrich, for his part, took great umbrage at the suggestion, calling the reporter's question "ghastly and offensive."[25]

The Southern Poverty Law Center, which used to focus on the Ku Klux Klan, now tracks militia and patriot groups; it also follows the activities of over 200 racist and neo-Nazi groups. Its Militia Task Force monitors over 800 militias and other groups "espousing extreme antigovernment views" through scrutinizing Web sites, publications, law enforcement reports, and media accounts. In 1996, according to the task force, there were 858 Patriot groups, with 370 identified as "militia." There were also 488 Patriot support groups, such as common-law courts, identity churches, radio broadcasters, separatists, and publishers. In Ohio alone there were 51 Patriot groups identified on the Web. In addition to Ohio, eight states had over 30 groups, including California, Texas, and Florida.[26]

Surprisingly, the Oklahoma bombing did not reduce the rhetoric, neither Gingrich's nor that of nationally syndicated talk show host G. Gordon Liddy, who immediately took to the air to suggest to his listening public that in case of invasion by the ATF, people should shoot above the neck to avoid bullet-proof vests[27] and to be sure to kill the agents. Despite the public opprobrium from some quarters, Liddy remains on the air and was even honored several months later by his professional colleagues at a gala dinner in Washington, D.C., where he was awarded a freedom-of-speech award by the National Association of Radio Talk Show Hosts.[28] He was scheduled by the Republican National Committee for a similar congratulatory banquet, but the invitation was withdrawn after unfavorable publicity generated by leaders from the Democratic National Committee appeared in the news media. Gingrich also continued for months after the Oklahoma crisis to pump the bellows in the cause of anger, blaming "liberals" and their role in creating the welfare state for the ghoulish murder of a young mother and her children in November 1995, when two psychopaths who wanted a child ripped a live fetus out of her stomach. He was widely criticized for his gratuitous remarks, most notably by the family of the dead woman.

Gingrich and Liddy's "legitimacy" with the Republican Party, among their colleagues, and in the marketplace raises the question of whether political anger is manufactured and manipulated or merely a manifestation of current realities. To what extent is the public malaise created, or at the very least intensified, by politicians and their partners on the airwaves? Or to what extent are these players merely capitalizing on a deep-seated well of anger that already exists—and if it does, where does that anger originate?

## Anger and the Absence of an External Threat

Ironically, political anger is gaining momentum at a time in history when conventional wisdom holds that Americans have never had it so good: For the first time in two centuries no outside threat menaces the country; no wars directly involve the United States; no recession imperils the economy; and with the crumbling of the Berlin Wall and the Soviet state, the worst hazards of communism have evaporated. "Soviet missiles are no longer aimed at American children," as President Bill Clinton so frequently points out. At the same time, all the economic indicators that for political scientists have always determined electoral outcome—inflation, the unemployment rate, the deficit, and interest rates—are the lowest they have been in over a decade.

The real dilemma we face as a nation concerns not just the nature of political anger but how we deal with it as citizens, as leaders, as a polity. What are the implications for governing when so many citizens are angry, alienated, or apathetic—especially at the government itself? What does it say about the quality of democracy when there is so much anger and yet so much success, particularly in terms of economic indicators? Do we really need an outside enemy, such as a cold war, to draw us together, keep anger under wraps, and keep our national purpose clearly in view? And is there a positive, creative aspect to citizen anger today that can be tapped if only we recognize it rather than reject it?

In other words, if things are so good, why are Americans angry? Many reasons can be summoned to explain the current wave of anger, beginning with profound historical changes besetting America as it approaches the millennium. The nation has just emerged from a long period—from the 1930s to the 1990s—in which Americans, particularly white Americans, believed that the system worked because incomes rose and enemies from Nazis to Communists united the nation. In the nineteenth century, the United States defeated foreign predators, closed the frontier, and saved itself from splitting asunder. For most of this century Americans have prevailed against the most daunting of challenges: two world wars, the Great Depression, the turmoil and urban riots of the 1960s, and for the past fifty years, the Cold War with its constant threat of nuclear peril. Americans unite in times of crises, which have an equalizing effect: Nearly everyone suffered in the Depression, and in World War II, citizens all pitched in to defeat the Nazis. Everyone was in the same boat. Of course, there was plenty of anger during the depression, and the anger in World War II was harnessed against our military foes.

A nation's internal problems burn more brightly in the absence of a truly perilous domestic or foreign risk—a war, an epidemic, an economic crisis, or a natural disaster—to the nation's survival. Does that mean democracies need an external threat to survive? Without an impending danger to their survival, Americans seem to have turned inward, free to indulge the political and psychological emotions that they have successfully kept pent up in the past in the interest of survival. In other words, anger is a luxury we can now afford. Although it is tempting to conclude that democracies need a unifying threat even more than a unifying theme to survive, the reasons for public anger go beyond that and revolve around the upheaval caused by the widespread denial and rejection of beliefs that have sustained the nation and the culture for two centuries.

One answer holds that without an external threat, American pluralism no longer works, as the Founding Fathers intended, to hold the nation together. In their view, the multiplicity of interests would compete freely with each other before settling down to negotiate the common good. Instead, today it appears that those interests have proliferated and hardened into extreme positions, with the concept of mutual sacrifice for the common good all but disappearing from the political scene. Such polarization of interests leaves a void in the middle of the spectrum with no one to mediate or moderate the differences—a bipolarity that bodes ill for pluralist democracy. Meanwhile, political anger continues to grow as those interests strain a nation-state that is getting harder to hold together in the absence of a common enemy. The accelerating trend toward decentralization, the allocation of ever more power to the states, has imposed even greater stresses on the national system.

## Mad As Hell

As myths involving the economy, government, and values become increasingly polarized, public confidence in government continues to drop; indeed, it has dipped lower than it has been since the Watergate and Vietnam era. Forcing issues into extreme positions oversimplifies them and also makes them relatively easy for politicians to manipulate in their own interest.

Remember Peter Finch flinging open the window in the movie *Network* and screaming, "I'm mad as hell, and I'm not going to take it any more!" The question of the decade is, What happens now that the window has been opened? Will this period of political anger result in healthy changes, or will it just feed unwholesomely on itself?

Is anger bad or good for society? Both sides boast a long lineage of defenders through the ages. Aristotle regarded anger as a creative force, acknowledging its value in *Nichomachean Ethics:* "Anyone can become angry—that is easy. But to be angry with the right person, to the right degree, at the right time, for the right purpose and in the right way—this is not easy."[29]

It is not easy primarily because most people feel they are not able to effect change, to use anger as a creative force through the political process. In this increasingly anonymous, transient society, voters have become invisible, which means they feel virtually powerless. The anchorman in *Network* grew angrier when he realized he couldn't change his situation. Impotent rage seized the scientist in H. G. Wells's *Invisible Man,* who grew ever madder as he began losing control.[30] Ralph Ellison's *Invisible Man* expressed a similar message about the status of American blacks, linking invisibility to hopelessness and the absence of a feeling of efficacy.[31]

Both sides of the anger dilemma have advocates. The conservatives tapped into and mobilized voter anger; others scorned it, as ABC anchor Peter Jennings did when he compared the voters of 1994 to a bunch of two-year-olds having a tantrum. Even after their shattering losses at the polls, leading Democrats scoffed that only one-third of those eligible voted, forgetting that elections are won and lost on the margins. But political anger goes far deeper than many Democrats admit and should not be viewed by any serious political leader as merely a temporary fit of pique. Anger has become the "number one issue of our times," and will follow us well into the next century, according to sociologist Amitai Etzioni, founder of the communitarian movement.[32]

Government has become a victim of its own success in providing layers upon layers of benefits—Social Security, medical care for the aged, the minimum wage, and the regulation of banks and the securities industry, to name a few—that ensured a stable economy and a middle-class safety net. People hate government because they expect more than government can possibly deliver, particularly in this era of budget constraints. As economic and cultural anxiety boils over into political anger, we can see that people expect government to keep providing benefits they have grown used to at the same time they force their leaders to impose budget cuts that will virtually guarantee the impotence of the public sector. No wonder people feel their "contract" with America has been broken; but how can this contract be repaired if political leaders keep withholding resources from the people in response to their demands for less government and "no new taxes"?

What is left after government as we know it has shrunk beyond recognition? Deregulation, privatization, and rugged individualism leave nothing but market forces in their place. Where did this misplaced confidence in the marketplace come from? Does the public really trust the Ford Motor Company to prevent future Pinto disasters or the states to deliver fair and equitable services without someone peeking over their shoulders? Some politicians look back at voter anger, grateful to be out of the business of politics. "I no longer have to lie to the voters and tell them I can do something about crime and pollution, when I can't," admitted former California governor Jerry Brown, now a talk radio host.

In this era of broken promises and shattered beliefs, pluralism no longer works to unify the nation, as it was originally intended to do. The myths that incomes will rise and values will stay constant relied on a certain homogeneity that has not existed for over a hundred years. Anger is all about communicating, and Americans have communicated a set of very strong feelings through the ballot box.

In the best of circumstances, current expressions of political anger will guide political leaders to channel this powerful emotion into constructive directions instead of clinging to the more reactive, poll-dependent mode of leadership that has guided this generation's political leaders. For democracy at its best provides ample outlets for absorbing the pent-up rage of any era. In fact, leaders who succeed in channeling political anger will own the next era. As unsettling as many find California's 1994 anti-immigrant Proposition 187, which denies benefits to illegal immigrants, it has proven salutary in forcing the issue of how the state is going to deal with increased numbers of people on its welfare rolls.

What follows is an examination of the major factors causing public anger to crest in this generation: historical, psychological, economic, cultural, and political. All of these elements have combined to produce the public turmoil that continues to puzzle political leaders and scholars. The final challenge is to harness political anger in the interest of enduring political progress and stability. For as Winston Churchill said, "Democracy is the worst system, until you've looked at the alternatives."

Today's angry citizens have the capacity to deal with the nation's problems, just as anger at King George III provoked the American colonists to throw off the yoke of colonialism. This means that today's anger needs to find new outlets beyond the "mad as hell" variety, although that is a good start. Democracies need to prove that they do not need threats such as wars and depressions to survive. How they deal with their problems and the anger that arises from those problems will determine their future.

# 2

---

# America and Its Discontents

## *The Roots of Antigovernment Anger*

When have we ever debated violence as a political strategy?

—Ann Lewis

············································································

When General Colin Powell declined to run for president in early November 1995, he vowed to "help bring more civility into our society." Civility goes hand in hand with a "sense of shame," he said, and without it you get the "incivility that we see in our national debate and in our political debate." Was Powell's decision influenced by the incivility he knew would only accelerate against him if he ran for president? By a strange coincidence both the *Philadelphia Inquirer* and *Newsweek* reported a week before his long-awaited announcement not to run that his wife had been treated for depression for the past decade. Some alleged the depression stories were planted by members of the far-right wing in an attempt to keep him off the Republican ticket.[1] Powell was also deeply affected by the assassination a few days earlier of Israeli prime minister Yitzhak Rabin, whose wife, Leah, blamed the inflammatory rhetoric of the Likud Party and religious zealots flourishing in the political mainstream for his death.

Powell's short-lived candidacy drew much of its support from public manifestations of political anger. Even though Powell had never held office, many political analysts believed he would win the presidency by significant margins against the two front-runners, including the president—assuming, of course, that he didn't have to enter the primaries. "None of the above," ran the message from voters so alienated from the current crop of political leaders that any candidate would do—any attractive candidate, that is, *not* associated with politics. Curiously, neither the military nor the Pentagon bureaucracy, where Powell spent his entire professional life, counted as government in the minds of the voters.

Powell answered the need for a hero at a time when politicians and ignominy were practically synonymous in the American mind. The public viewed him as a hero even though he had never engaged in the military equivalent of storming the beaches of Normandy or charging up San Juan Hill; he did, however, engage in combat in Vietnam, where he was wounded. In marked contrast to the stereotype of macho military heroes, however, the record showed that as a proponent of evaluating American interests rigorously before entering foreign entanglements, he frequently took a contrarian position to the administration—as he did when he initially opposed U.S. entry into the Gulf War or further U.S. engagement in Bosnia.

Voters starved for heroes and personal character in their leaders projected their needs onto Powell. Unburdened by a voting record, he quickly became a dream candidate whose views mirrored the majority of today's voters: fiscally conservative and socially moderate. He also conveyed an image of honesty, intelligence, humanity, and hard work—a model of what the American dream can deliver for an African American boy with immigrant parents born into the dire poverty of the South Bronx. He was precisely the kind of leader, many believed, who could heal the nation's growing racial tensions. When Powell declined to run, the anger reverted to a political process that discouraged such worthy candidates from pursuing public office.

Powell never allowed his own anger to engulf him or to impede his upward mobility in life or professional progress in the U.S. Army; on the contrary, he turned his anger at racism into a positive force. "I did not intend to give way to self-destructive rage, no matter how provoked. . . . I felt anger; but most of all I felt challenged. I'll show you."[2]

Political leaders such as Powell who long for more civility in the national discourse would find cold comfort in the experience of their predecessors, even predecessors enshrined today as heroes. Incivility has always enlivened elections, worried politicians, and flooded the media with lively material. Respect for the office of president has always been a problem, back to the time when the father of our country, George Washington, threatened not to run for president if the newspapers didn't call a halt to their vile diatribes against him. President Herbert Hoover knew his reelection campaign was over when angry citizens pelted rotten eggs through the windows of his campaign train in 1932. "I see the handwriting on the wall," he said. "It is all over."[3] In retrospect, it is hard to believe that his much-lauded successor, Franklin Delano Roosevelt, was also routinely trashed by the media and by his well-heeled peers, who called him "a traitor to his class."

## The Psychology of Political Anger

But the anger against government that we are now experiencing has seldom been as all encompassing or grassroots based as it is today. An examination of some of the historical and psychological antecedents of today's antigovernment anger may lift some of the fog from the landscape. Following are some examples.

### Injustice and Deprivation

A major source of personal anger stems from deprivation, or "a sense of what one has in terms of what one thinks others have." The psychology of deprivation raises questions of fairness and bears the strongest relationship to the backlash over entitlements: "If we feel deprived . . . the anger and resentment generated will first contaminate our relationship with those who are depriving us and later be extended, illogically, to those who are given more than we are in the same situation," according to psychiatrist Willard Gaylin.[4]

Deprivation leads to feeling "cheated," an emotion that quickly turns into the "smoldering anger of political resentment." *Ressentiment*, analyzed in the work of Max Scheler, goes beyond mere resentment to an "explosive rage that can destroy any society."[5] The extent of the anger depends on the discrepancy between what society promises and what it can deliver; the wider the gulf, the greater the anger.

Why do Americans, the most privileged population on earth, feel deprived? The answer is that deprivation is a relative feeling: "Even in the best society . . . the deprived [can] feel resentful and angry." In fact, one of the dirty little secrets of our society is how "we have within the last forty years . . . in America managed to perversely maintain our deprived minorities while making our privileged majorities feel deprived."[6]

Before people feel angry or aggrieved about an injustice, according to psychologist Carol Tavris, they must (1) want what they don't have and (2) feel they deserve what they don't have. A third condition involves the anger that comes from unkept promises, a common feeling among voters when politicians fail to fulfill their campaign pledges.

Anger spawned by deprivation has been called a "relative" emotion because it is so highly dependent on culture.[7] An islander on Bali may feel hardly any sense of deprivation, for example, whereas a suburbanite from Winnetka, Illinois, can work up quite a froth over half a percentage point increase in his local real estate tax. Isolated cultures, such as the Amish in Pennsylvania, and less developed nation-states in Africa and South Asia experience only a fraction of the anger now measured in the United States despite the fact that in absolute terms their citizens experience far more actual deprivation than Americans. Diminished media opportunities to see how others live and limited expectations of government in most parts of the world tend to reduce envy and anger in other cultures. "We can endure the fact that we do not have something unless we feel that something has been taken away from us. We will then experience a sense of violation. . . . The smoldering rage which comes from being cheated [will be extended] to the society which allowed us to be so cheated."[8] As communications improve across the world, and citizens from other nations can see with their own eyes via the Internet, television, and greater travel opportunities how others live, we can expect levels of anger to rise. In 1998 the Asian financial crisis spawned the revolution in Indonesia, which overthrew the Suharto regime, in addition to heightened levels of anti-Americanism in many other countries.

Imagine the rage against government when it takes back resources it has already given away! Most Americans feel they are entitled to jobs, health care, and a minimal standard of living. As budget austerity programs continue to slim down entitlements to which people have become cumulatively accustomed, we can expect the negatives to rise and political anger down the road to loom much larger than now.

Witness, too, the language of deprivation that inundates current political life. "Takings" legislation, an antiregulatory issue, conveys in a very visceral sense the idea that government is removing the very birthright of U.S. citizens.[9] The term "welfare cheats" grew proportionately with the economic squeeze on Americans. The existence of a vodka "queen" who was using food stamps to pay for liquor—an anecdote widely used by Ronald Reagan on the campaign trail—attracted an enormous amount of resentment and anger even though no one could ever find either the queen herself or the liquor store or, in fact, any liquor store that accepted food stamps.

## Blame and Scapegoating

Blame also involves anger, specifically the kind of anger that finds an easy outlet in scapegoating, an all too common thread in legislation, political rhetoric, and public budgeting choices. Witness the increase in congressional reprimands directed at members who succumb to the temptation of orchestrating public anger into inflammatory rhetoric. Blaming others helps individuals escape from accountability for their actions. At times, people tend to blame themselves if something goes wrong with their lives. Encouraged by Madison Avenue, they can change their deodorant or their mouthwash, read Dale Carnegie, and improve themselves and their lives. But for many these days, the reverse is true: "In our secular age, . . . the issues of blame and moral judgment have yielded to a more lax form of discourse . . . one in which personal accountability is transmuted into something abstract and nonwilled."[10]

A rash of scapegoating has emerged to take the place of self-criticism; personal responsibility is viewed by many as irrelevant in view of the magnitude of problems faced by voters grappling with overcrowded schools, street crime, and diminishing benefits. Blame quickly fills the void, especially when no one seems to have ready solutions: Blame the victims, blame the leaders, blame immigrants, blame anything visible.

Scapegoating directs blame to the wrong source. A classic example of blaming the victim occurred with California's resounding vote in 1994 in support of

Proposition 187, which prohibits illegal immigrants from receiving public welfare benefits. Widely criticized throughout the nation for their anti-immigrant passion, voters also revealed the close connection between economic hardship and the flowering of ugly xenophobic emotions, which lurk very close to the surface of our society. In California, local services were being severely stressed (by immigrants and other groups living below the poverty line), and no government entity bore the responsibility for relief. Indeed, referenda remain the last resort for people responding to wide cracks in our federal system, which in this case allowed illegal immigration to flourish while granting universal fiscal absolution from its consequences.

If unchecked by law or culture, blame quickly catches fire, engulfing everything around it. Most notable are the state-based gay-bashing amendments that surfaced in the 1990s, the anti-immigrant scapegoating in border states such as Texas and California, and the escalating growth of conspiracies such as those given recent expression by the militia movement. In early February 1998 voters in Maine went to the polls to repeal their state's bill guaranteeing civil rights and civil liberties to gay citizens. "This effort establishes the Christian Coalition of Maine as a major force in the democratic process of the state," read a statement at the coalition's website after the referendum. Despite being outspent 8 to 1 by supporters of the 1997 bill, the coalition's drive at the grassroots level paid off: The group distributed 240,000 voter guides to 900 churches, ran local radio ads, and mailed 100,000 get-out-the-vote brochures.[11]

You don't have to look too far for even more threatening examples of blame's progenitors in contemporary American or European history. Franz Neumann relates anti-Semitism in the 1920s and 1930s in Germany—the country "least likely to have spontaneous anti-Semitism"—to mass anxiety manipulated by leaders who needed a handy scapegoat for their political troubles:

> The Protocols of the Elders of Zion [was] a forgery . . . but led to a lot of anti-Semitism [because] the leaders need[ed] an enemy worse than other countries [and because of] . . . their inability to understand the problems causing real anxiety: inflation, depression, [a] non-functional political system . . . [and] moral, social and political homelessness." The only way to integrate people was "through hatred of an enemy."[12]

Why blame the Jews? According to Neumann, Bolshevism, big business, and the Catholic Church were too strong; only the "Jews remained" sufficiently weak politically. Witness the nation's current crop of scapegoats: immigrants, welfare mothers and children, seniors on Medicaid, the poor and the disabled.

All these groups share the problem of political impotence, as evidenced by their low rates of voting, the dearth of well-financed interest groups ready to spring to their defense, and the easy targets they offer to those claiming to speak for mainstream America. The handwriting on the wall couldn't have been clearer than the original budget offered by the 104th Congress in terms of the future for these groups, most especially the destitute, the disabled, the elderly, pregnant women, and children. Steep cuts in Medicaid, which covers health care for the poor and long-term care for the elderly poor; reductions in Medicare, which guarantees medical care for retirees; and enormous changes in welfare as we know it all place the nation's poorest and most dependent groups in a state of permanent uncertainty.

And why blame the government? Far more family farms are gobbled up by the forces of agribusiness, timber, and mining interests than by wetlands legislation. Why isn't Weyerhaeuser as tempting a target as the Interior Department? Probably because people can do something about government, whereas it is virtually impossible to vote out the chairman of the board or change corporate policies. Government is also more visible and more prominent in the consciousness of Americans than economic forces, which do not have a name or a face against which to direct anger. Also, with attacks from right, left, and center, government is now perceived as weak and unable to impose penalties— hence the public increasingly blames political leaders and bureaucrats. But although government remains the scapegoat of choice, Americans still remain skeptical about capitulating to blind faith in the marketplace.

The need for enemies has long occupied students of international politics; today, these concepts also relate to domestic politics. Blame always worked well as a staple of foreign policy, where the identification of an enemy elevates the self to a position of moral superiority, warranted or not. The philosophy guiding U.S. policy throughout the Cold War, for example, rested on positioning the Soviets as the enemy, an "evil empire"; thus we justified our entry into wars as well as the expenditure of enormous amounts of money to compete with the Soviet military and retain our influence as a superpower throughout the world. These "assumptions tend to produce grandiose feelings of power, invulnerability and strength" and combat the confusion so prevalent in the postwar world.[13] The notion of an enemy is also necessary to manage conflict, since conflicts of all kinds are dependent on "reciprocal antagonisms." Governments have long realized that "the manipulation of symbols is easier than the destruction of foreign armies," wrote international relations specialist Quincy Wright.[14]

The demonization of an enemy supports the manipulation theory of anger, since it rests so heavily on rhetoric and images. Witness the Nation of Islam's term "White devils"; the National Rifle Association's term "jack-booted thugs" for ATF agents; or, from America's many enemies abroad, "Yankee imperialists." The Nation of Islam's leader, Louis Farrakhan, amazed critics with his Million Man March on Washington on October 16, 1995. The march was peaceful, the numbers larger than expected, and its themes espoused the renewal of family and individual responsibility among African American men. Why, then, did Farrakhan feel the need to scapegoat Asian Americans and Jews as "blood-suckers"? Was he merely repeating the timeworn patterns of the past, generating anger through blame to create a following? Or does he not care about what ultimately happens to political and social goals, however worthy, when they are conceived in hatred?

Free-floating anger can have a deleterious effect on physical as well as mental health, according to Drs. Redford and Virginia Williams, coauthors of *Anger Kills,* a riveting book on the psychology of anger. "About 20 percent of the general population has levels of hostility high enough to be dangerous to health," they claim in support of their thesis and prescriptions for assuaging anger. In the light of their data, it comes as no surprise that "road rage" has become a serious problem on the nation's highways, with the roads around Washington, D.C., among the most dangerous.[15]

Anger and blame offer many people a way to deal with disappointments that occur in their everyday lives. In 1994, Hillary Rodham Clinton attributed the high negatives in her polls to those who blamed her for problems in their own marriages and personal lives. Blame as a component of xenophobia also resurfaces periodically, along with myths that perpetuate anger: Communists were a subspecies of humanity; Catholic presidents would call Rome for instructions, charged a group of John F. Kennedy's opponents in the 1960 election campaign; and from Republican presidential candidate Pat Buchanan, 1 million "Zulus" would have a problem assimilating in the state of Virginia "compared with a million 'Englishmen.'" Buchanan also blamed "promiscuous homosexuals [who] appear literally hell-bent on Satanism and suicide" for the AIDS epidemic.[16] Public humiliation also generates feelings of blame and punishment: Jimmy Carter was booted from the presidency primarily because he was unable to effect the release of the fifty-two American hostages held by Iran from 1979 to 1981, and Clinton was damaged in 1993 by the spectacle of Somali warlords dragging an American soldier through the streets of Mogadishu. Americans vastly prefer the Teddy Roosevelt style of charging up San Juan Hill as a public response to humiliation: In that way, the leader is expressing the nation's indignation and is responding from a posture of conqueror, not supplicant.

## Betrayal and Public Trust

Democracies rest on trust, according to political theorist Judith Shklar. "Freedom creates a whole new range of complexities. . . . Not the least important reason for this is that a Lockean political society depends on trust more than does any other. . . . Yet it may well lack the means to enforce it, if it is to remain free . . . that is, politically trustworthy."[17]

Feelings of betrayal have emerged as a significant factor in the anger of the 1990s. Ironically, in this context traditional loyalties often are turned inside out. In a switch from their typical stance as law-and-order types, Republican members of Congress curiously led the charge in hearings involving the role of agents from the ATF at Waco and from the FBI at Ruby Ridge. People expected the STASI, the former East German secret police, to kill or frame innocent people; they don't expect this kind of behavior from the police forces in New Orleans, Philadelphia, or Los Angeles, much less from federal law enforcement officials.

Congressional hearings in the fall of 1997 and the late spring of 1998 on the Internal Revenue Service's intrusion on individual rights also evoked considerable public anger. After the first set of hearings the agency's director promised that the IRS would be more sensitive in its dealings with people in the future. Special prosecutor Kenneth W. Starr also drew high negatives for his Whitewater investigation of President and Mrs. Clinton for similar reasons: the public's perception that in the course of his work he was trampling on the rights of U.S. citizens. One prime example of his prosecutorial excess involved his issuing of subpoenas to two bookstores in Washington, D.C., (Barnes & Noble and Kramerbooks) to uncover the book purchasing habits of a potential witness, Monica Lewinsky.

## Anger, Confusion, and Political Change

In *The Protean Self*, Robert Jay Lifton relates political anger to the massive confusion of contemporary life: bewilderment about values, politics, family, and human relations. Political anger, he explains, is a way of seeking fundamental truths, "all in the name of a past of perfect harmony that never was."[18] Since anger and fear are so closely related, anyone who offers solutions to the problems of crime, unemployment, poverty, and failure also offers the hope of assuaging those fears. For this reason, so many people in our country and throughout the world adhere to fundamentalist movements for the certitude with which they decipher the unexplainable and the solutions they offer to dispel the public's feelings of helplessness, frustration, and inefficacy. Their answers may fail to address the problems, but they soothe the anxieties of the multitude, at least for a while.

The psychological roots of anger—feelings of deprivation, injustice, confusion, and betrayal—appear throughout history. Periods of great societal upheaval generate enormous quantities of public anger, which in turn release unforeseen political changes in their wake.[19] Tax revolts based on injustice and deprivation occurred well before the Boston Tea Party. Politicians have long been viewed as betrayers of the public trust, and today's scapegoats can trace their ancestry to untold groups of Americans—slaves, Catholics, and successive waves of immigrants, to name a few—who bore the brunt of a wider public's anger rooted in societal upheaval and uncertainty.

The anger of the 1990s should be regarded as a signal that we are in the midst of an era of major change and not, as many would have us believe, merely experiencing an isolated fluke that can be remedied by inventing ever more imaginative political slogans. Psychologists warn that anger should be treated as a serious sign that important needs are not being met; that they deserve immediate attention; and that ignoring or repressing them will lead to serious consequences.[20] But when we look at responses by fearful political leaders, it is obvious that although political anger is being manipulated for political success, it is not being addressed in terms of either its root causes, its wide swath across demographic lines, or its sustained momentum.

A glance backward would prove today's leaders shortsighted. Political anger throughout history has always signaled profound change, for better and for worse. In the American experience, the forces unleashed by anger over taxes led to the revolt in Massachusetts Bay known as the Boston Tea Party, which became the prelude to the American Revolution; the abolitionists' anger over slavery led to its eradication after the Civil War; and the privations suffered by citizens during the Depression steered the nation toward federal government protection of stocks, bank accounts, and labor unions. The latter occurred during the New Deal and is a good example of how political anger led to positive, proactive, and effective government actions. But anger can just as easily turn regressive: In the period most similar to our own, the 1890s, anger turned into third-party movements, anti-immigration backlash, and other forms of political expression that reflected public anxiety over rapid social and economic change.

Unleashed anger can tear down the pillars of freedom, as it did in Weimar Germany and in the McCarthy era in America in the early 1950s. Anger fueled

Political rallies offer one outlet for citizens' anger. Photo by Maura Boruchow; courtesy of *The Hill*.

the rise of the Ku Klux Klan, the Khmer Rouge in Cambodia, and the rebellion that incited the Russian Revolution. History shows how much a nation's political culture determines the response to popular discontent that has metamorphosed into anger. Authoritarian cultures such as prewar Germany and the former Soviet Union typically treated public anger as illegitimate, and officials worked hard to suppress it.

Democracies also try to quell uprisings; but the movements that give rise to rebellion—and the anger that propels them—have more room to evolve in a democracy, and many of their themes eventually become absorbed into the mainstream. Ancient Greece, the first of the world's known democracies, kept the violent side of anger at bay through a practice called *agonism,* or contests. Known as a "contest society," the Athenians made everything into some sort of public contest—sports, debates, events of all kinds—creating outlets for anger at the same time they imposed strong prohibitions against violence.

As a nation, the United States has shown a marked ambivalence toward anger that has led to both repression of the factors that lead to anger and a national glorification of anger in crime literature, campaign slogans, and spectator sports.[21] "We like our Green Bay Packers to be mobile, agile, and hostile," fans are fond of saying.

# Between the Centuries:
## *Anger and Its Populist Roots*

The closest counterpart to our own era is the 1890s, when the nation also faced rapid industrial change and societal upheaval at the approach of the new century. Economic changes wrought by industrialization fueled rebellions that crested in the 1890s and formed the basis of the Populist movement. Encouraged to "raise less corn and more hell," farmers formed the Granger movement and joined with business groups, Greenbacks, and antimonopoly groups to mobilize their anger into a very potent third party, the People's Party, which captured the Democrats in 1896.

One of populism's major themes, the fear of change, sounded a familiar ring; people resisted the advent of change because they didn't know how it would change their lives. Nor could they begin to sort out a minimalist government's role in cushioning the worst effects of change. In that era, many people viewed rural America as a superior way of life; they fiercely opposed industrialization, just as today many resist the onset of the postindustrial era. Between 1870 and 1900 the economy went through a wrenching modernization with the arrival of national transportation, financial, and communications systems. As family farms and small enterprises were replaced by an economy dominated by giant corporations, farmers, merchants, artisans, and small manufacturers were all squeezed in the maws of change. People were also subjected to frequent financial "panics," or minirecessions (some of which we might today even consider depressions), in the business cycle that shook the markets and roiled the economy. These events were used by Populist and later Progressive leaders, all of whom hit political pay dirt criticizing the rapacious behavior of railroads and big business for mergers that led to firings of employees and the disappearance of smaller enterprises. When you add the attacks on big business for spending money to corrupt the political process, you get a sense of déjà vu in light of today's wave of downsizings, merger mania, and campaign finance reform.

As the previous century drew to a close, the economy was also becoming more involved in international trade—hence the interest of Wall Street financiers in upholding the gold standard, which many Populists viewed as a plot against ordinary people. Bitter debates raged then as now over issues long forgotten but riddled with the passion of class warfare. The fight over "free silver" and the gold standard turned so bitter that it was said that "gold was the only metal ever wept over."

The 1890s also resembled the 1990s in their relative freedom from major domestic and international threats. Recovered from the worst physical and emotional ravages of the Civil War, 1890s Americans enjoyed the luxury of finally dwelling on their own internal problems, which always seem worse in peacetime. They bear an eerie resemblance to Americans recuperating from Vietnam and the Cold War, freed at last from external threats only to turn inward in anger.

Anti-immigrant violence also erupted during this period, becoming one of the nation's most troubling domestic problems. Then as now, the changing economy brought with it the onset of relative deprivation for many indigenous groups who felt displaced by "foreigners." Rapid industrialization created the need for more labor; in response, the nation opened its doors between 1890 and 1910 to the largest wave of immigration in its history. Clashes between immigrant groups and the relatively homogeneous culture that dominated America at that time were as ferocious as the "diversity" clashes affecting a growing multicultural nation today.

Harking back to this earlier era, Newt Gingrich as well as voters and politicians of every stripe openly identify themselves as "populists." Modern devotees of populism should take another look. Romanticized in later years, populism also displayed a decidedly ugly side with undercurrents of "provincial resentments . . . suspiciousness, and nativism," according to the noted historian Richard Hofstadter. Anti-Semitism ran rampant in Bryan's free-silver movement; speakers inveighed against Wall Street and the Jews of Europe, offering such examples as the House of Rothschild, along with Shylock and other "usurers."[22] Progressivism, which came a few years later, also emanated from widespread social and economic discontent. Forming their own political party in reaction to the Democratic Populists, Progressives drew their supporters primarily from disaffected, middle-class Republican insurgents and later supported Theodore Roosevelt for president in 1912 under their banner, the Bull Moose Party. Those waxing nostalgic about third or fourth parties should remember that they were relatively short lived.[23]

If we can take heart from the 1890s, it is because even though society seemed weighed down by anger over moral and social degeneration and anxious about the possible eclipse of democratic institutions, the nation did not give way to despair. Instead, it drew on its unique political culture of optimism to regenerate. Out of this era of anger came an era of hope, for just as "the sinner can be cleansed and saved, so the nation could be redeemed if the citizens awoke to their responsibilities," wrote Hofstadter.[24] Current political anger has not yet been dissipated despite the efforts of both political parties to tamp down the public's fury by absorbing the issues that produced it. What the Populist era shows, however, is that the issues that survive current fads will eventually be assimilated by the political system; what form they will take depends on the results of future elections and the flexibility of the two major political parties.

## The Legacy of Violence and Distrust

Events crowding the century sandwiched between the 1890s and the 1990s also contributed to today's angry political mood. In that era, U.S. citizens were sharply awakened to their global involvement and against George Washington's advice spent the rest of the century fighting on foreign soil and in foreign wars. The twentieth century held the dubious distinction of being the first century of mass death and dangerous ideological movements—namely communism, fascism, and Nazism—that seriously threatened the existence of American democracy. In World War I and World War II, the death toll climbed into the millions, and genocide became part of our vocabulary.[25] In Vietnam, 58,000 American and 3 million Vietnamese lives were lost; the toll in the two world wars and the Korean War ran much higher. Americans also find themselves still reeling from the brutal assassinations of three of the nation's most promising leaders—the two Kennedys and Martin Luther King—which occurred in the space of only five years, 1963–1968.

Recent history has also shown that federal government has more than earned the public's distrust. The Vietnam War period exposed lying as a routine government activity. Lies about the progress of the war, body counts of dead Americans, and the reasons for fighting there in the first place were commonplace from the highest echelons of public leaders—generals and cabinet secretaries right up to the president. In fact, the controversy over former defense secretary Robert McNamara's book *In Retrospect* focused on his tardy admission that it was a monumental mistake for our nation to become involved in fighting a ten-year war without either a clear threat to the nation or any definable American interest.[26] McNamara, who went on to run the World Bank and receive several major peace prizes, was not alone in misjudging America's entry into the war: Congress and two presidents willingly participated in conducting an undeclared war whose purposes still remain a mystery to most Americans and which was a clear violation of the U.S. Constitution, since Congress is the only branch of government empowered to declare war.

The Watergate scandal continued to fill the annals of distrust with revelations about how President Richard Nixon and his aides subverted the CIA, the

FBI, the IRS, and other government agencies for their own political purposes, not to mention the lead role of the White House in directing criminal activities involving the break-in at the Watergate headquarters of the Democratic Party. Still processing Watergate and Vietnam in their minds, the American people then confronted the Iran-Contra scandal, in which high-ranking officials from the Reagan administration were caught lying to Congress to cover up the fact that they were conducting their own private war in Central America in clear violation of legislative directives from Congress.[27] Lies and cover-ups continue. In April 1996, the *Los Angeles Times* revealed that in 1994 the Clinton administration had secretly approved arms shipments from Iran to Bosnia at the same time it publicly supported the United Nations arms embargo. Needless to say, neither Congress nor the American people knew about this duplicitous policy.

More serious charges dogged President Clinton during his second term. The Whitewater scandal, involving a land deal in Arkansas that led to the indictment and conviction of several partners of President and Mrs. Clinton, continued to occupy the independent counsel, Kenneth Starr, as well as the media. Added to Whitewater were additional charges of illegal money raising from foreign sources—primarily Asian—much of which was eventually returned to the donors after party officials admitted that accepting the funds had been a mistake. Unanswered questions that percolated throughout Clinton's second term stemmed from the 1996 presidential fund-raising efforts: What did the foreign donors receive in exchange for their contributions? A night in the Lincoln bedroom? Special trade favors? Ignoring human rights violations in China? Just what was the China lobbying connection?

To top off the fund-raising investigations, inquiries into the president's sex life now burgeoned from the Starr inquiry, namely, the Monica Lewinsky scandal, which occupied official Washington often to the exclusion of other matters of state. The question of Lewinsky, a former White House intern, went beyond Clinton's past extramarital affairs; it involved whether the White House, led by the president, tried to influence Lewinsky's testimony before the grand jury in the Paula Jones sexual harassment case by arranging a job for her in New York. The mystery of the Clinton presidency was why his poll ratings continued to soar despite all the scandals. The Lewinsky scandal caused a considerable uproar when the president, who had initially denied a relationship with "that woman," finally confessed seven months later, in August 1998, that he had engaged in behavior that was not "appropriate."

No wonder the public now believes the worst about government; why shouldn't it, since it has been lied to so much in the recent past? But the public has gotten the facts mixed up: The lies have come more often from *political leaders* than from the *bureaucracy,* for whom the public has reserved most of its contempt. "The ship of state is the only vessel that leaks from the top," noted James Reston, the late *New York Times* columnist. Alas, however, the bureaucrats have all too often served as handmaidens to leaders who have acted in violation of their oaths and, when not scrutinized, have occasionally acted in violation of basic human ethics. Imagine the justifiable fury of those leukemia-afflicted citizens living in Utah and other states who were subjected without their knowledge to government-run atomic testing programs during and after World War II. The pattern persists even today, according to the White House–appointed Advisory Commission on Human Radiation, which revealed that "one out of four participants in current, federally funded medical research projects at hospitals around the United States are taking part without their knowledge."[28]

Ironically, cynicism toward government coincides precisely with the very reforms emerging from the Watergate era, which forced government open to public scrutiny through the Freedom of Information Act, inspectors general, special prosecutors, independent counsels, and sunshine laws. Clearly, proximity to government only bred more contempt and anger.

## Issues Born in Anger and Their Antecedents

Capitalizing on the atmosphere of anger, politicians maintain its momentum; few politicians are courageous enough to confront the issues, and most capitulate to the temptations of bipolarism. Senate Majority Leader Robert Dole, seeking the Republican presidential nomination in 1996, moved quickly to the right on issues such as gun control, abortion, the influence of Hollywood on public morality, and regulatory reform after announcing his intention to seek the Republican nomination. Unfortunately for the GOP, Dole was unable to capitalize on public anger, and repeatedly asked, "Where is the outrage?" during his unsuccessful campaign. Perhaps the voters had unconsciously identified him as part of the problem and were unwilling to follow his recent conversion to bipolar politics. They became especially cynical at some of his solutions. For example, as one of his remedies for attacking the drug problem in the nation's cities, he admonished, "Just don't do it." Another presidential candidate, Pat Buchanan, tried to convince voters that under his leadership, the Republican Party would be a "party of conviction, not consensus." For their part, conservative politicians claim that it is merely their turn to capitalize on political anger; liberals dominated the 1960s, they claim, with their angry anti–Vietnam War slogans of "burn, baby, burn" and their accusations of "baby killer" leveled at the White House.

## Entitlements

Along with term limits, one of the most potent issues in the anger portfolio, especially over the past decade, involves clashes over—with apologies to John F. Kennedy—*what government should do for me.* This relates right back to theories of deprivation, the feeling of anger that stems from what people perceive others have that they do not. In this context, democratic government has become a victim of its own success, responding as it has to the needs of successive groups with layers upon layers of benefits ranging from Medicaid for disabled children to capital gains tax breaks for wealthy investors. (See Table 2.1.) The result? Everyone feels entitled to government benefits, then victimized when those benefits don't meet their heightened expectations. White males feel victimized by affirmative action policies, minorities and women consider themselves victimized by affirmative action policies that fall short of addressing their needs as well as by white males and their restrictive power structure, the middle class feels victimized by tax and spending policies that keep its earning power stagnant, and business owners feel victimized by onerous regulations that they presume reduce their profit margins.

Polls show utter confusion on this issue even among blacks, who are split on the question of whether the government has helped or hurt them with federal affirmative action programs: Fifty-two percent of blacks interviewed for a *Washington Post* poll in 1995 indicated they supported affirmative action programs; 46 percent did not. (Those African Americans negative about affirmative action felt that white colleagues believed their professional success was based on preferential hiring, not merit.) Other salient issues share similar divisions, often depending on how the questions are asked. If you ask a white male if he cares to relinquish his job to a black woman to redress past wrongs, he will likely respond negatively. Does this mean he opposes equal opportunity or affirmative action?[29]

In this environment of anger it is no wonder that the issue of welfare reform has flourished, especially since Democrats as well as Republicans have promised for years to end welfare as we know it. Whether "reform" will also reduce illegitimate births, find jobs for the needy, or improve the economy is anyone's guess. Governor Pete Wilson of California, formerly of the 1996 Republican presidential candidate pool, drew some initial mileage for his attack

**TABLE 2.1**

**Top Entitlements**

Mandatory spending programs account for more than half the federal budget. Their sheer size makes the biggest of them tempting targets for budget cutters, but the critical factor is how fast they grow. Medicaid and Medicare combine size with an explosive growth rate that makes them the two most serious budget problems in the short run. Social Security will become a similar problem when the baby boomers begin to retire early in the next century. The following are the top 12 entitlements, ranked by size. (By fiscal year; dollar amounts in billions.)

| Rank/Program | Actual 1991 Outlays | Annual Average Percent Change | |
|---|---|---|---|
| | | 1985–91 | 1991–97 |
| 1. Social Security | $267 | 6.2 | 5.8 |
| 2. Medicare | 114 | 8.6 | 11.6 |
| 3. Deposit insurance | 66 | NA[a] | NA[a] |
| 4. Medicaid | 53 | 15.0 | 15.8 |
| 5. Federal civilian retirement[b] | 37 | 6.2 | 6.9 |
| 6. Unemployment[c] | 25 | 8.0 | 0.7 |
| 7. Military retirement | 23 | 6.6 | 5.7 |
| 8. Food stamps[c] | 20 | 8.1 | 4.0 |
| 9. Supplemental Security Income | 15 | 9.1 | 9.4 |
| 10. Family support | 14 | 7.8 | 5.3 |
| 11. Veterans' benefits | 14 | 2.4 | 4.6 |
| 12. Farm price supports | 10 | −9.0 | −1.4 |

[a]It is misleading to calculate the year-to-year change in deposit insurance outlays. The savings and loan crisis forced Congress to supplement deposit insurance—ordinarily funded solely by premiums from covered institutions—with huge sums of taxpayer money. The annual amount of taxpayer funds depends on the vagaries of congressional politics.

[b]Includes civil service, foreign service, Coast Guard and other retirement programs, plus annuitants' health benefits.

[c]Unemployment insurance and food stamps are "countercyclical" or "automatic stabilizer" programs designed to counteract the effects of an economic downturn. Much more than most other entitlements, their year-to-year growth rates and total spending are dictated by the health of the economy. *Source:* Congressional Budget Office, Washington, D.C.

on welfare policy, which [paraphrased] argued that people who are working hard so that they can afford to have children must now pay for those who break the rules and are rewarded. (Given his views, it was no surprise that Wilson lent considerable support to Proposition 187.) Wilson's presidential campaign eventually floundered, many said, because of its spiteful, negative tone;

angry as Americans are about affirmative action, it wasn't a big enough issue to carry a candidate into the White House.

Eventually the issue grew bigger than the candidate. In 1996 a majority of Californians voted to approve Proposition 209, a referendum designed to abolish affirmative action. Directed primarily at the state's universities and couched in civil liberties language, the amendment specifically states that "the state shall not discriminate against, or grant preferential treatment to, any individual or group on the basis of race, sex, color, ethnicity, or national origin in the operation of public employment, education or public contracting."

The other side of the victim coin is the complex question of corporate entitlements; some are convinced that they are entitled to wheat subsidies or other government goodies but resent other groups who feed at the public trough. A hopeful sign for those who fear that this era of entitlements bears too close a likeness to the social Darwinism of the past century is that along with benefit cuts to the poor, "welfare for the rich," or "corporate welfare," has also angered the populace. These benefits abound for all kinds of reasons relating mostly to the political clout of the recipients: mohair subsidies for TV star and multimillionaire Sam Donaldson's ranch, corporate tax breaks, agricultural subsidies for rich farmers, real estate tax benefits for country houses, and other special tax subsidies for oil and mining interests.

When the entitlements of the past half-century are tallied, no wonder almost all groups feel wedged in the gulf between promises and expectations, some groups more than others.[30] James Baldwin wrote that to be black and relatively conscious in America meant being in a perpetual state of rage; Ellis Cose quoted former New York mayor David Dinkins: "A white man with a million dollars is a millionaire, and a black man with a million dollars is a nigger with a million dollars."[31]

Indignation rises with each media exposé divulging what the public sees as blank checks to [often] hostile foreign countries, rich American landholders, mining companies, and undercover intelligence agents. It becomes easier to understand how citizens working three jobs to make ends meet feel hostile, especially when they are told that their country can't afford health care, public television, and school lunches at the same time that mining companies remain entitled to drill for minerals on federal lands for a pittance.

## Taxes

Taxes present another hot-button issue providing new sources of anger to the polity. If public wrath over taxation goes back before the founding of the republic, why, after 200 years, are we now experiencing the worst tax revolt since the Boston Tea Party? Two reasons: broken promises and the widespread perception that taxes have become disconnected from the public's well-being.

On the question of shattered promises, George Bush broke his pledge on taxes ("read my lips; no new taxes"), as did President Clinton, both presidents mistakenly believing that the public would rather have them "do the right thing" than keep a promise. Fueling the anger against taxes, Majority Leader Dick Armey (R–Tex.) called for the elimination of the withholding tax on paychecks at a congressional hearing on February 21, 1995. Why would a political leader suggest something that could cost the Treasury billions of dollars? Because, he said, if people had to write a check every month for their taxes, the government could never have grown as large as it has. Only by taking people's money before they ever see it has the government been able to raise taxes to their current high level without sparking a revolt.[32]

Shays' Rebellion in 1786 in western Massachusetts was spurred by farmers who didn't see the relationship between heavy taxes levied by the state legislature to pay debts from the Revolutionary War—primarily to speculators—and their own safety, security, and well-being. Similarly, the Whiskey Rebellion eight years later in western Pennsylvania set up a direct challenge to the brand-new federal government's right to impose excise taxes on whiskey makers, who had become used to cashing in on their lucrative business without worrying about taxes. In light of our nation's longtime aversion to taxes, no wonder the United States could not enact an income tax until the twentieth century.[33]

Commentator Kevin Phillips also links the tax revolt to the widespread perception that taxes are not linked to the public good. He warns that current inequities in the tax system show all the signs of a nation in decline, like Spain and Holland in the eighteenth century and Great Britain in the nineteenth.[34]

The tax issue seized voters during the 1996 presidential primary season with candidate and publishing mogul Steve Forbes forcing the issue of the flat tax onto the campaign agenda. Widely debunked by pundits and economists everywhere and never seriously debated by Congress, the idea nevertheless caught on: a tax of 17 percent on all wages, salaries, and pensions; the elimination of existing deductions for mortgage interest and charitable deductions; and personal exemptions keyed to helping families with dependents and indexed for inflation. Forbes was matched in Congress by Majority Leader Dick Armey, who introduced a bill along the same lines.

The flat tax issue dissipated in the late 1990s, primarily because of the reduction of the deficit, a victory widely attributed to the unusual and short-lived spirit of bipartisanship—namely, the Clinton administration's leadership and the Republican Congress's willingness despite partisan pressures to work with the Democrats in the White House and in the legislature toward their shared goal. The success of the budget reduction surpassed everyone's expectations. By 1997 the budget deficit was posted at $22.6 billion—down from $290 billion in 1992—and by 1998 estimates from the White House and the Federal Reserve Bank were so optimistic that projected budget surpluses ranged from $10 billion to $75 billion. If these expectations are realized, 1998 will be the first year since 1969 that the government spent less than its posted earnings. Despite these buoyant numbers and the equally surprising number of surpluses in a great many state capitals, many Republican members of Congress and candidates for local office still press for tax reduction. Whether they are fearful of the future or are capitalizing on the success of past antitax campaigns is anyone's guess.

The Viacom issue also gave new meaning to the issue of taxes and inequity, proving that despite all efforts at reform, special privileges were alive and well. Viacom, a New York–based media conglomerate, teetered on the edge of selling its cable division to a minority-controlled company. The company stood to save nearly $400 million in taxes before negative publicity quashed the deal. The problem? The so-called minority-controlled company was a phony; and the front man for the purchaser coincidentally wrote the discretionary tax rule in question, providing tax breaks for minority companies when he worked in the Carter administration.[35]

Other issues confront the public daily, leading to the growth of what can only be described as cognitive dissonance. Taxpayers react with shock and horror at the lack of respect shown by government toward their pocketbooks. Consider the reaction that greeted the revelation that Energy Secretary Hazel O'Leary had hired a consulting firm to rank reporters on the basis of their coverage of energy issues. The expenditure was minimal—less than $200,000, or to put it in perspective, a nanosecond of what it takes to fund the Pentagon. But the specter of tax dollars funding this kind of public relations frippery provoked appropriate outrage. O'Leary also angered voters by taking dozens of aides on overseas trips at government expense.

Anger comes from frustration, or more specifically, from the growing realization that we are unable to control our immediate environment. After all, democracy rests on the principle that we the people undergird the political system. Phrases like "public support," "the popular will," and the "people's court" reflect the view that government should work for the people, not vice versa. Events from Vietnam to Hazel O'Leary's luxury travel prove that has not always been the case. The difference today is that people are more sophisticated about what constitutes legitimacy in government spending and have escalated their demands on political leaders to change their profligate ways. Politicians can no longer claim ignorance or the inability to act: It is unlikely, for example, that in this era two presidents could preside over a ten-year war without public support.

Nothing drives Americans to the ballot box and to the airwaves as much as their heightened awareness of where their tax money is being spent, an awareness that becomes especially acute as they feel the economic noose tightening around them. But this anger is healthy because people are expressing their will through the only channels open to them. The real danger to democracy comes when people give up—when their expectations of government become dashed by one disappointment after another and when the same forces that lead to anger result in apathy, evidenced by declining voter turnout.

## Political Anger: *A New Paradigm*

Political anger assumes greater importance when it is recognized and treated seriously as a precursor to revolution. The "emotional states of discontent, anxiety or anger," wrote Ted Robert Gurr, one of the preeminent scholars in the field, are what create "the revolutionary state of mind."[36] This consideration more than justifies the speedy and positive resolution of those issues most connected to public wrath, particularly those linked to deprivation: entitlements, budget allocations, political corruption. The quest to prevent social upheaval, to keep the nation wedded to evolutionary, not revolutionary, patterns, has occupied Americans since the founding of the republic, whose leaders knew all too well the factors that give birth to revolutions.

Over the ages political anger—that is, anger expressed through the political system—has always preceded revolution, although anger doesn't always lead to revolution. The knowledge that anger is so mercurial, that it occupies the penultimate stage before revolution, and that with little provocation it can be guided in the wrong direction has tipped the scales in favor of the prevailing view of anger as a negative force. Experience probably explains why most leaders adhere to the more common view of anger as a force for evil that will lead to revolution, violence, destruction, and aggression unless it is suppressed or ignored. One of the earliest proponents of the darker side of anger, the ancient Roman sage Seneca, called anger the "foe of reason," arguing that it would "cease and become more controllable if it finds that it must appear before a judge every day."[37] Plutarch also believed that anger only exacerbated a situation, that tempers are "more readily fanned into flame by what people in that state do and say."[38] The Old and New Testaments of the Bible reinforce the fear of anger; both books warn repeatedly against anger, defining it as an undesirable emotion to be curbed at all costs in the interest of peace. Influenced by literal interpretations of the Bible, the early colonists also viewed anger as socially deviant behavior, one of Satan's evils, which justified in their view their horrific treatment of women "witches," whom they identified by such characteristics as uncontrolled anger.[39]

The Bible relegated anger—along with greed, lust, pride, envy, sloth, and gluttony—to the loathsome company of the seven deadly sins. Remember that in the Old Testament, the Hebrews were denied entrance to the promised land because Moses lost his temper at God. Taking this view to heart thousands of years later, the psychologist B. F. Skinner sought to eliminate anger from his utopian community by the systematic training of emotions in young children. No wonder, given this long history, that so many politicians today are more concerned by the emotion of anger than the substance of what it signals.

Other ancient guides argue for assuaging anger through such devices as mediation, negotiation, and recognition. The same Bible of fire and brimstone that rails against expressing anger also calls for constant mediation, warning not to let the sun set on anger. Seneca presaged the passive-resistance approach, calling the "mark of true greatness" the ability "not to notice that you have received a blow."[40] Jesus also preached in favor of turning the other cheek and loving one's enemies, a pattern later used to great effect by Mahatma Gandhi in India and Dr. Martin Luther King Jr. in the United States.

St. Thomas Aquinas defended the "legitimacy and usefulness of anger," pointing out that even though scholars tended to juxtapose anger and love, anger's opposite was really indifference.[41] To be angry you have to care; in other words, anger in this mode precedes creative thinking, an individualistic process very much in evidence today. Flooded with information, Americans find they are no longer slaves to long-held myths about government: that it will always protect the individual, be fair, and represent progress. Court TV has exposed the advantages offered by the judicial system to those with the money to hire superior defense teams; the plethora of national and specialized news shows have revealed in living color the acts of rogue cops planting evidence, beating and torturing suspects, or reaching too quickly for the trigger at Ruby Ridge and Waco. Ironically, widespread anger over these events shows the American people as more respectful of civil liberties than their leaders, and as more willing to oppose these flagrant abuses in the system.

By recalling the noble rage of Achilles, Aquinas offered another view of anger that virtually justifies revolution given the right circumstances: knowing which side to select between just and unjust wars. Aquinas vindicated the "rightness of revenge," believed revenge to be the central feature of anger, and called the "failure to use anger under just circumstances . . . a sin of omission."[42] Depending on the context, this is a theory that could be subject to considerable abuse; after all, how often do leaders or citizens ever admit to fighting unjust wars? (Only afterward, as in postwar France, do you find the kind of selective memory in which everyone recalled himself as a member of the Resistance, fighting the Nazi-controlled Vichy government.)

In a democracy elections can be considered the political equivalent of revenge: The elections of 1992 and 1994 both expressed vengeful [toward government] and punitive [toward politicians] themes, which continued into the primary and general elections of 1996. The Bill of Rights guarantees of free elections, free speech, free press, and the freedom to petition have provided democracies like the United States ample outlets for political anger that act to prevent full-scale revolution. The writ and rights of *habeas corpus,* with us since the time of the Magna Carta, allow citizens to rest secure in the knowledge that they can engage in lawful protest activities without fearing illegal arrest. When legislators in the 104th Congress attempted to restrict the rights of *habeas corpus* in the interest of speedier trials, Senator Daniel Patrick Moynihan (D–N.Y.) protested that if "I had to live in a country which had *habeas corpus* but not free elections, or vice versa, I would take *habeas corpus* every time."[43] The restrictions were ultimately incorporated into the antiterrorism bill passed by the 104th Congress and signed into law by President Clinton in April 1996.

The unique character of American democracy with its emphasis on individual rights of protest explains in large part why the United States has not reacted to political anger as forcefully as have other cultures and other nations. American leaders have relaxed in the knowledge that their own unique democracy has provided ample channels for angry citizens to blow off steam without resorting to more anomic forms of behavior; one exception was the Civil War, which erupted into a full-scale revolution when normal outlets no longer worked.

Charles Maier argues that the reasons for anger are deeper: They are rooted in "civic discontent" or "moral crisis," which reveals a "broad distrust of political representatives regardless of ideology." How else, he asks, "should one make sense of the malaise that currently sours public opinion in the countries of Europe, in Japan and North America." In other words, basic economic needs are being met, while others, in the realm of spiritual and community needs, are not.[44]

The gap between political anger and public violence has narrowed recently with such antigovernment, cataclysmic events as the Oklahoma City bombing, as well as the growing dangers attached to what used to be regarded as the rights of peaceful protest. "The bishops lit the fuse of anger [on the choice issue] and the fire's gone all the way to the top," noted Ann Lewis, recalling her experience as vice president of policy for Planned Parenthood. "When have we ever debated violence as a policy strategy? That is what is different today," she added, referring to the incident involving the murder by an antiabortion activist of Dr. David Gunn. Successive bombings of abortion clinics have indicated that passions on this issue have not abated; on the contrary, the volatility of reproductive choice as a bipolar issue continues to worsen, as indicated by increased violence and by the growing dearth of clinics.

The antigovernment character inherent in today's political anger includes all the elements on which students of revolutionary societies have long focused: the plethora of "enemies"; the need to scapegoat; the increase in terrorism and violent acts from within society; and the widespread protest movements, rigid in their goals, unwilling to compromise, and in a permanent state of resistance with no place to go. Political theorist Harry Eckstein, analyzing the etiology of internal wars, differentiates between "precipitants" and "preconditions," some of which seem roughly parallel to our own polity: the disruption of political legitimacy and social harmony, some blockage in channels of social mobility, and rapid changes in demographics.[45]

Scholars of American political rhetoric, most notably Murray Edelman, have linked the power of words to political action; in the 1990s, Edelman's theories have seen even fuller expression. He links fear, confusion, powerlessness, blame, and anger, as well as the need to create heroes and enemies: "Political opinions help 'externalize' unresolved inner problems," particularly in times of depression or anxiety.[46]

Eric Hoffer identifies the unifying agents for discontented groups: hatred, imitation, persuasion and coercion, action and suspicion. In other words, "discontent by itself does not invariably create a desire for change. Other factors have to be present before discontent turns into disaffection."[47] All of these other factors are preconditions for organizing the emotion of anger that leads to what recent analysts would call the kind of "empowerment" that leads to positive or negative change.

An important dimension to anger involves an examination of the era of postmaterialism, discussed by Paul R. Abramson and Ronald Inglehart. Economic security in industrialized nations, they argue, has led to a set of new goals, in which "an emphasis on economic security gradually fades, and universal but often latent needs for belonging, esteem, and the realization of individual intellectual potential becomes increasingly prominent." In order to understand current social movements and emotions like anger in politics, it is necessary to understand the newer sets of needs that propel groups to organized action.[48]

Today we need a new paradigm that differentiates the many manifestations of anger in current political life from its cousins: anomie, apathy, revolution, and violence. All of these relatives remain ready to unite with anger, which can erupt at any time; anomie and apathy lead to anger, and violence and revolution can develop from it. Scholars of international politics have always paid special attention to anger and its relationship to revolution; now that anger occupies such a growing portion of the domestic spotlight, it is time to bring the different indicators and etiology of political anger into sharper focus. U.S. political leaders have taken particular notice in the 1990s because "the anger factor" has upset the apple cart of political power. Their concern: When and at what point does anger impact on the political process? To answer this question, they must focus on the mobilization of political anger and its impact on elections, political parties, national movements, and legislation. Perhaps this explains why the defection of the white male drew such an inordinate amount of attention after the 1992 and 1994 elections. Women and minorities also organize, join parties, and raise money; but their financial clout and—in the case of minorities—voting rates still fall well behind those of white men. What factors have led up to these pockets of anger? Which new groups will enter the fray? What will the future bring in terms of the capacity to deal with political anger? Will the political system's usual coping mechanisms prove adequate for absorbing new layers of anger from all the groups defined by gender, ethnicity, and race that fall outside the white male circle of concern? And finally, will the two major political parties as well as the political system be sufficiently flexible to absorb the crushing demands emanating from the questions of entitlement, deprivation, and the allocation of resources?

Political anger has affected the polity in new and different ways in the 1990s, indicating that it will grow before it declines or becomes absorbed into the mainstream. The steady erosion of entitlements, the new patterns of deprivation and blame feeding into the political system, and the antigovernment philosophy taking hold, all spell a new and very different era before us. Many of the outlets that U.S. democracy has traditionally provided for protest have now been capped and are in jeopardy. Thus fewer positive channels exist for the explosive anger that characterizes the political system today, and new dilemmas have arisen for leaders who must cope with its consequences. No wonder Colin Powell declined to plunge into this uncertain and volatile environment to run for president.

# 3

················································································

# The Visible Ceiling

## *Economic Uncertainty and Political Anger*

The problem is that some Americans are getting rich,
but most Americans are getting nowhere. It is like the
taxidermist and the veterinarian opening up shop
together. Their slogan: Either way, you get your dog
back.

—Representative David Bonior (D–Mich.)

**W**HY NOW? Why are people so angry when they've never had it so good? Why is the country experiencing the worst tax revolt since the Boston Tea Party when Americans are paying the lowest taxes of any industrialized country on earth? Are the problems getting worse, or is the awareness of them more acute? Many political leaders and economists find the anger of the "anxious class" grossly disproportionate to reality; after all, Americans are living better than ever, they say, and a family's inability to upgrade the Jeep Cherokee hardly constitutes what you would call financial hardship.

If you believe in the magic of numbers, they look remarkably healthy. By 1998 economic indicators literally glowed with health, growth, and stability:

- Unemployment had fallen to 4.2 percent.
- The deficit had been reduced by 63 percent during Clinton's first term, and the budget was almost in balance by the middle of his second term.
- 13.7 million new jobs had been created.
- The median U.S. household income was $35,492 by 1996, according to the Bureau of the Census.
- The prime rate, at 8.5 percent, was the lowest it had been in years.
- Inflation was way down.
- The United States was designated by international organizations as the most competitive of all the industrialized economies.
- The Dow Jones average had surged to the 9000 mark, although it dropped later in the year below 7600 in a massive market "correction."
- The nation's economic growth rate had climbed to 4.2 percent.

For political scientists, such figures have long served as surefire predictors of political optimism, partisan vitality, and certain victory for the president in power. A prime rate that hovered around the 20 percent mark in 1980, the last year of the presidency of Jimmy Carter, contributed mightily to Ronald Reagan's defeat of a sitting president. Does that mean voters appreciate today's low inflation and low prime interest rates or that the Democrats can count on holding on to the White House well into the next century? Don't bet the ranch on it. Party leaders from both sides of the aisle no longer take any of these economic indicators for granted and recall the anger of the first half of the 1990s over economic conditions as the worst conundrum of the decade. They know that any fluctuation in these figures could trigger comparable results at the polls, as voter expectations rise and fall with the Dow Jones figures. Moreover, not all anger is attributable to general economic indicators; other factors, some of them not economic, have a role as well. But when political anger is generated from economic causes, usually it has to do with how individuals or groups are faring, rather than how society as a whole is performing.

## The End of Optimism

Well, what about "It's the economy, stupid," the slogan that dominated the first Clinton campaign for president? Why are so many Americans angry despite low inflation and low unemployment? And where will the disparity between the deteriorating condition of individual lives and the rosy scenarios Americans have been conditioned to expect lead us politically? The fifty-year-old who has just lost his job at IBM doesn't really care about the prime interest rate. The Dow Jones Industrial Average may surge to well above the 9000 mark, as it did in early 1998, but many Americans felt that they were not reaping the benefits, even though their pension plans were doing very well on the bullish market. President Clinton recognized this in his 1995 State of the Union address when he admitted that the "rising tide has not lifted all boats." In successive years, however, he emphasized the figures that buttressed his administration's achievements, particularly the declining unemployment rate and the balanced budget.

The real dilemma for Americans is that the numbers no longer mean what they used to mean. Or perhaps we are just looking at the wrong numbers. In fact, the figures used by politicians to tout their achievements fall into aggregate categories. The unemployment rate, for example, covers the entire nation but doesn't probe into the reasons a fifty-year-old "lifetime" employee has lost his job at IBM. If he hasn't reported to the unemployment office, he probably isn't even factored into those numbers, which partially explains why they are so low.

These "macroeconomic" figures fail woefully when it comes to explaining to individuals and their families why some people benefit while others suffer. The unemployment rate may be the lowest it has been in years, but tens of thousands of middle-aged Americans have been thrown out of work thanks to downsizing, outsourcing, exporting jobs abroad, and other recent phenomena loosely attributed to the "postindustrial world." Are there holes in the statistics, or have these workers restored their lost jobs with "replacement" jobs? Actually, both. Many have supplanted their lost jobs with new jobs—another reason the unemployment rate looks so bright—but the problem is that most of the new jobs pay lower wages and offer far fewer benefits.

The tide may be rising, but more people are navigating in rowboats while others ford the same waters in yachts. In this climate, bipolar issues such as term limits would lose much of their steam were it not for the underlying motif driving political anger in this generation: the sharp dichotomy between *economic setbacks* and *genuine progress*.

One of the greatest myths sustaining the nation—that incomes will rise along with economic opportunities for those who work hard—was cruelly shattered in the past decade. For the first time in history people see the ceiling, according to startling poll results first reported in *U.S. News & World Report*'s 1994 election-day cover story, headlined "Why Are You So Angry?"[1]

The newly visible ceiling spells the "end of optimism," particularly for so many middle- and lower-middle-class families forced to work two to three jobs to pay the bills. No wonder 75 percent agreed with the statement that "middle class families can't make ends meet" and 57 percent regarded the economy as "stagnating." Two-thirds of those surveyed worried that their children wouldn't live as well as they did, and a majority believed the American dream was now out of reach for most families.[2] Most respondents did not see the vaunted economic recovery showing up in their household budgets, and by 1995 signs were beginning to appear that indicated people were beginning to accept the economic ceiling as a condition unlikely to change.

The *Wall Street Journal* identified this group as "have-less whites," referring to the vast number of Americans who have suffered a 12 percent decline in real income over the past two decades and who have clearly not shared in the nation's rising productivity. The *Journal* accused the liberal elites of ignoring this group, reminiscent of the congressional leaders who neglected to share their own focus groups [on political anger] with fellow Democrats before the 1994 elections.[3] No wonder the polls showed middle-class voters expressing recurring disappointment and frustration and a majority of them believing themselves in a recession long after the recession was over. As expected, their mental state also worsened as time with their families and leisure activities decreased.

The most striking change is that Americans' expectations are changing: Today, many middle- and lower-middle-class people expect that they will have to work longer hours to make ends meet; they may even have to work two or three jobs to pay medical expenses that are no longer covered, or retire later

The truth about new jobs. © 1995 MacNelly—Chicago Tribune. Reprinted with permission.

than they had planned. Most important, they no longer rely on government to provide security; why should they, when serious policy discussions were underway by 1998 to privatize Social Security? At least three-quarters of the nation's younger generation of workers believe that social security will not be around when they are ready to collect it.

While the rich are getting richer and the poor, poorer, the middle class tries to find its niche and discovers that it is off the charts. How come? Members of the middle class have worked hard, studied hard, and heeded all the mantras of the 1980s: free trade, free markets, deregulation, and privatization. Still, they remain behind the curve. Or their children have fallen behind the curve. No wonder they are angry. And they vote.

The current anger attributed to the middle class comes primarily from the fear of slippage. "You are talking about the guy making $32,000 threatened by the guy making $18,000," asserted a Democratic staffer on Capitol Hill. "He knows the pie isn't getting any bigger." Blaming the boss also no longer works as well as it did when unions wielded more power; in fact, globalization and technology have both forced union membership down, from its peak in 1968, when 28 percent of the labor force was unionized, to 14.5 percent in 1997. Today, when middle managers or blue-collar workers lose their jobs they blame government even though when pressed they can not think of what specific role government played in influencing decisions by Xerox or Mobil or IBM to downsize their workforces or move factories to Mexico.

As it has in each era, improved technology has led to wrenching job losses at all levels of employment. "When I started working for AT&T more than 30 years ago, we used to get sent off to training to learn the math, learn the calculus, learn the logarithms, learn all about electronics. There's no need to do that anymore, because the software will allow the kinds of testing we did by hand to be done by computers," said Jim Irvine, a skilled technician.[4] Technology has replaced telephone operators, engineers, and a host of other telecommunications workers, and globalization has moved the production of telephone equipment to low-wage countries. Unfortunately, comparable policy and management innovations have not occurred at the same time to solve the problem of displaced workers caught in the vise of change.

"Anger stems from economic decline over a period of years," recalled former senator Jim Sasser (D–Tenn.), who reaped a whirlwind of voter anger in his losing 1994 campaign. "It is mainly blue collar . . . trade union members, people who are unemployed having lost their assembly line jobs. Now they are doing crummy service jobs. In my campaign it was anger at Washington. They blame government because they have been conditioned over the years to look to government for solutions. Government is just coming up with the wrong answers."

Specifically, people blame government spending decisions and high taxes. A *Business Week*–Harris poll in late spring 1995 found that 73 percent of Americans blamed government spending for stagnant incomes; 61 percent also blamed high taxes. Stagnant wages led two-thirds to conclude the American dream was harder to achieve than it was a decade ago.[5]

A year later, in 1996, the *New York Times* published a series based on a national survey that addressed the question of why people were so insecure in a period of relative economic prosperity. The data revealed the basis of what forms the economic disconnect: The number of people concerned about their own jobs had not changed one iota, despite the rising number (67 percent) that believed the economy was improving. Why? Because widespread layoffs were no longer an abstraction; despite a booming economy, three-quarters of all American households have witnessed a friend, relative, family member, or neighbor lose a job. In other words, downsizings had become a way of life, with almost as many people losing jobs as fast as the economy was creating them.[6]

When the polls reveal figures that speak to the loss of control over the nation's political sovereignty or national destiny, they also reflect the feelings of individual loss of control that come from the lowered economic ceiling. If you have lost your "lifetime" job with IBM, that colors your whole view of society as a much bleaker place than it was before. The decline of American optimism about the economy also conveys the unpalatable reality that America might well have entered a new era that economist Jeffrey Madrick calls an "end to affluence." Although he agrees that America is "still the most productive and richest nation per capita in the world," the nation seems "unable to marshall these advantages." Otherwise, we would not be facing the lowest growth rate in recent history, as well as "lost jobs, falling and stagnating wages, eroding markets, closed factories, rising level[s] of poverty, insecure pensions, and reduced home ownership."[7]

The nation's political leadership responded with alacrity to what their pollsters told them had led to such widespread public anger: taxes and the burgeoning deficit. Deficit reduction became a jewel in the president's crown, and by 1998 President Clinton confidently predicted that by the millennium the deficit would be down to zero. But other, scarier figures lurked at the peripheries of the public radar screen, including a national debt of $5 trillion and a rising trade deficit.

Also in response to public anger, Clinton fulfilled a 1992 campaign pledge to change "welfare as we know it," ending the decades-long attempts by both Democrats and Republicans to reform the nation's obsolete welfare system. His welfare bill, which passed handily, was criticized by the left as too draconian and by the right as too little, too late. Although the bill created conditions of extreme hardship for many welfare recipients, the legislation fulfilled its goal of shifting the welfare problem to the states.

## The Wage Gap

The economic upheaval facing the nation over jobs, taxes, and global change pales against the yawning earnings gap between rich and poor, a development that is way out of sync with the nation's bedrock tenet of ongoing economic progress. Americans in this winner-take-all society can no longer take their individual economic growth for granted, wrote the highly respected Urban Institute scholar Isabel V. Sawhill:

> Between 1973 and 1992, the incomes of the wealthiest one-fifth of the population increased by 11% while the poorest one-fifth saw their incomes decline by 13%. The result is a widening gap between those at the bottom and those at the top. . . . The postwar baby boom generation is the first to have not done better than their parents [and] the prospects for the next century are not encouraging.[8] (See Figure 3.1.)

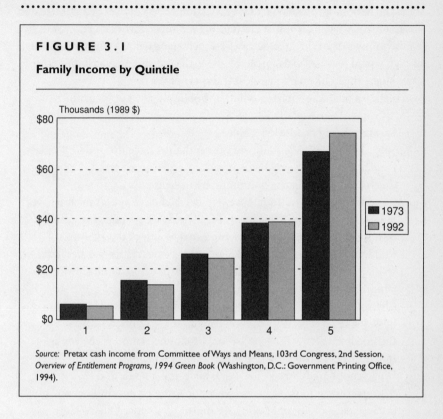

**FIGURE 3.1**

**Family Income by Quintile**

Thousands (1989 $)

1973
1992

Source: Pretax cash income from Committee of Ways and Means, 103rd Congress, 2nd Session, *Overview of Entitlement Programs, 1994 Green Book* (Washington, D.C.: Government Printing Office, 1994).

America has emerged as the only industrialized country where the income gap has actually grown wider, and it has grown significantly, particularly for working-class Americans, according to the Federal Reserve Bank.[9] Additional awards from the dubious-achievement category designate the United States as the most "stratified of industrial nations," wrote *New York Times* economics reporter Keith Bradsher, with "economic inequality on the rise since the 1970s and child poverty four times worse than the average Western European nation."[10] Even when compared with class-conscious Great Britain, America emerges unfavorably, a rude awakening that contradicts the nation's image of itself as an egalitarian, progressive society: In the United States 1 percent of households with a net worth of over $2.3 million control nearly 40 percent of the nation's wealth; in Great Britain, the richest 1 percent own about 18 percent of the wealth, down from 59 percent in the 1920s.[11]

A microcosm of this exaggerated "banana republic" pattern was reported in a study designating Manhattan as the county with the greatest income disparity in the nation, surpassed only by a collection of seventy households situated "near a former leper colony in Hawaii."[12] Even those fortunate enough to live on the sunny side of the income gap find their standard of living eroding, such as highly paid professionals forced by the high cost and unavailability of child care to take their children to work at least part of the day.[13]

A plethora of studies bolsters what the public already knows instinctively:

- Earnings have become less stable.
- Since 1970, real wages adjusted for inflation have dropped by more than 20 percent.
- Chances of escaping the "bottom" have decreased.
- Conditions at the "bottom" have worsened while people at the top have noticeably improved their lot in life. The top 1 percent, for example, owns over 60 percent of the newly created wealth of the 1980s.
- Children from poor families in Sweden and at least fifteen other industrialized countries are more likely to prosper than children of poor families in the United States.
- Chances of a young male's attaining middle-class status by age thirty have dwindled regardless of race, parents' income, or education.
- Income inequality has become more pronounced among the young.
- Individual bankruptcies have substantially increased.
- High school graduates in the 1960s were still able to find high-paying manufacturing jobs, whereas today, the same group finds fewer jobs because technology and trade have drastically reduced factory jobs.
- Median income adjusted for inflation is declining. In 1979, for example, the median household income totaled $38,250. By the mid-1990s, that income dropped over $1,000.
- Productivity is rising at about twice the rate of pay and benefits.

Libertarians such as William Niskanen of the Cato Institute claim that Americans should not worry about rising wage inequality. He argues that the income gap has nothing to do with government policies and that the yawning gap will eventually narrow and bring about long-term growth for the economy. The reason: Such income distribution, however inequitable, leads to enhanced growth and less debt passed on to future generations.[14] (See Figure 3.2.)

Another contrarian view comes from Robert J. Samuelson, who argued in *The Good Life and Its Discontents* that Americans' sense of entitlement has led to social angst and that by historical standards, we have never had it so good:

## FIGURE 3.2

### The Young Face Tougher Times and the Poor Move Up More Slowly

Percentage of men who had earned a middle-class income before turning 30 in each period.[a]

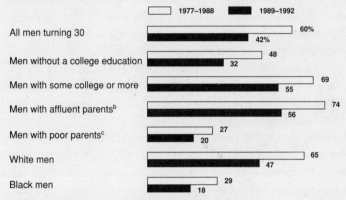

| | 1977–1988 | 1989–1992 |

All men turning 30 — 60% / 42%

Men without a college education — 48 / 32

Men with some college or more — 69 / 55

Men with affluent parents[b] — 74 / 56

Men with poor parents[c] — 27 / 20

White men — 65 / 47

Black men — 29 / 18

[a] At least $23,042 in 1993 dollars, or twice the poverty level for a family of three.
[b] Household income equal to four times the poverty line or more.
[c] Household income equal to one and a half times the poverty line or less.

The poor are more likely to stay poor and the affluent are more likely to stay affluent.

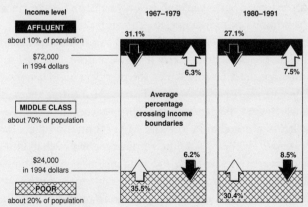

*Note:* All figures are for household after-tax income, including wages, salaries, and some government assistance programs like food stamps.

*Sources:* Greg Duncan, Northwestern University; Timothy Smeeding, Syracuse University.

"We have achieved unprecedented prosperity. . . . We are healthier, work at less exhausting jobs and live longer than ever." So what is the problem? "By now, it's obvious that we can't have it all. . . . By making more promises than it can keep, government creates distrust. . . . Instability and excess are inherent in business."[15]

Others argue that nothing can alter the trend toward income inequality, because inexorable forces propel the nation toward a fate over which it has no control: economic decline. America's trajectory spells doom for its unique political culture of equity and progress, in part because of what Michael Lind calls the phenomenon of "Brazilianization"—a new and permanent oligarchy that monopolizes power, income, and resources at the expense of the poor and middle class.[16] Some counter this argument by insisting that there are vast differences between the United States and Brazil: in the United States a rising stock market affects the pensions and purses of a broad swathe of the population, not just a thin layer of elites.

Most agree, however, that our rapidly changing cultural patterns have produced even more poverty, especially among young children, who have suffered disproportionately from altered family patterns, namely the dramatic increase in one-parent families and out-of-wedlock births. "The trend away from marriage accounted for about half the increase in child income inequality and more than the entire rise in child poverty rates," wrote Robert Lerman of the Urban Institute.[17] Again, the United States fares poorly in comparison with other industrialized nations, many of which have experienced the same cultural trends; the United States ranks above only Israel and Ireland in a comparison of the condition of children in eighteen nations.

Children and their parents also suffer greatly from America's trend toward declining public benefits, particularly if they are poor. The actress Whoopi Goldberg, once a welfare mom, lobbied the president and Democratic members of the Senate on behalf of welfare benefits. Exhorting them all to stop GOP welfare "reform," she generously credited government help for turning around her life. "I'm proud of it," she said. "The country was there for me, and the system worked for me."[18] She knew from experience what all the studies say, that child poverty rises with the widening income gap and plunging benefit levels and that even in Italy, where the median income is much lower than in the United States, children are better off because of free or low-cost health care.[19]

Clinton's former secretary of labor, Robert Reich, called the widening income gap "our greatest remaining challenge," that is, if we intend to bridge the gulf between the nation's macroeconomic prosperity and the "home economics" by which people live. The earnings of most Americans, he acknowledged, are "either stuck in the mud or sinking," with millions of white- and blue-collar workers joined together in a "common category [of] frayed-collar workers in gold-plated times."[20]

Americans could endure the most dire poverty if they felt they were making some progress toward climbing to the top of the pyramid. They have even been conditioned to accept the most exaggerated symbols of the earnings gap. After all, movie stars always made astronomical salaries compared to average folks, CEOs drew salaries many times that of their workers, and authors with the widespread appeal of Danielle Steel invariably drew advances in the neighborhood of $12 million. The optimistic nature of American capitalism explains why so many Americans buy lottery tickets despite overwhelming odds against winning the jackpot and also why a Marxist movement never took root in this country. People cling to the belief that even if they labored for a lifetime in a factory, their children could one day become rock stars or investment bankers or CEOs; if they were lucky, those offspring could really hit the jackpot, like Disney's Michael Eisner, whose 1993 pay package totaled $203 million. In fact, CEO pay continues to skyrocket, increasing to new heights every year. In 1996, CEOs from the thirty companies with the largest announced layoffs "saw their salary, bonuses, and long-term compensation actually increase by 67.3 percent. Among 365 major companies, CEO pay increased by 39 percent; if options were included, the figure soared to 54 percent. In contrast, during the same period, factory workers' pay increased by only 3 percent."[21] The absence of a rigid class system in America helped perpetuate the hope that anyone's child could achieve the status of royalty, American-style, in politics, entertainment, or business. What is different today is the winner-take-all philosophy, which glorifies inequality, reduces hope, and pits groups against each other in the struggle for a diminishing pool of resources.[22]

## The Jobs Dilemma

The public isn't stupid, as elected officials often learn to their grief. You can fool people for a while, but they eventually figure things out, particularly when they are being manipulated by phony figures. Take the 13.7 million private-sector jobs created between 1992 and 1998.[23] Why are some people angry about that otherwise upbeat figure? Because voters know that with the decline of manufacturing, many of those jobs are in the nonsupervisory category and many pay lower wages than the jobs they lost, that they are working harder for less, and that benefits to which they have long been accustomed—such as health care and stable pensions—have become either sharply reduced or nonexistent.[24] If we follow the psychohistorical pattern of anger, economic conditions provide a perfect trajectory, moving from entitlement to deprivation to political anger.

"No wonder people are angry," asserted David Bonior (D–Mich.), minority whip of the House. "We were telling them we were creating jobs, yet [polls showed] 60% of the people thought they were in a recession right before the [1994] election. If the stockholders are happy, everything is *not* O.K. It's like the taxidermist and the veterinarian opening up shop together. Their slogan: Either way, you get your dog back. The problem isn't that some Americans are getting rich but that most Americans are getting nowhere."

"Where have all the good jobs gone?" asks Robert Kuttner, coeditor of *The American Prospect* and the author of the classic work *The End of Laissez-Faire*. Identifying the culprits as technology, global trade, deregulation, and weak unions, Kuttner concludes that the shift from factory to service-sector jobs has left us with "growing part-time and temporary hires, low-wage jobs in services, especially retailing, and dismal starting wages." The Bureau of Labor statistics confirm this view; the occupations that generated the most new jobs over the past decade were fast-food worker, janitor, and retail sales clerk. Better jobs in management follow the 50–50 rule: If you are over fifty or making over $50,000, your job is in jeopardy.[25]

The anxiety and anger generated by the raft of mergers, acquisitions, and downsizings have hit the electorate like a cyclone. Like Nero's Rome, the revelers celebrate without thinking of the future or of those suffering outside the palace gates. They revel in what they call "corporate efficiency": Stocks climb higher, shareholders are happy, lawyers and investment bankers draw millions out of the deals, and out-of-work CEOs parachute gently into gilded retirement. Even convicted felon Michael Milken, barred from the securities business for life, was to be rewarded with a fee of $50 million for giving advice to corporate giants involved in the Time Warner–Turner Broadcasting merger. Only the families of the fired workers—the detritus of tough love in the marketplace—grieve about the future. Little mention was made of the 12,000 people slated to lose their jobs when Chemical Bank and Chase Manhattan merged or the 40,000 workers from AT&T who found themselves out of work through "restructuring" or the 3,000 who joined the unemployment lines after Colgate Palmolive closed a few of its plants.

Separately, the numbers don't look like much, but in the aggregate, they add up to substantial job losses. In the first nine months of 1995, over 300,000 jobs

Representative David Bonior (D–Michigan), Minority Whip of the House. Photo by Pamela Hazen; courtesy of *The Hill*.

were lost, according to the outplacement firm of Challenger, Gray & Christmas.[26] Frank Woolsey of the accounting firm of Deloitte & Touche predicted that in retail banking, 450,000 jobs would disappear, the result of new mergers as well as the consumer and the industry's increased reliance on electronic banking.[27] Similar horizons loom into view for other merging industries such as transportation, health care, pharmaceuticals, consumer goods, defense, entertainment, and media. Downsizing in the defense industry, prodded by cuts in the procurement budget, was capped by the merger of Martin Marietta and the Lockheed Corporation (now called Lockheed Martin). Following their corporate parents, unions have also begun to merge: The United Rubber Workers, for example, has joined forces with the steelworkers' union.

Public dissonance reaches a new level of cacophony when voters hear they are being fired at the same time the economy is hunky-dory or when they learn that the Dow fell 171 points after the Labor Department in spring 1996 announced rising employment figures—Wall Street's reaction to good news! Unlike other periods in history when job losses reflected a weak economy, today the nation is experiencing job losses simultaneously with an expanding economy. The downsizing by AT&T, which eliminated more than 13 percent of its 300,000 member staff, sent shock waves throughout the nation. It was the fourth largest downsizing in recent memory, following IBM's 60,000 layoffs in 1993, General Motors 74,000 layoffs in 1991, and Sears Roebuck's 50,000 layoffs in 1993.

Downsizings continued throughout the late 1990s, with company leaders blaming pressures from Wall Street and global competition for the loss of jobs. The biggest layoff occurred right before Christmas in 1997 when Eastman Kodak added 6,600 job cuts to the 10,000 announced the month before. Previously known as the Great Yellow Father in Rochester because of its paternalistic policies, Kodak expects to shave off 10 percent of its work force by 1999; the company had already eliminated 40,000 jobs since 1983. George Fisher, Kodak's CEO, defended his actions by saying that they spared the company further cuts of up to 20,000 people, and proclaimed that the current "restructuring," combined with a reduction of $150 million from its research budget, would save the company at least $1 billion. Kodak pointed to its loss of market share to Fuji, a Japanese company that undercut Kodak's prices abroad and successfully fended off Kodak's unfair trade competition case. The strength of the dollar also hurt Kodak's sales abroad.[28]

Layoffs continued into 1998, with 2,250 job cuts scheduled at the Chase Manhattan Corporation, the nation's largest bank, and the closure of eleven plants in four states by Levi Strauss. Plans to eliminate yet another 2,250 workers at Chase accompanied plans to freeze hiring and to abandon the use of management consultants—a savings of $70 million a year. Analysts blamed Chase's problems on its overexposure to the instability of Asian markets, the questionable soundness of some of its loans, and pressures from its new partner, the Chemical Banking Corporation.[29]

Job losses of such truly massive proportions wreak havoc on society and the economy. Why, then, are they routinely greeted by applause from Wall Street with rising stock prices following each layoff announcement and by fat rewards for the CEOs wielding the ax? AT&T's layoffs, for example, followed record profits posted at $4.7 billion. Called "corporate killers" and "hit men" by a *Newsweek* cover story in February 1996, the CEOs of these companies drew salaries that even by conservative estimates would be called stratospheric: Robert Allen, the CEO of AT&T, earned $3,362,000 in 1996; Louis Gerstner of IBM, $2,625,000; Robert Stempel of General Motors, $1,000,000; and Edward Brennan of Sears, $3,075,000.[30]

Acting in their own defense, the CEOs argue that what seems an abdication of their responsibility to their workforce is really an act of survival; if they didn't chop jobs now, the companies would risk eventual extinction. Despite the problems, the trend continues. The American Management Association (AMA) found that over 50 percent of the firms it surveyed—representing one-quarter of all U.S. employees—were reducing the number of their workers. Even highly profitable firms cut staffs to satisfy shareholder demands and trendy notions of sound corporate governance.[31] The AMA also found, incidentally, that morale and productivity suffered drastically with downsizing and that companies that reduced their workforces tended to repeat the experience with even deeper cuts the following year. Plummeting morale and a palpable sense of fear grips the workplace as employees wait for the next ax to fall.

Even the government, long viewed as the employer of last resort, joined the march toward "cutback management." In the National Performance Review, led by Vice President Al Gore, one of the strategies to reinvent government involved the elimination of 272,000 "unnecessary" jobs. How did the panel arrive at this number? The government needed to show it was sharing the pain with the private sector, admitted one of the plan's architects, Hale Champion, at a Washington meeting of the National Academy of Public Administration.

## International Realities and Political Anxieties

Numbers are especially tricky in the global arena, depending on which figures you believe; some are simply pulled out of a hat. Let's take the hat tricks first and look at jobs. No government agency or private economist knows within even a simple margin of error just how many jobs have been lost or found by the internationalization of the economy, although figures for both sides are offered in abundance. The most recent figures support the view that more jobs have been lost than gained in the short run as a result of NAFTA (North American Free Trade Agreement, the major trade pact between the United States, Mexico, and Canada), passed in 1993 despite great opposition from labor unions. Republican presidential candidate Pat Buchanan claimed that 300,000 jobs were lost in the first two years that NAFTA was in effect; the president and his Democratic and Republican allies who voted for NAFTA in Congress defend their decision on the basis of all the jobs that were created in spite of the 1995 peso crisis.[32]

Public wrath also depends on which numbers matter to the public and which do not. Unlike the budget deficit, international trade did not provoke much reaction—despite the enormous impact of U.S. trade policy on the public—until the candidacy of Pat Buchanan. His message of economic nationalism—connecting the issue of job loss to trade policy—drew votes and attention during the 1996 Republican primaries. "We didn't plan it this way. I didn't realize that jobs and trade and what makes America work would become a big issue in the last days of this campaign," admitted Robert Dole, woefully, the night before Buchanan won the New Hampshire primary. "Where has he been?" retorted Buchanan.[33] Stung by the numbers, Dole and the other Republican candidates quickly began discussing international trade issues in the hope of stealing some of Buchanan's thunder.

Polls seem to conflict on voters' views of international trade: Americans by a 3 to 1 margin favored tariffs against countries that ran a trade surplus with the United States, according to a poll conducted by the firm of EPIC/MRA Mitchell. But other polls reflecting consumer interests indicate just the opposite, that Americans are unwilling to pay higher prices for imports even in the interest of national sovereignty.[34]

Public opinion may also change as corporations, political leaders, and unions begin to tell the public the truth. Corporations, for example, are finally beginning to admit publicly the impact of trade policy on their decisions: For the first time since passage of the trade treaties, a major company blamed NAFTA and GATT for its decision to close six plants and lay off 3,200 workers. "What you're seeing is the cumulative impact of NAFTA and GATT," said a spokesman for Fruit of the Loom, the nation's largest underwear manufacturer. Nearly 100,000 textile workers lost their jobs in the first nine months of 1995 as the result of agreements lowering the barriers to textile imports.[35]

The early returns indicate that globalization has engendered a new form of anger that relates to the public's feelings of injustice, betrayal, and blame. Angry Americans feel the effects of downward spiraling, revealed most vividly when they find themselves compared with their global trading partners and allies; reports may call the United States competitive, but few individual citizens see the benefits at close range. Instead, they feel cheated when they realize that although Americans pay lower taxes than any other industrialized country, their health and education benefits fall well below those of their counterparts. They also know that the jobs lost through trade agreements and downsizings will never be recovered, that most of the newly created jobs touted by political leaders who supported NAFTA and GATT pay lower wages than the jobs that were lost, and that they are now working harder for less. Ironically, the issue of jobs has typically been ignored by trade negotiators anxious to reach closure in international agreements; in NAFTA, for example, jobs (together with the environment) were dealt with in side agreements and not in the body of the treaty.

A startling shift in the political climate in the area of international trade rivaled El Niño's impact on rainfall. It should not have surprised the president, who won NAFTA in 1993 by only sixteen votes and the U.S. entry into the World Trade Organization several years later, but in 1997 Congress did an about-face on trade and reversed a half century of abdicating trade policy to the White House. "Fast-track," a bill that would have given the president virtual carte blanche on trade agreements, was never brought to the floor, since its sponsors realized they were 30–35 votes short of winning. At any other time in history, "fast-track" would have sailed through Congress, but this time public pressure on the ravages of globalism finally reached Congress—much to the consternation of America's trading partners. Increased union strength helped convey voters' concerns and finally "released the anger within the liberal wing of the Democratic Party toward the centrist, 'New Democratic' politics of President Clinton and his Capitol Hill allies."[36]

Rising amounts of PAC money from organized labor also helped; increased PAC contributions to Democratic candidates rose from $29.8 million in 1992 to $37.3 million in 1996. With the defeat in 1994 of so many moderate Democrats, the Gephardt wing of the party had grown stronger; in addition, since its standard-bearer, Representative Richard Gephardt (D–Miss.), harbored aspirations to run for president in the year 2000, he was more than ready to promote his longtime interest in trade issues in the legislative arena.

Confusion over the economy and its uncertain impacts for the future bear a greater relationship to political anger than any other factor. Fearful of being labeled Luddites, people can't quite figure out their role in the postindustrial age. They bought NAFTA because the labels read "free trade." They can't openly oppose "progress" or technological advances and certainly don't want to be labeled "protectionist"; but neither can American citizens figure out their place on the factory floor or in the executive suite of the "virtual corporation." And what about those unable to design software packages, create a new Microsoft, or raise the money to gobble up Turner Broadcasting? Are they doomed to flipping hamburgers at $5 an hour?

# The Boeing Strike:
# Globalism and the Visible Ceiling

"If you are a worker, and you are unpacking a crate, and it has Chinese calligraphy on it, and it is a job you used to do, you don't have to be an economist to see where the jobs are going," argued Barbara Shailor, international affairs director of the International Association of Machinists and Aerospace Workers (IAM).

In its second longest strike in history—the longest took place in 1948—24,000 machinists, riveters, painters, crane operators, and other blue-collar workers took to the barricades in October 1995 to protest the export of their jobs, among other grievances over salaries, hours, and benefits. Most important, this was the first time in recent memory that workers had actually struck over their company's corporate global policies and the first time the rank and file had actually viewed globalization as contrary to their interests.

The union leaders understood the significance of the numbers and inserted the issue on the agenda two years before the contract was up for renewal. "Up to 250,000 jobs are at risk in aerospace and related industries in the year 2000," said a study on the eroding aerospace industry, "and up to 469,000 in 2013."[37] They also understood the effect of globalization on their members' wages, benefits, and work conditions.

Traveling back and forth to China, Shailor saw what was happening to the industry; the Chinese demanded more and more offsets as the price of opening up their market to U.S. aerospace companies. The Chinese insisted on "building the back end of the 737 [a commercial aircraft]," recalled Shailor. "This means bringing in engineers, upgrading their old military factories, bringing in equipment, teaching them how to use it, and giving them the 'how-to.' This is not about trading products. It is about trading an industry. We've traded away an industry, with no debate."

Shailor was also struck by the incongruence of Boeing executives negotiating with two ministerial level Chinese agencies: "You have a private company dealing [directly] with the Chinese military; this is not voted on, not talked about, and not understood." In other words, no U.S. public sector presence sits at the table representing America's national interests.

Globalization happens slowly, but the consequences for the workers are very real. Naturally, companies want to manufacture close to their buyers and take advantage of the low wage rates in so many countries. Cheap labor forms one of the few "comparative advantages" that countries like China offer in the race toward global competitiveness. In the aerospace factories, workers make the equivalent of $50 a month, or 35 cents an hour; they live in barracks in "secure" military facilities. "If they dare to form a union, they are immediately imprisoned," observed Shailor, "if not worse." But as a country bursting with potential buyers, China offers firms an enormous market; in fact, beating their international competitors is the real reason so many American companies are ready to give away their technology and sacrifice their workers.[38]

Losing members by the thousands—in Seattle, Hartford, Cincinnati, Wichita, Portland, and Southern California—IAM president George Kourpias met with President Clinton in September 1995, according to Shailor. Kourpias reminded the president of his campaign promise in a speech before Boeing executives and employees in Seattle to "grow" the aerospace industry. "Since you have been in office," he told Clinton, "we have lost 18,000 workers." Shocked by the figures, Clinton ordered a National Economic Council review of administration policy. The union offered specifics, but the beleaguered White House offered little in the way of concrete help, fearing the political ramifications of practicing "industrial policy."

"We were on strike for 69 days," recalled David L. Clay, the shop steward for District Council 751 and a skilled machinist at the Boeing plant in Everett, Washington. "We have lost 27,000 jobs in the last four to five years. At my plant we had 19,000 people back in 1989; today we have nine to 10,000."

Clay marched on the union's picket line with his wife and child, bearing a sign that read "Stop Off Loading Our Jobs." How did he know jobs were being off-loaded? "On a daily basis I saw my jobs going out the door," he said. "I saw more boxes coming in from China, from Australia, Korea, Italy. Tools on the shop floor were removed and sent to those vendors to assemble. They took our tools and were building [the products] there. The best example was the wing tips for the 747 [a wide-bodied transport aircraft]. . . . They ripped the tools off the floor and sent them to Daewoo, in Korea. Daewoo is using our tools to build the wing tip. Boeing's Number One core technology is wing technology. When they sent that tool to Daewoo, that was technology transfer. Daewoo is now part of a consortium building an Asian airbus with India and China. Now they have Boeing's core technology."

Clay argued that the strategy was deceptive and that Boeing workers were being used to make the company look efficient. "A lot of the work is substandard. On the 777 airplane, the doors are made in Asia. We've got a shop working full time just to get the doors straight, at great cost to the company. It takes six people working three weeks just to fix a door. When we redo, they don't charge the vendor. It makes it look like we're inefficient."

Why does a firm, interested in the bottom line, engage in such wasteful practices? "In some cases, it is economic blackmail," explained Clay. "They say, 'If you don't give us part of the airplane, we're not going to buy your airplanes.' Our answer: 'Let them go elsewhere to buy the 747, or the 767, or the 777. You're buying a Mercedes, not a Ford. I don't know why the company succumbs to this kind of blackmail. We can't get a drill press or a new grinder, but they're spending $750 million in China."

David Clay (right foreground) and other striking Boeing ma-
chinists and their families march through Seattle's South Park
(October 1995). Photo by Betty Udesen; courtesy of the
*Seattle Times*.

Union leaders also offered concrete suggestions for dealing with the problem. One of their targets, the Export-Import Bank, is a government agency involved in insuring companies that invest in politically unstable countries like
China. In this case, the agency was actually "financing . . . U.S. aircraft sales to
foreign countries (China specifically) where the sales of aircraft have been conditioned on offset arrangements as a result of market access requirements,"
wrote President Kourpias to bank president Kenneth Brody. The continued
deindustrialization of America should not be funded by the U.S. taxpayer,
union leaders argued. Brody answered that he would collect data from other
agencies to "make a fully informed decision." Other ideas involved using
China's interest in joining the World Trade Organization as leverage and en-

forcing the 1992 memorandum of understanding between the United States and China that was intended to bar restrictive trade practices.[39]

Getting little satisfaction from either the company or the White House, the Boeing production workers spurned their union leaders' advice and voted two days before Thanksgiving to reject the company's offer. By this time, the issue of internationalization took second place to the wage gap. Their angry mood was exacerbated by an announcement that very same Tuesday of $2.5 million in bonuses to the company's five top executives, including the chairman and chief executive officer, all of whom were being rewarded for rising stock prices. The timing of the bonuses could not have been worse, since at the same time the company's executives were receiving fat bonuses, the union was being asked to make concessions on salary and health benefits.

When the workers were finally offered a settlement at year's end, the best they could extract from the company on the issue of exporting their jobs was a promise to "consult" with the union on future global strategies. "Disappointing," said Clay. "There is no definition for exactly what we're going to grieve about in terms of what [jobs] are off-loaded. They can say there are no jobs. For production and tooling guys, there is no protection."

## Ignoring the Gap: *The End of Bliss*

The jobs issue stymies American leaders. They are mystified by market forces and can't figure out viable solutions. So they take the easy way out, lurching from one policy to the next without factoring in the impact of those policies on workers. Real jobs have been ignored in trade agreements, deregulation policies, and even in programs designed to create employment. Trade deals go by the rationale that an international free market will create jobs, the more unfettered by protective language, the better. Federal jobs programs designed specifically to retrain workers have met with insufficient political success over the years to justify their enormous costs, although some analysts believe they can work if the goals remain modest.[40] And various "adjustment" subsidies designed to offset the worst consequences of trade or deregulatory policies often find their funds lost in a disappearing act before they can make much of a difference.

Political leaders have also largely ignored the growing income disparity despite the increasing polarization of society and numerous warnings about the consequences of ignoring the middle class in favor of more tax breaks for the rich. They know all too well who votes and who pours big money into their campaigns. "The single most important characteristic of voting in the United States is the economic bias of turnout patterns," wrote Thomas B. Edsall, author of *The New Politics of Inequality.* "In every survey of voter participation, those at the top end of the income scale turn out in far larger numbers than those at the bottom end. . . . There is . . . little doubt that politicians are responsive to those who vote: voters determine who is elected; nonvoters do not."[41]

Ignoring the classes with low or nonexisting voting rates, politicians risk consequences unconnected to the ballot box. The "GOP's concentration on the rich is playing with economic and social fire," cautioned columnist Marianne Means, who blamed the "business-tilted Reagan years" for policies that doubled the share of income for the richest 1 percent while allowing the bottom 40 percent to remain stagnant.[42] Actually, the trend toward the burgeoning overclass started before Reagan's presidency, in the middle 1970s, when the polarization between the classes began to emerge. Before the 1970s, in the quarter-century after World War II, the middle class actually got richer and poverty was reduced.

The middle class forms the bulwark of democracy. Its members buy the houses, pay taxes, populate the schools, and keep the economy flowing. Democrats have attempted the impossible task of pitching their economic message across class lines, but their battle map doesn't seem to work in the field, perhaps because the middle class can't see where its fate is tied to the poor. The Republicans have enjoyed the political advantage of a narrower economic constituency and fewer groups to please, although this appears to be changing. The poor remain largely ignored by both parties, which are all too aware of continued low voting rates among the disadvantaged: Those with incomes of more than $60,000 a year had voting rates of over 60 percent in the 1994 elections; those below the poverty line dropped from 30 percent in 1990 to 23 percent.[43]

The gap has also been ignored with relative impunity because of the dichotomy between elites and the rest of society. A set of figures first emerged on foreign investment in the late 1980s, for example, showing wildly differing perspectives between the nation's elites (editorial writers, political leaders, corporate elites) and the rest of the public: Seventy-eight percent of the public believed that foreign investment in American assets should be screened for security reasons compared with 13 percent of the elites. No doubt the public was reacting to a massive surge of foreign investment—particularly Japanese investment—during the last half of the 1980s, when foreign investors bought large shares of American assets, including hundreds of high-technology companies, trophy real estate, agricultural land, movie studios, an enormous hunk of the U.S. national debt, energy resources, banks, and even a baseball team, the Seattle Mariners. So anxious were the elites to continue the flow of money that a policy vacuum ensued and some issues were ignored, such as the lack of reciprocity among our trading partners on investment issues; the problem of Americans fresh out of the Pentagon, Commerce, White House, and State Departments who betrayed U.S. strategies and trade secrets by representing foreign governments and foreign companies; the paucity of meaningful trade data; the enormous subsidies states were giving to foreign companies, for example, $325 million from Kentucky to lure Toyota to the state; and the significant outflow of U.S. technology and diminished national sovereignty.[44]

The feeling on the part of elites that others should sacrifice because they, the elites, are right has created an idea gap that perpetuates the economic gap. Corporate leaders fight quietly for government protection for their own industries, for example, while advocating free trade for everyone else. The press identifies closely with elites on the issues of downsizing and trade, as James Fallows suggests in his book *Breaking the News:* "Most media coverage of GATT and NAFTA," he wrote, "made it sound as if the [job] losses would be nonexistent—as indeed they would be in the world that most big-time reporters saw every day."[45] And many college professors who are unwilling to give up lifetime tenure to put their jobs on the worldwide free market feel very differently when it comes to sacrificing aerospace workers on the altar of "free trade."

The opinion gap also helps leaders get the rest of their colleagues off the hook when the public doesn't care enough about a policy to get angry. When the $40 billion Mexican bailout surfaced after the 1995 peso crisis, a *Los Angeles Times* poll revealed that an overwhelming 82 percent of the American people opposed it.[46] So did a hefty majority of the Congress. Yet the president and congressional leaders forged ahead with the public's opposition papered over, and members of Congress were delighted to slip off the hook on the bailout.

When it comes to what makes voters angry, some economic indicators count and others scarcely make a dent. President Jimmy Carter drew considerable voter wrath for high interest rates and rising inflation. His opponent, Ronald Reagan, whipped the public into a frenzy over a budget deficit of $59 billion, although ironically, by the time Reagan left office it had soared to well above $200 billion—resulting from his successful efforts to lower taxes and double the defense budget. Also, in 1982, during the Reagan presidency, the nation was pushed off its perch as a net creditor nation to become a net foreign debtor to the tune of nearly $1 trillion when he left office; curiously, the public never expressed any real rage about that figure thanks to elite indifference.

The distance between the elites and the rest of society has grown as wide and as deep as the income gap, which partly explains why voter reaction appears so disconnected from the nation's buoyant economic indicators. The elections of 1992, 1994, and 1996 showed an angry electorate, but the anger was random and not focused on some of the concrete problems that will follow us clear through to the next century. Some examples:

- Cutting the budget deficit and national debt makes people feel good but will do little in the near term to soften the blows on those individuals struggling to meet their monthly bills.
- Freeing up trade with Mexico has led to a trade deficit where we once had a surplus and to an increasing loss of jobs as companies flee across the border to take advantage of low wage levels and weak unions.
- Immigration policies allow companies such as IBM to hire programmers from India on special visas; these workers settle for much lower wages than their American counterparts.[47]

Only after pollsters alerted politicians that the income-gap issue was hurting them did they finally sit up and begin to grapple with the problem, although viable solutions have yet to emerge from their agonies. Democratic pollster Stanley Greenberg told leaders of both parties as they entered the tumultuous election year of 1996 that "nearly all recent elections have been decided by 'downscale' voters, who swing between Republicans, Democrats and Ross Perot in a desperate search for an answer to their declining economic fortunes."[48]

Finally, who is going to sustain America's competitive edge in the world economy? If the wage gap leads, as expected, to "soft demand," where will we find the consumers to buy the goods produced by the world's most competitive economy? In global markets? Perhaps, but judging from offsets and other restrictive measures practiced without penalty by some of our leading trading partners, this prospect remains, at best, uncertain. A major reason for American workers' lowered standard of living in spite of their rising productivity is the nation's hapless trade policy: Since 1981, the United States has accumulated a trade deficit of more than $1.6 trillion with no change of direction in sight for the annual $100 billion outflow. "This is the greatest unilateral transfer of wealth in the history of the world," concluded Dr. Pat Choate, an economist who ran for the vice presidency on the Perot ticket in 1996.[49] "Put another way, each billion dollars' worth of lost trade equates roughly to 17,000 to 20,000 jobs. As production is shifted offshore to lower wage locales, there is an irresistible demand to lower the wages of those who remain behind. This is what has happened to our living standard."

Clinton had argued that his administration had created over 13 million new jobs, thanks to a boom in exports. What will happen to those jobs if exports continue to decline, as they are expected to do, given the gloomy trade prognosis? Witness the trade deficit, which widened significantly in 1997 and l998, despite the otherwise optimistic economic figures. The trade deficit for 1997 rose to $113.7 billion, the worst showing in nine years. One of the reasons was that imports climbed above the $1 trillion mark for the first time in history. If the January 1998 trade imbalance of $12 billion—mostly in goods—continued at that rate for all of 1998, the annual deficit would rise to a record $144 billion. The figures in February 1998 showed no sign of abating; in fact, the deficit had risen to $12.1 billion, and U.S. exports began to fall. Many blamed the 1997–1998 economic crisis in Asia for the trade gap, especially since a jump in deficits with China (of 25 percent, to $49.7 billion) and Japan (17 percent, to $55.7 billion) accounted for most of the problem. By January 1998 the trade gap with Korea, America's fifth largest export market, had also climbed to $856 million, more than double its December level. But trade gaps with Korea, China, and Japan are not unusual; the United States has tolerated deficits with those nations on the grounds that they made no difference in the health of the economy, a view that is slowly changing.

The unique economic conditions of the 1990s have set the stage for new manifestations of political anger. There are new jobs, but they pay lower wages and offer less security. Citizens fear for their jobs and for their children's future. In fact, many argue that the high level of political involvement over the budget deficit was generated primarily from the public's growing concern for future generations.[50] Other figures emerge alongside the optimistic numbers, presenting a confusing view of the economic picture. The U.S. debt, for example, now totals $5.7 trillion, according to the Office of Management and Budget.[51] Many economists caution against too much optimism, fearing that irrational exuberance could cause lenders to become "too complacent about evaluating repayment risks," in the words of Alan Greenspan, chairman of the Federal Reserve Board. Consumer debt has also risen above the danger line, with people shrinking "the margins of safety that they otherwise might maintain," warned Lawrence Meyer, a Federal Reserve Board governor. Mortgage borrowers have also overextended themselves, often taking out mortgages equal to more than 90 percent of the selling price of their homes. No wonder mortgage delinquency rates—normally down in good economic times—have risen, while personal bankruptcies have hit an all-time high.[52]

Americans are unaccustomed to decline. This is the first time in the nation's 200-year history that the economic future does not look brighter than the past. The visible ceiling justifiably frightens those who have been led to expect an unlimited horizon by their political culture, by Madison Avenue, and by a world that views their nation as a superpower. Was the unparalleled growth of the past half-century an anomaly to begin with? Or was it perhaps the result of our military victory and speedy recovery from World War II? And if the economy fails to roar ahead, will psychological feelings of deprivation continue to feed the nation's growing political anger? What are the solutions?

Capitalism in the United States represents more than an economic ideology. It forms the vortex of democracy, with political stability dependent on a certain degree of economic equilibrium. In the 1990s, that delicate balance has been disrupted by a form of predatory capitalism characterized by cavalier attitudes toward jobs, wage equity, societal benefits, and the less advantaged. The result, a sharp rise in economic anxiety, can only lead to the exacerbation of political anger.

# 4

---

# The Cultural Divide

## Zones of Intolerance on the Battlefield of Values

The tygers of wrath are stronger than the horses of instruction.

—William Blake[1]

I N THE WANING DAYS of the Bush presidency, Murphy Brown had a baby. Not an actual baby, of course, but the staged version was sufficiently authentic to convey the real experience. She wasn't the first sitcom heroine to feature her fecundity on live TV; the trail was blazed decades earlier by Lucille Ball. But she was the first prime-time superstar to produce a baby without benefit of matrimony and baggy maternity garb. Just as Lucille Ball and Desi Arnaz personified—falsely, as it later turned out—the two-parent marital bliss that Americans idealized as the perfect cocoon for child-rearing, Murphy Brown symbolized an alternative household with which viewers could also identify.

The show's writers penned a season's episodes on the travails of pregnancy and single parenting, prettied up by baby showers featuring real-life TV anchorwomen as guests. Attending Murphy as she panted through labor pains and childbirth stood her versatile house painter, Elden, who cheerfully added baby nursing to his decorating duties. The situation retained its high ratings as a comedy thanks to Murphy's other genuine and fictional attributes: beauty, glamour, brains, wit, professional security, and unlimited wealth.

Did the show glorify out-of-wedlock births? Would viewers rush out to copy Murphy's lifestyle? Were Hollywood writers taking the place of home or religion and unduly influencing family values in America? Few agonized over these questions until Vice President Dan Quayle weighed in with his views: "It doesn't help matters when prime-time TV has Murphy Brown—a character who supposedly epitomizes today's intelligent, highly paid, professional woman—mocking the importance of fathers by bearing a child alone and calling it just another lifestyle choice."[2] The vast majority of single parents did not earn megabuck TV-star salaries: nor was single-parenting nearly as glamorous as Murphy Brown's TV experience made it seem. On the contrary, single parents find themselves rapidly impoverished by the needs of their children.[3]

Quayle's attack created a firestorm, as he probably knew it would. Here was the vice president crossing the line between politics and entertainment and venturing into battle against the influence of television on social values. Was he acting sincerely or merely trolling for votes? It didn't matter; whatever his motive, Quayle was ridiculed by his critics and scorched by the media, which made *him* the issue, not single parenting.

"If the vice president thinks it's disgraceful for an unmarried woman to bear a child, and if he believes that a woman cannot adequately raise a child, then he'd better make sure abortion remains safe and legal," responded Diane English, the creator and executive producer of the show.[4] Even many of Quayle's allies questioned the propriety of his action. After all, Murphy Brown was strictly a fictional character. Was it not beneath the dignity of the vice president to become involved in real debates over imaginary predicaments? And what about the first amendment? At what point should political leaders such as Quayle hesitate before crossing the line that separates the power of the state from art forms that rely on the Bill of Rights guarantee of free speech?

One presidency later, political life shifted into reverse, starting a trend that continued well into the late 1990s: the increasing tendency to mix morality with politics. In retrospect, Quayle's diatribe against Murphy Brown's gestation pales in comparison to the campaigns launched by Republicans and Democrats against popular culture. First in line was Senate Majority Leader and presidential candidate Robert Dole's attack on gangsta rap, which he instigated following efforts by black activist C. DeLores Tucker, chairwoman of the National Political Congress of Black Women. Fast on Dole and Tucker's heels followed former education secretary William Bennett, author of the best-selling *Book of Virtues*. Bennett's campaign against the "sick" morality of daytime TV talk shows ("trash TV") was introduced at a press conference, where he was joined by Democratic senators Joseph Lieberman of Connecticut and Sam Nunn of Georgia.[5] These leaders shared the view that much of today's deviant social behavior could be blamed on popular culture—movies, television, magazines, books, paintings, music, and even the Internet.

Other politicians soon entered the fray, such as Representative Steve Stockman (R–Tex.), who assailed the Kinsey Report on human sexuality. He labeled the report a fraud that called into question the previous half-century's attitudes toward "sex education, sex outside marriage, and tolerance of homosexuality." Stockman's efforts mirrored criticisms of the report by members of the Kinsey Institute, who faulted the study's reliance on limited samples of pedophiles and prison inmates as the basis for its findings.[6]

So strong is the nexus between politics and public morality that political critics today find they can attack even as powerful a medium as television without fearing the public pillory. Why such a sudden change in so short a time? Look back at the election returns of 1992, 1994, and 1996, when political anger manifested itself in full force. Spurred by the Christian Coalition but not exclusively, voters today organize around pillars of support that blend social values into their political agendas.[7] Representative Stockman's involvement, for example, was promoted by an interest group known as the Family Research Council, which endorses a strong religious agenda. Without congressional involvement, which catapulted the issue onto the front pages of the national press, the Kinsey Report issue would have remained mired in a dry, scientific debate. From the election results and from the growing power of groups like the Christian Coalition, it appears that the need to reassert values most closely associated with religion takes precedence over another, conflicting American tradition: the wall of separation between church and state.

Thanks to the explosion of technology and the growing accessibility of media outlets, those who support a conservative social agenda can tune out Murphy Brown and tune in a panoply of offerings. One nonprofit religious organization that has successfully utilized modern communications and business technologies, Focus on the Family, operates a conglomerate of media operations that runs ten radio programs, including a syndicated radio show that plays to 2,000 stations across the country; publishes eleven magazines and best-selling books (such as *Dare to Discipline*, a child-rearing manual that sold 2 million copies); produces films and videotapes; and sends mailings to a list of 2.1 million subscribers. The organization runs on an annual budget of $101 million and is headed by a former professor of pediatrics, Dr. James Dobson, who is also the author of *Dare to Discipline*. Viewers and listeners know they are buying into an active political agenda that embraces opposition to abortion, support for constitutional protection for "some forms of school prayer," and other "moral issues." "What takes us into the political arena is not politics," explained Dr. Dobson, "but moral issues. There's no other way to defend the unborn children but to take the battle onto the political battlefield."[8]

A world of difference separates Murphy Brown from gangsta rap, but the basic issue is the same: the legitimization of political influence on American values. Quayle became a bellwether for what was to come in the culture wars. Even if some felt he trivialized the issue, at least he could take some cold comfort in having paved the way for the explosion of morality in politics. Today's arbiters of popular culture insist that they, too, have First Amendment rights, although they say they hold those rights as individuals, not as representatives of the state. But surely they must see the inconsistency between their pose as average citizens and the power they bring to bear by virtue of their political position. Average citizens can't hold press conferences, get their views published on op-ed pages, or sway public opinion as effectively as senators or former cabinet secretaries. The message for those who oppose political intervention in the arts or who long for the swift public retribution of the Quayle era is that they will have to get equally involved as a counterforce—if only to hold the line against the potent mix of religion and morality in politics.

The dilemma for today's leaders is how to bridge the growing cultural divide besetting Americans who have sustained their nation on a belief system that emphasized unity. That unity was one based on faith in a democratic nation-state and specifically did not mean unity of religion, culture, or traditions. (Remember, the nation was founded by individuals escaping countries that forced citizens to practice an established religion.) What has happened to our heritage of tolerance for others' beliefs and our legacy of unity in the face of diversity? Today's leaders must find a way to resolve the yawning cultural divide and point the way back to the greatness of our historical traditions.

## Back to Basics:
### *Public Anxiety and Cultural Rifts*

"Why are we arguing about funding National Public Radio if we can't walk the streets in safety?" asked William C. Adams, professor of public administration at George Washington University. Crime has shot to the top of the charts in the 1990s. Parents feel especially abandoned by government when their children are forced to pass through metal detectors just to go to school.

Issues such as crime fuse public anxiety with public anger and aggravate the nation's real dilemma over process. Everyone agrees that crime has gotten worse, yet the conflict over what to do about it prevents government from effectively addressing the issue. The public faults government for not putting tax dollars to work even for the most rudimentary of its functions, providing security. But the issue of crime also presents a classic value conflict—the right to bear arms versus the right to walk the streets in safety—that offers almost no room for compromise. How, for example, can leaders solve the nation's crime problems without regulating the purchase and ownership of guns? Do gun owners really need AK-47 assault rifles to shoot deer or to protect their homes against marauders? And how can leaders balance the value of personal security against the equally dearly held value (codified in the Second Amendment to the Constitution) that guarantees the right to keep and bear arms? In Europe and in Japan, for example, there were fewer than 1,000 murders per year in the 1990s—contrasted to 13,000 per year in the United States. One major difference: Handguns are regulated in those countries, whereas practically anyone can purchase a Saturday Night Special in almost any location in America.[9]

Crime is basically a local issue that is best addressed at the local level, where people feel its effects most forcefully. In Oxon Hill, Maryland, parents had long complained to school officials about lax security around their local high school; frequent fights often disrupted classes, and violent attacks around the school were on the rise. Their grievances were met with deaf ears until a seventeen-year-old student, Charles Lewis "Chuckie" Marsh, was struck by a bullet and killed on school grounds while waiting for a bus. Too late for Marsh, the district administration finally replaced the principal and installed security measures.[10]

In response to the reported escalation of hate crimes, President Clinton convened a White House conference on November 10,1997, that outlined steps his administration would take to prevent these crimes and toughen existing law enforcement. "Teenagers and young adults account for a significant proportion of the country's hate crimes," he said, . . . which "leave deep scars not only on the victims, but on our larger community."[11]

Many other conflicts follow the pattern of the crime issue, indicating that the anger common to this era is not amorphous but focuses on distinct themes all rooted in social values: affirmative action, abortion, taxes, gun control, term limits, and entitlements. Each theme spawns narrower, more tangible subordinate issues that reveal serious frictions within society: Should Murphy Brown have a baby out of wedlock? Do Robert Mapplethorpe's photographs represent obscenity or art? Should government prohibit late-term abortions or leave those decisions to physicians and their patients?

Massive shifts in values that used to be regarded as eternal verities have increased public anxiety, primarily because Americans are very uncomfortable with ambiguity: They want answers even when they are wrong or elusive. Following are some of the specific rifts involving core values.

## Traditional Values Versus Relative Morality

Those who adhere to established religious or cultural beliefs—particularly on issues such as gay rights and single parenthood—pit themselves against those who prefer a more secular approach. The reaction to President Clinton's order involving gay rights in the military surprised even political experts, who failed to predict the intensity of public reaction to this issue. Battles among groups conflicting over values now occur with increased frequency as more people take courage from the 1992, 1994, and 1996 elections, and from school board elections, plebiscites, and other victories on the local level. Debates over creationism versus Darwinian views of evolution have also popped up in selected localities across the country to the dismay of those who thought this debate was put to rest decades ago. Many jurisdictions, in fact, have mandated the teaching of creationism and prohibited discussions of evolution in biology curricula, a trend that was officially attacked by a report issued by the National Academy of Sciences in 1998. And states such as Michigan have begun to reassess their no-fault divorce laws on "moral" grounds, questioning whether the national trend toward easier access to divorce has hurt or helped society, particularly children. Their advocates will probably not succeed in turning back the clock on divorce, but the debate over core values will continue to crowd legislative agendas for a long time to come.

## Permissiveness Versus Discipline

Another theme dividing Americans relates their fear of crime to a fairly universal feeling that no one is minding the store. Witness the home school movement, which boasts a growing number of parents who have chosen to educate their children at home rather than subject them to the values and violence of the public schools. No one knows for sure how many parents have chosen to educate their children at home, but estimates indicate that there are 400,000 to 1 million home-schooled children in the country. Although home schoolers do not use the public schools, they have not opted out of the political system; on the contrary, home-school advocates are vigilant in protecting their rights. When the House of Representatives was about to pass legislation that home schoolers thought would require them to be certified by the government, "thousands of angry religious conservatives . . . besieged members with phone calls, letters and faxes for over a week, browbeating them into killing a mandate actually aimed only at public school teachers."[12]

## Government Intrusiveness Versus Free Markets

A deep-seated value conflict also plagues this issue: the rights of the individual against the rights of government to act on behalf of society. A virulent antiregulatory movement, which seeks to unravel government protections developed over the past century, has recently gathered steam in Congress. The "takings" bill, which came close to passage during the 104th Congress, mandated that the government compensate private companies for financial losses attributable to regulatory action, particularly those actions involving public goods: clean air, public safety and health, clean water, pure drugs and meat. The fiscal ramifications of takings legislation were daunting: The bill required the federal government to ante up big bucks any time a company or an individual could prove that its profits had been reduced. This meant that if the government decided to ban the export of certain kinds of weapons, for example, the manufacturers would be paid *not to produce*; similarly, polluters would be paid not to pollute and insurance companies not to raise rates.[13]

Although the conflict over government has been with us since the founding of the republic, what is different now is that anger at government intrusiveness crosses economic and ideological lines. A common complaint links environmental regulation and agricultural land. One minute someone owns a farm that has sustained his family for generations; all of a sudden government calls it "wetland" and appropriates it. The flap over unfunded mandates also arises from the public's anger over the imposition of federal regulatory burdens on states and localities with nary a thought about who pays the price. For the first time, much of the anger seems propelled by the belief that the nation's laws and social values have careened out of control, escaping all boundaries of common sense.[14]

Ironically, the very groups that oppose government control over the economy seek *more* government control over social values. The same Congress that deregulated the telecommunications industry, for example, imposed a requirement on the television industry to include a feature known as a V-chip that would allow owners of television sets (parents) to screen out material they considered violent or obscene. The V-chip was strongly supported by the president in a rare show of executive-legislative comity. And the same 104th Congress that brought ten antiregulatory bills close to passage saw fit to pass legislation—subsequently vetoed by President Clinton—prohibiting third trimester abortions regardless of a physician's judgment concerning threats to the mother's life or the health of the fetus.

## "Us" Against "Them"

Nowhere is the bifurcation of society more evident than in the debate over multiculturalism. The verdict in the O. J. Simpson case bared for the first time in almost three decades what the Kerner Commission concluded after the race riots of the 1960s, that the nation was divided into two societies, white and black. Since that time, the racial issue has been studied to death, but the divisions are deeper than ever. Buried in the topsoil of today's debate on welfare, for example, lies the simmering hostility against paying the tab for unwed black teenage mothers—despite the reality of welfare, which is that the majority of the funds go to poor whites. On other levels, ample evidence reveals the continuing racial divide. Look no further than any college cafeteria and you will observe students dining together by race or ethnic group; few dare to bridge the gap.

The rights of gays and lesbians have become another leading issue in the us-against-them portfolio. Indeed, many have asked why, with all the problems besetting society in the 1990s, one of the leading issues to emerge in the 1996 Republican primaries has been whether to allow homosexual marriages. The battles over English only versus bilingualism in the schools, the allotment of scarce resources to affirmative action goals, and a host of other issues have led to an increased sense of balkanization among the American people, who used to take pride in the melting-pot character of their society but now watch helplessly as their society continues to divide along ethnic, gender, and racial lines.

## Anger Unbound:
### *Do the Media Reflect or Manipulate Values?*

As anger accelerates, so does criticism of the media for exacerbating the problem. Do the media reflect political anger? Or are they merely messengers of bad tidings? And just as value conflicts continue to mystify so many people, so have new developments in the media outpaced political leaders' ability to master them. This is particularly true in the realm of the expanded segmentation of media markets, where a plethora of channels now compete for audience attention and market share. In this new environment, where should political candidates spend their time and money for maximum impact—television, radio, print media?[15]

Another by-product of this new environment is expanded media attention, often focused on the same body of information. This creates what political scientist Larry Sabato wrote about in *Feeding Frenzy,* a study of the relationship between an increasingly aggressive press corps and the polity.[16]

Recent scandals have shown the new media to be far more invasive than their predecessors in the practice of "pack journalism." Many predicted the problems that were bound to emerge from the explosion of media, media markets, and the need to fill the gaping information voids. Increasing public hostility to the media was almost inevitable, although the cause remains a mystery. Is the antipathy directed toward the message or the messenger? Studies from the Pew Center for the People and the Press point squarely at the messenger: "The public's assessment of press performance has grown increasingly negative in recent years. A majority (56%) now say news stories and reports are often inaccurate, up more than 20 percentage points since 1985, when a similar majority (55%) said news organizations get the facts straight." The report went on to say that nearly two-thirds of the American people now believe that television news programs invade people's privacy.[17]

Scott Keeter argues that the media's focus on negative stories distorts public perceptions toward politics, government, and ultimately the media itself. For example, on the issue of environmental protection, poll data show that 57 percent of the American public believes that air quality today is significantly worse than it was twenty years ago, although that is obviously not the case.[18]

The explosion of the Internet has also changed the media in ways that are still being discovered. Anyone with a modern home computer can gain access to the Internet for as little as a few dollars a month. Compare that with the price of a newspaper, magazine, or books, and the conclusion is obvious: Consumers suddenly have a wider world open to them at minimal cost. The websites of newspapers and radio shows get thousands of "hits" a month, indicating that their audience has expanded well beyond initial expectations.

The quality of news has also changed, in terms of the speed of delivery as well as its content. The Monica Lewinsky scandal, for example, was an Internet-driven story, having first appeared on the Drudge Report, an electronic gossip sheet originating in Hollywood. The Drudge website gets 6 million "hits" a week; the White House claims 29 million. The "Net" is interactive— people can talk to each other and respond; it is expansive—the whole world is linked; and it is cheap—making it the most democratic of all media. But unlike the more establishment media, the "Net" doesn't discriminate; it doesn't censor; and it doesn't screen stories for truth and legitimacy.

## Television and Narrowcasting

Television has been around for a long time. In 1950, my gadget-loving father bought our family the first television set on the block in Queens, New York, where each week the entire neighborhood crowded around the tiny screen to watch the comedian Milton Berle on the Texaco Star Theater. Today, the screens as well as the audiences have expanded, along with television's impact on society. Hundreds of channels compete for audience share, and the public can now choose among a broad selection of news and entertainment offerings.

According to some media critics, the problem rests with the lack of separation between entertainment (and gossip) and straight political news. Before 1980, 80–90 percent of the public depended on the three major networks for news; today the figures are down to 56 percent. What is the rest of the public watching? CNN? Movies? The Family Channel? Soap operas? With most people now choosing their own media cocoon, news is no longer what the three networks and newspaper editors from the mainstream press decide it is going to be. That is why the term "broadcasting" has been replaced with "narrowcasting" to reflect the narrow segmentation of the electronic media market.

To some extent, increasing segmentation of media markets isolates people, cordoning them off from society and its problems much like the detached and controlled environment of the nation's growing number of "gated" communities. The reverse, however, could just as easily occur: Narrowing the market connects people to other like-minded folks; it widens their choices about what to watch; and more important, it gives them more control over what their children will watch. Segmented markets also make media less expensive and, therefore, more accessible to a wider range of advertisers. The same goes for political candidates, who can often avoid beaming their messages out to three different states to reach just one congressional district.

Anger also assumes a much larger role in this segmented environment as networks react to their diminishing share of the market by increasing their use of shock value, innuendo, and investigative material—all in the name of becoming more competitive. Investigative journalism relies for its success on the "drumbeat" of government distrust, alleges Mark Melman, a Democratic pollster and consultant. "ABC-TV highlights government waste all the time. How often does ABC tell the public when their money is being spent wisely? There is one segment each week [*Your Money, Your Choice*] on how the government is screwing up. This is a relatively new phenomenon. [As a result] more people have the sense that government is reaching into their wallets, that government spending is a rat hole, that they are getting nothing back." (ABC-TV actually ran a story on January 15, 1996, on how the government saved money for taxpayers by selling off defunct silos for use as homesites and schools in Topeka, Kansas.) "If you listen carefully," added filmmaker Charles Guggenheim, "you can often hear correspondents on the network news finish off their sixty-second presentation with a question; that query introduces a sense of distrust, warranted or not, and sparks up an otherwise boring segment."

The immediacy of television also tends to exacerbate anger. It is a "hot medium," say political consultants, who advise their clients to counter its force by lowering their pitch. "When people see things visually, they tend to get angry about them," asserted former CBS correspondent Marvin Kalb, who now heads the Shorenstein Center for Press and Politics at Harvard University. "TV elevated a lot of people; it also agitated them. If television had been around the Israelites might never have escaped from Egypt, since their leader, Moses, stuttered and was afflicted with a harelip. What would have happened if Moses were forced to go on television and explain everything? TV makes us confuse eloquence with leadership and intelligence."

Television has also raised the cost of politics, tipping elections more than any other known factor toward those with access to money. In 1990, Ann Richards's gubernatorial campaign in Texas cost $13 million with 85 percent going to pay for television advertisements. Her opponent, George W. Bush, spent $22 million four years later and won.

But even with all these negatives, television, particularly cable television, has contributed to a vast improvement in the nation's political education, opening new worlds to millions of Americans—particularly those in rural America—who would never before have been privy to such a wide range of university courses, legislative deliberations, and political commentary. Thanks to Speaker Newt Gingrich's (Contract with America) promises delivered in the first hundred days of the 104th Congress, even committee hearings are now televised; voters all over the country can now watch members of the Ways and Means Committee debate taxes or the Agriculture Committee discuss farm subsidies. In the final analysis, this is a great boon for democracy: full sessions of Congress, accessible to all, courtesy of C-SPAN! It no longer matters if folks are sitting in living rooms in Hattiesburg, Mississippi, or Washington, D.C.; television has enabled all citizens to share equally in the legislative process.

Television has also changed congressional behavior, charged Representative Marcy Kaptur (D–Ohio) before a town meeting in her district on February 12, 1996. "People change when TV cameras are in the room. Congress was never intended to do major work on the floor [of the House]. On Medicaid, we had one day of hearings. This affects 36 million Americans. On Medicare, there were no hearings. [Congress] is no longer operating on the committee level. Issues like Medicare and Medicaid are too boring for the cameras. We used to have extensive hearings. Now the entertainment medium dominates proceedings. TV has infected us in a way that is nonproductive. That has to heal. It is creating partisan divisions, causing a lot of people to leave Congress."

In the best of all possible worlds, opening up the process should reduce public anger; under the harsh glare of the klieg lights, government would find it awfully hard to mobilize a cover-up, lie about a secret war, or impose more new taxes.[19] Also, armed with more information, voters find they are better equipped to make informed decisions about their elected representatives; no longer are they forced to rely on franked newsletters, press releases, and other sources of predigested information.

Why, then, does the reverse occur so often? Does harsh reality generate anger? Most definitely. Media watchers complain that such openness hurts the negotiations process. No one wants cameras recording the sordid details of political bargaining, and moreover, if television had existed in Philadelphia in 1789, the Constitution would never have been written. Openness denigrates public institutions, particularly Court TV, which destroys the "majesty of the law."

In the final analysis, demystifying institutions through television doesn't necessarily mean vilifying them. Close scrutiny can also lead to a healthy sense of outrage over what isn't so "majestic" about the judicial system, the president, or Congress; and that outrage can just as easily produce reform as it can generate apathy or cynicism. Coverage of the Vietnam War, the first war reported regularly on television, made it much harder for the government to lie about the darker side of the war than had been the case in the past. The murder trial of O. J. Simpson, watched each day by an insatiable audience, uncovered problems in the judicial process that cried out for future attention, particularly jury selection and sequestration, as well as police misconduct. And after the Waco hearings on television riveted the public's attention, pressures to reorganize the Bureau of Alcohol, Tobacco, and Firearms made more sense than ever before. "It's a foregone conclusion," admitted former White House chief counsel Abner Mikva privately.

## Talk Radio

Nowhere is the correlation between the media and anger more evident than in the explosion of talk radio shows with their steadily increasing market share of audiences across the nation. Endowing new meaning to the act of political participation, talk radio has broadened the nation's interest in politics and heightened its sense of anger over politics as usual. In the process, it has elevated anger into a badge of citizenry and validated it. Regardless of their political views, talk show hosts offer people an outlet for their anger, encouraging listeners to express themselves openly by conveying that public anger is authentic and socially acceptable. Most important, they give people the sense that they matter, that their views count, and that they are being heard—even if their words are soon dissipated over the airwaves. The relatively new medium of talk radio projects itself as accessible, immediate, and sympathetic to a growing group of Americans who feel that were it not for the open lines of talk radio, no one would hear them. Talk radio also provides information on issues that are largely ignored by other media.

Chief among the practitioners of this craft is Rush Limbaugh, whose impact on the 1994 congressional elections was incalculable; in fact, some of his pre-election material was culled from a daily fax that came from Newt Gingrich's office. "Rush Limbaugh was a significant force in the 1994 election," recalled Jim Sasser, who lost his Senate seat in Tennessee. "He really worked me over.

He mimicked my pronunciation." Confident, irreverent, opinionated, sexist (he coined the terms "femi-nazis" and "liberalmediaelite") and ardent in his criticism of liberals, Democrats, and government, Limbaugh struck a chord that resonated especially well among a substrata of white, middle-class males, many of whom congregated in Rush Rooms—downtown havens in major metropolitan areas for fans who wanted to eat their lunch without missing his program.

The fire and brimstone invoked by Limbaugh and many of his fellow hosts risks losing some of its punch because the decibel level is beginning to deafen listeners to the *message du jour*. Watch *Crossfire* or *The McLaughlin Group*, good examples of this genre transposed to television. Appearing on NBC on Saturday evenings, host John McLaughlin, a former priest and White House official in the Nixon administration, screams questions at his guests, serious journalists all, who then yell back at the host and at each other almost in unison. In this cacophony, no one listens to anyone else, and the level of public dialogue plunges downward to middle earth. What is the message here—that as society becomes increasingly more anonymous, people feel they need to scream to be heard?

The upshot of these televised food fights is that public hostility only increases toward the media for many reasons. First of all, these sessions convey the impression that journalists are insiders, know-it-alls, who allow their biases to affect their work. Barely concealing their contempt for ordinary Americans, many of these journalists spend most of their time crafting *bon mots* that will keep up their franchises as camera persona at the ready for their weekly performances. Many have long since abandoned the more traditional shoe-leather reporting that has made the media such a valuable component of the political process. They know it is far easier and more lucrative to appear as guest pundits on the weekend chat shows than it is to research a story on a complex tax issue, dodge land mines in Bosnia, or travel around the country talking to actual voters.

Primal screaming also deafens the press corps, which sometimes covers the news as if it were following the races at the Kentucky Derby. The steady erosion of dialogue and the devaluation of ideas both feed into the process of turning policies that call for careful nuancing into mere horse races with winners and losers watched from the starting gate to the finish line. News analysts Edwin Diamond, Steven Katz, and Cara Matthews found this in press coverage of Clinton's abortive health care reform effort, where events were covered even in the absence of real developments: "This is John Cochran on Capitol Hill, where the noise level over health care is rising." Press critics also shared the blame for the demise of health care, concluding: "Journalism's traditional narrative model . . . proved enough to speed the demise of reform [with] stories . . . fitted into the political campaign narrative—a format organized by charge and rebuttal, attack and counterattack, and who's winning and losing in the metaphorical horse race."[20]

Aware of the public's aversion to anger, New York's Mayor Rudolph Giuliani called publicly for more civility among the citizenry of his city. Whether he hoped to pep up the dreary late winter doldrums of 1998, or whether like a good politician he detected his constituents' heightened sensitivity to the nation's acrid political environment is anyone's guess; what is certain is that despite the drubbing he took from the media, he stood his ground in asking for formalized classes in civility and a citywide campaign on civility awareness.

Talk radio has also provided a new avenue for recruiting political candidates, becoming in effect a modern version of the local clubhouse. No less than seven Republican candidates running for Congress in the 1994 elections got their start as talk radio hosts. One host, Stan Solomon, used his power over the microphone to branch out into political fundraising, forming his own political action committee, called SACKPAC, organized literally to "sack" the four Indiana representatives who voted for the Clinton budget in 1993.[21]

In reality, anger cuts both ways. Certainly the temptation to manipulate public anger for winning office and for successful governance is enormous. After all, it is much easier to manipulate symbols than it is to destroy a foreign army. But leaders could not possibly sustain such a high level of rage for very long, which means that whereas some anger is manipulated, most of it is based on genuine feelings of anxiety.

After the bombing of the federal facility in Oklahoma, the issue divided into two camps:

1. The media provoke anger, manipulating an already disillusioned public middle class via the hot media of electronic journalism.

2. The media merely tap into an "anger repository" by reflecting reality and rendering information accessible enough for people to make their own decisions.

Proof of the anger-repository theory emerged during the peso devaluation crisis in spring 1995, when radio host Chuck Harder asked his national radio audience what they thought of the president's plans to bail out Mexico. After getting no calls, Harder and his guest figured the subject was too complicated and they'd better move on. They soon found out that the reverse was true: So many listeners called in that they blew the station's 800 circuits in northern Florida.

"We validate what people are already thinking," argues Rush Limbaugh, who agrees with the anger-repository theory. Limbaugh reaches an audience of 20

Do the media provoke citizen anger or simply tap into existing anger? Doonesbury © 1995 G. B. Trudeau. Reprinted with permission of Universal Press Syndicate. All rights reserved.

million listeners. Just compare that for impact with even as influential an organ as the *New York Times,* whose circulation numbers about 1.2 million. Do these 20 million listeners really think the way Rush thinks? "The second violent American revolution is just about—I got my fingers about a quarter of an inch apart—is just about that far away," thunders Limbaugh. "Because these people are sick and tired of a bunch of bureaucrats in Washington."[22]

Others take the opposite view: Talk radio would talk itself out of business very quickly were it not that so many hosts incessantly fan the flames of public anger because they have more of a vested interest in maintaining high levels of anger than in transforming anger into constructive change.

Actually, talk radio can also encourage isolation, since people are more apt to brood alone than in groups. "People tend to be less angry when they have to interact with each other," wrote commentator Joe Klein. Otherwise, they become afflicted with "Information Age disorder," which Klein defines as the "product of our tendency to stew alone—staring into computer screens at work, blobbing in front of the television at home."[23] In other words, talk radio and its electronic mates can provide the illusion of connectedness but offer little in the way of interpersonal substance.

The work of Robert Putnam, based on research on civic associations in Italy, reinforces the importance of personal and community integration to effective democracy; he concluded that political activities were vastly improved by recreational networking.[24] A few years later Putnam extended his view to the United States. In a seminal article, "Bowling Alone," he concluded that the "vibrancy of American civil society has notably declined over the past several decades," citing such evidence as declining union power, low voter turnout, decreased PTA memberships, and loosening family ties. Addressing the nation's erosion of "social capital" and consistent "civic engagement," he questioned the impact of the nation's "electronic networks" on these staples of community life.[25] Ted Gurr's work correlating levels of civil violence to community organization also supports the view that civic organizations maintain societal stability. Speaking of the urban rebellions in the black communities in the 1960s, Gurr wrote that Watts, Los Angeles, an area still torn apart by riots, had "less associational activity and job-training programs than any other large Negro community." Similarly, the "comparative quiescence of mid-nineteenth century English workers vis-à-vis their French counterparts [is attributed] in part to the proliferation in England of new cooperatives, . . . building societies, and trade unions, which provided positive alternatives to violent protest."[26]

In the absence of readily identifiable communities, politicians increasingly turn to electronic town meetings to combat the influence of talk shows and deliver what they consider unabridged messages to the people. President Clinton brought this campaign strategy with him into the White House, hoping that he would be able to circumvent the national networks in attracting public support for his policies. Town meetings may cool anger for a short period of time, but there is little evidence that they create communities, improve the quality of debate, or enhance the quality of political support.

In fact, two of President Clinton's town meetings in his second administration turned into fiascoes. The first, on race, left all participants unsatisfied by the inconclusive and rambling nature of the discourse. The second, a meeting at Ohio State University in early 1998 that was supposed to drum up support for an attack on Iraq had the opposite effect: Clinton's national security team, which included Secretary of State Madeleine Albright, Defense Secretary William Cohen, and National Security Adviser Sandy Berger, looked extremely ill at ease as they were beset by hostile questions for which they seemed to have few adequate answers. For their part, White House aides met the hostile reviews with comments that the town meeting was not "controlled" as it should have been.

Few citizens find electronic communities, however sophisticated, preferable to the real thing: sustained interpersonal communication. Talk radio may provide a temporary outlet, but it cannot transform political anger into political change any more than throwing sacks of tea into Boston harbor was sufficient to create a nation. To achieve anything worthwhile, citizens need to commit themselves to the tedious process that is the essence of democracy—the face-to-face meetings, repetitive negotiations, suboptimal agreements, and constant sacrifice that it takes to reach some semblance of the common good. "Many forms of political interaction . . . involve mutual role taking," wrote Murray Edelman. "Each party observes from the other's perspective. . . . Adeptness at politicking depends on 'flexible role taking.'"[27]

These activities may not be as satisfying as sounding off on the airwaves or in cyberspace, but they are more nutritious and last longer. At their best, talk shows enhance democracy by involving citizens in political issues and inspiring them to participate in politics at the grassroots level.

# The Danger Zone:
## *Intolerance, Hate Language, and Political Blight*

The media-manipulation theory gained steam after the Oklahoma City bombing, when President Clinton asked the media to cool its "rhetoric." No doubt was left after the president's remarks about the linkage between the volcanic rhetoric of anger and the grisly event in the nation's heartland. Feeling the pressure, the Oklahoma senate urged radio stations to cancel G. Gordon Liddy's shows for airing "hate and violence," and three radio stations actually pulled him off the air. Many applauded this action, especially when the unrepentant former Watergate burglar talked proudly over hundreds of airwaves about how he'd used pictures of the president and first lady for target practice. Most surprising, however, was the public outcry on the other side of the issue that followed dropping the Liddy program: Calls flooding two of the three stations vigorously protested the annulment of Liddy's First Amendment rights!

Thanks to the First Amendment, speech of all kinds has always been protected in the United States, with periodic exceptions for sedition in wartime and pornography in peacetime. For this reason, Americans reserve a high tolerance for language, however odious, knowing that fringe elements can function freely in a democracy without tearing apart the fabric of society. Today the climate has changed: Some extremist elements now occupy the center of American politics, allowing hate speech to flourish often without the barest minimum of public opprobrium.

Hate speech escalated dramatically after the 1994 election, when open season was declared on liberal Democrats. Some attacks were striking not so much in their lunacy but in their mainstream sponsorship. "WANTED—Liberal Democrat Wanted Poster," read the headline of a poster labeled "Project 28: A Special Project of the National Republican Congressional Committee." Drawn to look like the most-wanted posters pasted on post office walls to identify criminals hunted by the FBI, the leaflet showed pictures of twenty-eight members of Congress, featuring a disproportionate number of women, blacks, and Jews. The poster advertised that these members were "wanted for voting against at least 7 out of 10 provisions of the Contract with America, and for aiding and abetting President Bill Clinton's big government, pro-tax, anti-family, anti-military agenda in the House of Representatives." (See Figure 4.1.)

"This nation is shocked by extremist campaign material produced by the National Republican Congressional Committee that suggests that Democratic Members of this House are 'Wanted' criminals just for disagreeing with the Republicans' Contract with America," charged an outraged Representative George Miller (D–Calif.) in a press release circulated on June 12, 1995. Miller also presented a widely circulated poster of mug shots of President John F. Kennedy, headlined "Wanted for Treason." Although no one claimed "credit" for distributing this leaflet, Miller called on Republicans as well as all members of Congress to repudiate what he termed "extremist rhetoric [that] endangers democracy and encourages the lunatic fringe."

# FIGURE 4.1

## Open Season on Liberal Democrats: The National Republican Congressional Committee's "Wanted" Poster

# —WANTED—

## LIBERAL DEMOCRAT WANTED POSTER

**WANTED FOR VOTING AGAINST AT LEAST 7 OUT OF 10 PROVISIONS of the CONTRACT WITH AMERICA** and for aiding and abetting President Bill Clinton's big government, pro-tax, anti-family, anti-military agenda in the House of Representatives.

DAVID BONIOR (D-MI)

JOHN DINGELL (D-MI)

BOBBY RUSH (D-IL)

RON DELLUMS (D-CA)

MAXINE WATERS (D-CA)

HENRY WAXMAN (D-CA)

LYNN WOOLSEY (D-CA)

NANCY PELOSI (D-CA)

HOWARD BERMAN (D-CA)

JULIAN DIXON (D-CA)

DICK GEPHARDT (D-MO)

BILL CLAY (D-MO)

THEIR LEADER
PRESIDENT
BILL CLINTON

ROSA DeLAURO (D-CT)

SAM GEJDENSON (D-CT)

JOHN LEWIS (D-GA)

CYNTHIA MCKINNEY (D-GA)

CORRINE BROWN (D-FL)

CARRIE MEEK (D-FL)

PAT SCHROEDER (D-CO)

GARY ACKERMAN (D-NY)

CHARLES SCHUMER (D-NY)

NITA LOWEY (D-NY)

CHARLES RANGEL (D-NY)

EDWARD MARKEY (D-MA)

BARNEY FRANK (D-MA)

HENRY GONZALEZ (D-TX)

RON COLEMAN (D-TX)

PAT WILLIAMS (D-MT)

**"PROJECT 28: A Special Project of the NATIONAL REPUBLICAN CONGRESSIONAL COMMITTEE"**
320 FIRST STREET, S.E. • WASHINGTON, D.C. 20003

Miller's challenge met mostly with silence, at least from Republicans. In the absence of much public censure, the level of hate speech continued to rise. Representative Robert Dornan, a conservative and highly vocal Republican member from California, criticized President Clinton on the floor of the House in late January 1995 for giving "aid and comfort" to the enemy as a Vietnam War draft dodger. Dornan, an air force pilot in the 1950s, was outraged by Clinton's State of the Union message that included a tribute to Jack Lucas, a winner of the Medal of Honor. The House rose to the occasion and censured Dornan for his inappropriate language, ordering it stricken from the *Congressional Record*. Dornan was also barred from the privilege of speaking on the House floor for twenty-four hours. Dornan was defeated in the 1996 election by Loretta Sanchez, a Hispanic woman, by a vote of 47,964 to 46,980. Since the numbers were so close, Dornan protested the election, but the dispute was finally resolved in Sanchez's favor.

Attacks on the president continued throughout his second term, one of the worst coming from Representative Dan Burton (R–Ind.), who publicly referred to Clinton as a "scumbag." In his capacity as chairman of the House Committee on Government Reform and Oversight, Burton told the *Indianapolis Star-News* that "If I could prove 10 percent of what I believe happened [with regard to the committee's investigation of campaign finance violations], he'd be gone. This guy's a scumbag. That's why I'm after him." Shortly afterward, the ranking Democrat on the committee, Representative Henry Waxman (D–Calif.), denounced Burton for remarks that he considered "repugnant" and criticized his fitness for leadership. Any semblance of comity between the two parties on that committee has long since broken down.[28]

Other examples of hate speech persist. House Majority Leader Dick Armey (R–Tex.) referred on the House floor to Representative Barney Frank (D–Mass.), an openly homosexual member of Congress, as "Barney fag." A slip of the tongue, Armey averred; he merely "blended the two words (Frank and harangue, which I pronounce with a hard 'g') in a way that made it seem as if I was using a slur."[29] This Freudian slip, responded Frank, revealed Armey's homophobia.

Homophobia, anti-Semitism, misogyny—it has been a field day for prejudice of all kinds, smack dab in the center of mainstream, Main Street American politics, on the right side of the spectrum as well as the left:

- Rap star Sister Souljah proposed a week dedicated to killing white people.
- At Rutgers University, feminists carried the banner "Don't F— With Us."

- Singer Michael Jackson's much-awaited album HIStory featured the phrases "Jew me" and "kike me."

"Everybody is an angry victim of some implacable force or other," wrote social commentator John Leo, arguing that these examples of incivility should not be justified as "Jeffersonian democracy in action."[30]

The indiscreet Republican political consultant Ed Rollins resurfaced in 1995 to call two Jewish members of Congress "Hymie boys." At a roast for newly elected San Francisco Mayor Willie Brown, Rollins quipped: "If [Brown were] elected mayor of L.A., he could show those Hymie boys, Berman and Waxman [Howard Berman and Henry Waxman, both Democrats from Los Angeles], who were always trying to make Willie feel inferior for not being Jewish." This time Rollins embarrassed the Dole presidential campaign; several years before, the campaign of New Jersey governor Christine Whitman reeled from his remark that campaign officials had paid off black leaders to keep their constituents away from the voting booths.[31]

Of the nation's political leaders, only Democrats seemed to confront the issue. At its annual convention, House Minority Leader Dick Gephardt (D–Mo.) openly challenged the decision of the National Association of Radio Talk Show Hosts to bestow its highest award on G. Gordon Liddy:

> We do not honor the First Amendment by honoring explicit calls to violence and bloodshed. That is why this organization's decision to give its Freedom of Speech Award to G. Gordon Liddy is not only wrong, but outrageous. And I urge each and every one of you to exercise your own First Amendment rights and boycott this evening's gala because of it. . . . Why can't we agree that Gordon Liddy [is] a convicted criminal who has openly advocated violence toward law enforcement. . . . You do not have to honor hateful speech in order to uphold Gordon Liddy's right to utter it."[32]

Physical violence directly stemming from hate speech has also risen well above normal levels. Just as Yitzhak Rabin's assassin believed the rhetoric that he was doing God's work, words truly can kill. Witness the fliers encouraging protesters to "burn and loot the Jews" that preceded the tragic fire at Freddy's clothing store in Harlem that killed seven people; the neo-Nazi literature consumed by the white soldiers charged with murdering two black servicemen stationed at Fort Bragg, North Carolina; the paranoid visions of the heavily armed and well-financed militia movement that fomented the disaster at the federal building in Oklahoma; and the drumbeat rhetoric of "baby killer" that fired up the killers of doctors and other innocents at abortion clinics. "The extremists love their country and want the best for its future," wrote Patrick Snare of Christiansburg, Virginia, in response to an arti-

cle on political anger by Dwayne Yancey of the *Roanoke Times & World News.*
"Circumstances have fueled a climate of hatred that poisons the public discourse. . . . We just want to talk about it. . . . Don't take that freedom away
from us."[33]

Many find the acrid environment that has sprouted around the zone of intolerance all too reminiscent of the McCarthy era, particularly for the ease with
which people today are branded by innuendo and association for their political views. Today's hate language—"femi-nazis," "baby killers," "liberals," "Barney fag," "blood-sucking" Jewish store owners—recalls that era when bigotry
reigned supreme and compromise was regarded as weakness or lacking in
principle. Hate language precludes society from engaging in dialogue that, if
successful, must be preceded by respect for the views of others.

The growing cultural divide afflicting this era impedes respect for others
and encourages incivility. How can it be otherwise when membership in ethnic, racial, and gender-based groups spills over the traditional boundaries of
pride and reinforcement to bigotry and intolerance? The real dilemma for
democracy comes from the growing connection between hate speech and
public policy. Does the language of hate deserve special protection? Where
are the guarantees that provide protection for the freedom to hate, and what
are the political effects of hate? The same week Armey called Representative
Frank "Barney fag," the Nebraska legislature prepared to ban adoption by
homosexual parents. Prior to that, anti–gay rights measures were passed in
Austin, Texas, and Cincinnati; in 1995 alone, well-funded groups in ten states
threatened to place antigay measures on the ballots. One of these measures
succeeded in defeating by referendum in Maine in February 1998 an
anti–gay civil rights law passed by the state legislature the year before. The
Christian Coalition claimed credit for defeating the law, which the group
said was part of their Families 2000 strategy: an attempt to recruit 100,000
church liaisons—or volunteer activists—to promote the Coalition's agenda
in all fifty states. To what extent did racial, gender, and ethnic prejudice
fuel Governor Pete Wilson's decision on June 1, 1995, to issue an executive
order opposing affirmative action programs in California, and the subse-
quent vote against affirmative action by a majority of the state's voters in
1996?

If a silver lining can be found in all this hate speech, it is the rising public
opprobrium that follows its escalation. Congress has applied various forms of
censure toward members who lose control of themselves; the perpetrators of
the horror at Oklahoma City were brought to trial and convicted, and their
views exposed; and some of the talk show hysterics are losing their ratings and
their microphones.

# Gangsta Rap and Trash TV:
## *The Objectification of Anger*

Hate speech emerges in yet another grotesque form: the musical genre known as gangsta rap. The lyrics of this so-called art form have recently achieved national notoriety for their explicit violence toward women and homosexuals—and for recent political attempts to censor them. Songs about cop-killing brought forth a rare surge of protests—primarily from police associations—against a rapper called Ice-T. One Baltimore deejay was fired the day after he refused to play songs with sexually explicit lyrics, including "First of the Month," a tune that glorifies the act of getting high and selling crack to welfare recipients.[34]

Black women have found themselves especially victimized by gangsta rap. "I'm an Assassin," part of the repertoire of a group known as the Geto Boys, warbles in praise of rape and mutilation: "I knew the girl was ready . . . but all was in my head was 'Kill the b—.' . . . I ducked between the chair and whipped out the machete. She screamed, I sliced her up." Another ditty from Masta Ace promised: "I'll slaughter your mother. . . . All we want to do is murder, murder, murder, kill, kill, kill."[35]

The objectification of women is not limited to gangsta rap. "One song by the [hard rock] group Nine Inch Nails describes a violent sexual act in the crudest language possible. So does a Snoop Doggy Dogg recording, which calls women whores and worse," wrote C. Delores Tucker and William Bennett in an article supporting their "education campaign" to alert the public to the "vulgar and misogynistic lyrics that glorify violence and promote it among children."[36]

Gangsta rap would have remained under wraps and outside the political mainstream had it not been for intense public pressure from Senate Majority Leader Dole, Bennett, and Tucker, later joined by Senators Lieberman and Nunn, who weighed in on the issue of "trash TV." Indeed, by today's standards the plotline of Murphy Brown looks like an episode from Mary Poppins, especially compared with the harsh lyrics of gangsta rap or with "women who marry their rapists" and other assorted samples of deviant behavior fed to the passive consumers of daytime TV.[37]

Tucker and Bennett hammered away until finally, powerful Time Warner bowed to their pressure and got rid of its rap music subsidiary, Interscope Records Inc.; this involved divesting its 50 percent share of a highly profitable $100 million corporation. It was a sweet victory for Tucker, who three years before had been arrested protesting outside Nobody Beats the Wiz stores. Time Warner's music division featured such artists as Snoop Doggy Dogg, a rap star tried and acquitted for murder, whose last record sold 4 million copies; and Tupac Shakur, in prison for most of 1995 on a sex-crime conviction but still reaping profits from "Me Against the World," which sold 1 million copies in its first four weeks, and "Strugglin'," which included the words "I'd rather use my gun 'cause I get my money quicker."[38]

Tucker and Bennett's campaign was unprecedented in its moral and financial victory over one of America's most powerful corporations. Procter & Gamble and other corporations also followed suit in pulling their ads from "trash TV" in response to public pressure. What a shift from past experience; formerly protests against Hollywood risked harsh political consequences from a community that could be counted on to present a united front against any form of censorship—even against gangsta rappers. Ask Tipper Gore, whose advocacy of self-censorship of record album covers derailed her husband's quest for the 1988 presidential nomination when Hollywood moguls withdrew their support from his race.

The rising popularity of "trash TV" has provided even more outlets for anger primarily by victimizing the disenfranchised and furnishing a forum for hate groups. On the *Jerry Springer Show,* for example, a typical theme has one guest coming on the set to degrade another, usually over sexual betrayal; all hell breaks loose, and a fistfight ensues. The show has risen swiftly in the ratings and ranks only behind *Oprah.* A recent video of the Springer show's outtakes, *Too Hot for TV* (featuring lots of profanity and nudity) sold 300,000 copies in the first few months of distribution; its producers expect to sell 3 million.[39] To everyone's surprise, few advertisers or parent groups have protested the rise of "trash TV," despite the proliferation of sexual content and violence on many shows running during prime time. One of the most popular shows, *South Park,* "features four dirty-talking third graders who poison Granddad, promote a boxing match between Jesus and Satan, and converse with a talking pile of stool called 'Mr. Hankey the Christmas Poo.'" . . . Another prime-time drama, *Dawson's Creek,* portrays "one of the lead characters, a high school boy, . . . [having] an affair with his English teacher; another boy, a football star, was mocked by the girls for being impotent."[40]

The popularity of "trash TV" and gangsta rap shows a facet of current political anger that has escaped observation: the objectification of anger onto distinct victim groups, sometimes referred to as scapegoating. This is particularly true of male black rage against black women and black rage against Jews. "These are the innocent victims of hatred" who suffer from bigotry imposed by those who have projected their feelings as a "way of handling" their own "diminished self-esteem." Instead of anger being directed toward "that segment of the majority who have actively persecuted them," it is instead being turned against the handiest objects of hatred, "thus making a bigot of the scapegoat himself" and "providing a built-in rationalization for all his failure."[41]

Another criticism involves the media's role in allowing some of its representatives to play fast and loose with the truth. "We've legitimized lying with radio and TV punditry, and with infomercials," recalled Betsey Wright, Clinton's chief of staff when he was governor and head of "bimbo control" in his presidential campaign. "The gimmick now is to get a London tabloid to run the story; then the media here rush to print it. Angry people now have leaders. These people mobilize, and in forty-eight hours they can flood the U.S. Congress with letters and phone calls. They whip up anger and hate and exploit people's fear. The Klan could mobilize, but what is different today is that it is nationwide; it is easier to coalesce and organize the 'anti's' because being mad is easier than education and persuasion."

"We had a situation where a fired Tyson's (the Arkansas chicken company) employee accused his boss of flying cash to the White House," Wright continued. "Reporters talked to every single pilot and co-pilot going from Little Rock to Washington and couldn't get a shred of corroboration for the story. But Clinton was put in the position of proving it didn't happen."

With White House backing, Congress finally responded to critics by passing legislation in late February 1996, requiring the television industry to help parents control their children's viewing habits. The daunting assignment: to put V-chips (for violence chips) in television sets that would enable parents to block out shows for sex and violence and a ratings system that would cover 2,000 hours of daily TV programming. The system won't screen out political lies or ethnic or racial scapegoating, but the message was clear: In an antigovernment era, a sufficient number of Americans felt helpless enough, and sufficiently angry, to seek Congress's aid in controlling the excesses of the television industry.

## The Tygers of Wrath

Blake knew two centuries ago that the "tygers of wrath [were] stronger than the horses of instruction."[42] Rage is always easier than education, constructive dialogue, compromise, or even the patience to wait and see if the events (as in Little Rock) that produced the anger really occurred. Gangsta rap, "trash TV," and infomercials reveal societal rage in its most primitive, objectifying, scapegoating form. In the long term, scapegoating is a "dangerous and destructive device for handling the rage, frustration and impotence generated by our society," according to prominent psychiatrist Willard Gaylin. "It solves no problems [and] it is rarely effective psychologically."[43]

Nor is free-floating anger satisfying politically. The great dilemma is that with virtually no middle ground left, how will today's leaders fashion solutions for the next generation? They may win elections by capitalizing on controversy, but the devil shows up to collect his half of the bargain the minute they take the oath of office. The problem is that the temptation to profit from public anger over value conflicts has far exceeded the rewards for reaching consensus through compromise—a message political candidates have absorbed and utilized.

The greater dilemma involves how to forge workable political solutions from the nation's growing diversity. Americans have always valued their rich ethnic, racial, and religious mix; history books extol the value of the nation as a refuge from European political persecution based on religious and cultural uniformity. Today, the focus on diversity and multiculturalism has opened up college curricula and forced changes on all levels of society.

But at the same time, growing evidence supports the view of Homi K. Bhabha, who believes that pluralism isn't working, that America's vision of absorbing divergent groups into a "melting pot" of a nation belies a myth that has no relationship to reality.[44] Instead, groups tend to impose their culture—including their view of nationhood—on the rest of society, where the melting-pot metaphor has given way to flavors that compete vigorously with each other to retain their own individual identity: the Christian right with its own notions of family; the antiabortion groups willing to use violence to force their views on the polity; and the Tucker-Bennett-Dole coalition, which has successfully produced its morality play on the public stage.

Forgotten are the sacrifices that went into successful nation-building; forgotten too are the acceptance of divergent views and the value of assimilating immigrant cultures, which have both strengthened and sustained our democracy.

Thanks to the increasing devolution in the late 1990s of federal power to the states, more rancor is now being recorded at the local levels. Examples of menacing physical and verbal violence abound. In Lake Forest, Illinois, protesters smashed mailboxes and made obscene telephone calls after a decision of the town council; in Arizona a tax protester shot and wounded a Maricopa County supervisor; and in one small town the president of the school board grabbed a fellow board member by the throat to contest his point of view. The obvious reason is that now "the stakes are higher as Washington kicks back more issues to local governments," and that "the presence of television brings dissent out into the open and often encourages high drama."[45] But the underlying cause is deeper, revealing a new level of acceptance among the American public of anger and incivility in political life.

The zone of intolerance continues to spread as political issues harden into state referenda on civil rights for gays; federal welfare reform with its own racial divide; efforts by members of Congress intent on preventing pornography through the Internet; campus battles over whether to read "dead white males" such as Shakespeare, Milton, and Chaucer as opposed to literature from other cultures; and racial strife heightened each day by such events as the verdict in the O. J. Simpson trial, the candidacy of former grand dragon of the Ku Klux Klan David Duke in Louisiana, the Million Man March, the fire in Harlem, and the burning of an Alabama high school after its principal barred an interracial couple from attending the spring prom.

Is there a connection between the rising tide of hate speech, cultural divisions, and public policies that would have been unthinkable a decade ago? The greater political environment is the connection: The power of words can galvanize armies, stir nations, sell products, and incite domestic and international terrorism. Clearly we face a dilemma. On the one hand, we want to preserve our First Amendment rights, individual liberties, and tradition of political compromise. On the other, we must protect ourselves from increasing incidents of physical violence that have emerged from the escalating eruptions of political anger.

# 5

# Raging Pol

## *Governing Angry Americans*

Hell, there is no center.

— Ambassador Jim Sasser,
former Democratic senator from Tennessee

TOLEDO COMES AS CLOSE to the center as you can get. Middle of the road in its politics, the city and its two surrounding counties, which make up Ohio's Ninth Congressional District, also occupy a central role in the nation's economy with thousands of acres of rich farmland devoted to raising grain, hogs, and vegetables and millions of square feet of factory floors humming with activity. Toledo wraps its arms around the nation's anger as well, as people grapple with an era of change more dramatic than anything they have coped with in decades.

Marcy Kaptur has represented Toledo since 1982, when at the age of thirty-four she wrested the seat from a one-term Republican who had won on the coattails of President Reagan. An urban planner and former Carter White House appointee, Kaptur proceeded to build a solid reputation in Congress for her steadfast advocacy on behalf of protecting jobs and preventing trade policy from continuing to harm the national economy as well as her district. A leading opponent of NAFTA, she predicted, correctly, that America would lose jobs from this trade bill.[1]

Kaptur travels the district without notes, written speeches, or a phalanx of aides telling her what to say, whom to meet, and how to think. As she listens intently, her constituents recount their problems, job insecurities, and fears about the future of the economy.

"In the last ten years, we've proven there's no such thing as job security," said Roy C. Grosswiler, an organizer for Local 8 of the International Brotherhood of Electrical Workers. "Toledo Edison just laid off a bunch of employees. They gave them buyouts. Now they are rehiring them as part-time employees, working the same number of hours; only now they have no health coverage or retirement benefits. A lot of that is happening around here."

Unemployment, or underemployment, also aggravates the racial issue. "Hardly a day goes by that I don't get a complaint, 'I tried to join the union and you only wanted minorities,'" added Grosswiler. "That's a cop-out."

Affirmative action joins gun control, immigration, foreign aid, and welfare programs in provoking an inordinate amount of anger across the district—from factory floors to legion halls to senior citizens centers. Passionate opinions pour forth from voters everywhere despite the fact that information about

Representative Marcy Kaptur (D–Ohio) meets with fellow opponents of NAFTA in Milwaukee (July 1995). Photo by Michael Halloran; courtesy of Michael Halloran and the office of Marcy Kaptur.

these issues is not always accurate. Special animus is leveled at the welfare system, especially from women, who bitterly resent the fact that they are working while others enjoy life on the dole. "That really frosts me," said Harriet Eckel, a diminutive, white-coated worker in a small office off the factory floor at Progressive Industries, Inc., an automotive metal-stamping company that makes hinges for car doors. "My kids had to pay for college. The government gives unwed mothers a free ride through college. They should have to pay even if it takes fifty years. My kids kept their noses clean. I had a friend who was laid off. She went on welfare and had her dental bills paid. I have to pay my own."

Her coworker, Betty Lewis, added: "I know one person who divorced her husband just to get the welfare benefits. He was making $21 an hour in a factory. Welfare was meant just to get people back on their feet. Not to permanently support people."

A deep sense of despair pervades the workforce about the government's inability to secure its future benefits. "We're giving all this money into Social Security," exclaimed Lewis. "We're never going to get it back. I won't be around."

Lewis, a Mormon like Eckel, has just adopted two troubled teenage girls, whom she has absorbed into her family of three other children, aged eleven to eighteen. Her husband works as a church custodian. "We felt we had a mission," she explained.

As expected, problems with Social Security abound at the South Toledo Senior Center, a recreational facility where over 500 people met to hear Kaptur speak at a Sunday lunch of roast pork, corn, and fried potatoes. Callous bureaucrats and the difficulty in dealing with them formed the bulk of the disputes. "My husband died three years and four months ago, and I still don't get any benefits," said Margie Perz, a retired official from the State Board of Education. "Social Security has been screwing me up, and I worked for twenty-seven years as a public employee." Perz's twenty-six-year-old nephew now lives with her, a former marine who can't get a job. "He went to Saudi Arabia and he came back," said Perz. "I'm disgusted. Immigrants get everything."

"The government has used Social Security money improperly," agreed John Owad, himself a former marine who retired after forty-one years from Libby-Owens-Corning, a glass manufacturer now owned by British investors. (Toledo used to be the glass-manufacturing capital of the nation.) Owad thinks the money is flowing out for foreign aid, a theme that echoed throughout the district. "They are giving up money to third-rate countries, who drag our troops through Somalia. We should take the money away from the UN. We can't play Santa any more."

"Medicine is our biggest problem," read a sign held up by a well-dressed woman in a red pantsuit. She leaned across her table and explained that Medicare doesn't pay for prescription drugs. "The golden years; where are they?" asked Eva Eronakowski. "We worked for everything we get. I fear for my children."

Kaptur listened carefully to their problems, addressed their questions, tried to put their fears into political perspective, and intervened when she could to solve their problems with government bureaucracy. The expertise of her aide, Susan Lowe, who holds a degree in gerontology, proved especially helpful at the senior citizens center. "There are 5,000 percent more millionaires per capita in the Senate than there are in the general population, and 3,000 [percent] more in the House," Kaptur told the senior citizens. "They don't know what the struggle is all about. They forget where they came from. The chairman of the House Budget Committee, John Kasich [R–Ohio], went to bed every night with a full stomach. Both of his parents worked for the Post Office. Gingrich's father was career military. He had full health coverage. This is an important year to pay attention."

Later as her car passed the boarded-up Toledo Glôve Manufacturing Company en route to the African American congregation at the Mt. Zion Baptist Church, Kaptur lamented the loss of industries and jobs in this depressed-looking neighborhood of unpainted buildings and vacant lots. "People here used to walk to work," she said. "There is a lack of hope here that anything will make a difference."

Despite their problems, the choir at the church sang "Victory Is Mine" with great gusto. "If we keep our hands in God's hands, it doesn't matter what government does," preached Sister Lillian Darrington. Kaptur reminded her audience that like her, none of them would have been able to vote at the founding of the republic. "We're still working toward a more perfect union," she remarked, "and we've done a better job of it recently." At the break, every member of the congregation came over to hug, kiss, and welcome Kaptur, along with the two other white women accompanying her. Later, several of them expressed their views. "I don't see how Clinton could have voted for NAFTA," said Ron Harris, a former textile worker. "How could he not see how employers would send jobs to Mexico? Congress doesn't care about the people's struggle. We agree that some welfare recipients are freeloaders. But you can't eliminate a whole generation. I grew up in this neighborhood. Look at the companies that have left Toledo: Champion, Toledo Glove, Interlake Steel. . . . Now the place looks like a bomb shelter. Like Beirut. A parent dies, leaves the property; nine out of ten chances the kids are unemployed or in jail. They lose the house, or it gets burned down. Dole and Gingrich are doing the Democrats a service, getting people out to vote who have never voted before."

Another parishioner, Sister Mary Cleveland, reluctantly revealed her own personal tragedy: "My husband is on Social Security. He's had three strokes. We're raising four grandchildren, two of them cocaine-addicted. Government has cut out subsidies. The black community has a terrible drug problem. Grandparents are suffering for it."[2]

Why did so many of Kaptur's constituents buy into the Contract with America? And why did so many of them vote Republican despite huge margins (a 75 percent majority in the 1994 election) for her? "Because the Democrats didn't solve their problems when they were in office," Kaptur said, "and the Republicans didn't solve their problems. They are losing faith in institutions." That means all institutions, including those in the private sector. "I went to a BP plant in Oregon, Ohio," she recalled. "BP had just announced it was putting $200 million into the plant, making it the flagship facility in the Midwest. Ordinarily, this would be cause for cheering. Instead, workers sat around in their chairs, their shoulders hunched in. . . . 'Can we really believe you?' they asked, looking at me in some disbelief. . . . 'Do you know how many times I've changed jobs?' asked one worker. 'Five times . . . Champion, Dana, BP . . . five times in all.'"

Kaptur also tries to offset all the antigovernment sentiment pervading her district by reminding voters everywhere of the benefits they enjoy from government. "Ohio has more people who use the GI Bill than any other state in the union," she told a hall full of veterans at the Diehn post of the American Legion in the town of Sylvania. Kaptur was responsible for erecting a monument in Washington to World War II, an idea that was generated at the Diehn post by a legion member named Roger Durbin.

Everywhere she traveled, voters voiced their disgust at the infantile behavior of Congress during the protracted budget battle. "The only thing missing from the Congress is a calliope; it's just like a circus," snorted Dwayne Austin, a warehouse man driving a forklift at Uritech International Inc., a firm that makes wheel covers, among other products, from processed chemicals. "Lock them in a room and don't give them anything but bread and water until they agree," suggested another gentleman. "Don't even let them go to the bathroom."

At a town meeting at the Eastwood Middle School in Freedom Township— the most Republican township in Kaptur's district—she explained how the current budget fight affected people from all corners of the district: "The Department of Labor can't fund long-term worker adjustment programs; they can't let contracts; railroad workers have found their retirement benefits cut; Peace Corps volunteers were left stranded without money; trips were canceled and people lost supersaver plane tickets because they couldn't get visas; classes that came to the capital couldn't get in to see anything because everything was shut down." This was reality, a harsh contrast to the view voters like legion member Matthew Dallas expressed of how irked he was at furloughed federal workers enjoying a "free vacation." After all, he said, "they will get paid."

Later at a meeting in Ottawa Township, Kaptur urged everyone to write letters of protest at the 44 percent cut in mass transportation slated for the district. Her background in public finance emerged as she ticked off the hard choices facing the country, focusing especially on Ohio. "Half the fight is over health benefits," she explained. "There are 10.5 million people in Ohio, and 1.5 million of them are on Medicaid; two-thirds of that goes to nursing homes. We're getting a 20 percent cut in Medicaid. With that kind of shortfall, where will the money come from? How are we going to take care of these folks? We aren't even talking about these issues." Kaptur blames income erosion for the shortfall in public benefits: "If workers have not had a wage increase in real terms for over twenty years, that means the revenue stream to Medicare is not flowing."

Gun laws also rank high on the anger list, with women as well as men viewing gun control as an assault on their favorite sport of recreational hunting. "I know I don't need 'em [AK-47 assault rifles] to hunt deer, but I like to collect them," said a plant manager. Ohio is known as the Buckeye State for the nuts that fall from trees, but the "buckeye" was so named because it looks like the eye of a buck—signifying the importance of hunting to the state.

Despite its passion for guns, Ohio has never developed much of a militia movement, according to Kaptur, although that view is subject to interpretation. The Southern Poverty Law Center has identified fifty-one Patriot groups in the state.[3] The state remains far more tolerant of diversity than other states, Kaptur continued: "Ohio is not as isolated; there is more respect for the organized military. We have a pluralistic tradition. [In my district] we have an Islamic mosque; three Jewish synagogues; every variety of Christian; Greek Catholic; Lebanese and Syrian Orthodox; and Hindu and Baha'i temples. We have farmers and labor union people. Our institutions have broader bases and greater outreach to people with different traditions."

Corporate executives also share their workers' concerns about the economy and have their own view of what is needed from Congress. "The tax structure favors larger business; I don't need the money from accelerated depreciation in five years, I need the money now," complained Scott Murray, CEO of Uritech. Before Goodyear sold the plant to Murray and his partner, it employed 700 workers; now the number is 100, but the new firm shares 10 percent of its before-tax profits with its employees. We also need "better long-term medical coverage," Murray added, as well as venture capital not exclusively in the hands of "legalized loan sharks" who take 35–50 percent of the profits.

This was a "tough year to be there [in Congress]," said Kaptur, who never wearied even at the end of a long day of grilling from her embattled constituents. "There is no spirit of cooperation between the White House and Congress. That is not right."

Toledo shows the dilemma today's political leaders face as they confront their angry constituents—the value conflicts, economic fears, and psychological distress that envelop political life. Everywhere they look they see:

- issues so bipolar in scope that no room is left for compromise,
- antigovernment sentiment so strong that leaders most inclined to compromise are leaving office in droves,

- groups and beliefs once relegated to the extremes now occupying the political center, and
- mainstream voters so alienated that they look outside the system for answers—and for fresh leadership.

## Bipolarity in Politics

The themes that made Toledo citizens so angry echoed throughout the 1990s. President Clinton turned the government shutdown into a compelling issue in the 1996 campaign, casting full blame for the furloughs on the congressional Republicans. The subject of international competition also accelerated quickly and became an enormous problem for the president, who was unable to convince the 105th Congress to go along with him on "fast-track" legislation. This would have been a "no-brainer" in past Congresses, which passed NAFTA and similar agreements dating back to World War II that automatically conveyed the power over international trade to the White House without much interference. Newspaper exposés in 1998 revealing the private fortunes of the Suharto family in Indonesia and Benazir Bhutto in Pakistan, not to mention the worldwide real estate holdings of former President Mobutu Sese Seko of Zaire, complicated the issue. As a result, legislative involvement accelerated, further linking foreign trade and foreign aid. The Asian financial crisis, coupled with greater public awareness of these vast fortunes, suddenly put the $18 billion appropriation to the International Monetary Fund (IMF) in 1998 in jeopardy, as voters began to question the IMF's role in relation to their tax dollars. In response to this sudden crisis, Clinton decided not to pursue the "fast-track" bill in the waning days of the 105th Congress in order to devote his full attention and political resources to the IMF, so that its leaders could continue negotiating the Asian economic crisis and prevent its fallout from affecting other regions. Health benefits also climbed to the top of the political charts, with increasing calls in Congress and in state legislatures for regulating health maintenance organizations.

"Hell, there is no center," declared Jim Sasser, one of the leading victims of the Republican sweep of 1994. The three-term senator from Tennessee and chairman of the Budget Committee was about to win a hard-fought contest for majority leader, making his defeat at the hands of a political unknown named Bill Frist all the more painful. At the time of his election Frist was a forty-one-year-old heart and lung transplant surgeon whose family had founded Hospital Corporation of America, today Columbia/HCA, the nation's leading private hospital company. On the advice of his pollster, Frist painted Sasser as a Washington insider whose liberal votes in the Senate cost voters their guns, their jobs, and their future. Some of Sasser's positions were "wildly at odds with most Tennessee voters," observed political analyst David Beiler, including his efforts to protect "social spending against enormous pressures to reduce the deficit" and his opposition to the renewal of the "patent of the Daughters of the Confederacy, a group founded in Nashville."[4]

"I was a centrist," Sasser exclaimed, bridling at the charge that his views veered off the charts of mainstream Tennessee. "Tennessee had a longer waiting period than the [Brady] bill. The NRA [National Rifle Association] went after me viciously. They ran TV ads using Charlton Heston and accused me of lying to the people. I had voted for the Brady Bill and for the ban on assault weapons. The NRA has 50,000 members in Tennessee. They controlled a whole lot of votes. All you need is a bunch of guys in the Goodyear plant bad-mouthing me."

If anything, Sasser's defeat proved how easily voters were manipulated into thinking of him as a left-leaning liberal. "They wrap you in the liberal mantra. He's going to take away our guns and give women and blacks your jobs."

"In my campaign," continued Sasser, "it was the anger of the white male. The anger at Washington from unemployed trade union members who had lost their jobs on the assembly line and were now doing crummy service jobs. They blamed affirmative action; they blamed blacks. Most important, they blamed women. . . . During the Thomas hearings [hearings on the confirmation of Clarence Thomas to the Supreme Court] white men kept calling in from the rural part of the state, which has a heavily black population, to support Thomas. Their accusations reaffirmed what was going on in their lives: women trying to run the show. Their masculinity is being threatened. I almost became majority leader. In ordinary times, people would have been proud. This year it worked against me. Public ignorance is the problem. Plus the skillful effort to manipulate that ignorance."

Sasser's experience also revealed how far right the mainstream had moved in a few short years, driving scores of senators and representatives from political office. "All the centrists are leaving the Senate," he concluded. "The newly elected people will be bipolar."

By early 1996 it looked as if Sasser's prophecy was right: Thirteen senators (eight Democrats and five Republicans) and thirty-five House members (twelve Republicans and twenty-three Democrats) all announced that they would not be running for reelection.[5] Like dominoes, they fell in rapid succession, one after another. Some cited the decline in civility; others blamed the media, political parties, and the harsh climate of politics. No doubt they all felt profoundly insulted by the overwhelming public support for term limits: According to ABC polling data, 73 percent of the general public supported term limits; 68 percent of those regarding themselves as liberals favored term limits.[6]

As of February 1998 the total number of GOP members who had announced plans to retire at the end of the 105th Congress was fifteen, including Representative Bill Paxon (R–N.Y.), who had planned to run for the leadership. At that point fourteen Democrats had also announced they were not running for reelection.[7] For those who remained in Congress, 1998 turned out to be an especially good year for incumbents. *CongressDaily* reported that with over half the filing deadlines passed, no fewer than 54 sitting House members—including 33 Republicans and 21 Democrats—could look forward to totally uncontested elections, that is, elections without a major party opponent. That means that "almost 22 percent of major party candidates [would] be getting a free ride in the fall."[8]

One departing senator, Alan Simpson (R–Wyo.)—widely respected for his role as the architect of immigration reform—flung some of the blame at the "unaccountable" media for their propensity to thrive on "conflict and controversy, not clarity." Speaking to a receptive audience in his hometown of Cody, Simpson also accused the media of damaging the hearing process in the Senate, as they did when they transformed Supreme Court nominee Robert Bork from a serious candidate who had never had a judicial opinion overturned into a "gargoyle." Curious especially in light of his hostility to them, the media turned into a virtual Greek chorus lamenting Simpson's departure from the Senate. Here goes yet another "moderate" abandoning the Senate, ran many of the stories. Had all those reporters forgotten his longtime reputation as an ardent conservative or his remarks during the Gulf War accusing CNN correspondent Peter Arnett of being a "communist sympathizer?" Or was this view of Simpson as a moderate—a label the senator himself would challenge—further evidence of the right moving to center stage?[9]

A genuine moderate, Senator William Cohen blamed the impasse over the budget in 1995 and 1996 as "instrumental in crystallizing this issue [whether to retire] for me."[10] The son of a baker, the author of eight books, and the only Republican to vote against his party's budget in 1995, Cohen experienced the sharp sting of bipolarism from his own party. The current pattern, he says, runs more along the lines of saying to leaders: "What we want is someone out there driving our flag into the ground saying, 'Here's where I stand. No compromise.'"[11] It is unlikely that Cohen's successor will be able to withstand the centrifugal forces in Congress to follow this three-term Senate veteran's politically independent record as a fiscal conservative and social moderate who steadfastly protected elderly Americans against his party's onslaught to unravel federal nursing home regulations. Cohen was appointed secretary of defense in Clinton's second term, the first and only Republican chosen by the Clinton administration for cabinet service.

If anything, the rash of resignations shows that the force of bipolarism will get much worse before the old traditions of compromise begin to kick in. The question is, Why does the public tolerate such high levels of conflict from its political leaders, particularly when those conflicts lead to legislative paralysis? Where was public pressure, for example, during the budget battle that dragged on throughout 1995 and early 1996 with two government furloughs and the specter of the U.S. government teetering on the edge of default?

The answer is that Congress merely reflects society, mirroring the conflicts that already roil everyday life; polls show Americans sharply divided on such hot-button issues as the federal budget, flag burning, abortion, late-term abortion, and affirmative action. No natural middle ground appears on the flag-burning issue, for example: People feel just as strongly in opposition to the act of burning the American flag in protest as their opponents view their constitutional right to dissent in any manner they see fit. In the summer of 1995, the public was evenly split between the Republican plan to balance the budget in seven years (45 percent) and Clinton's plan to balance the budget in ten years (42 percent), according to a *Washington Post–ABC News* poll. The survey called this division "gridlock in the electorate," which merely mirrors gridlock in the legislative process.[12]

Both parties actually worked so hard in 1997 and 1998 to reduce the deficit that their efforts reflected far more cooperation and consensus than gridlock. Also, by that time politicians were responding to intense public pressure to reduce the deficit and to prevent another shutdown; and both parties rushed to cover their bases on these issues. Republicans rightly concluded that one of the reasons they lost the 1996 presidential election was that Clinton had effectively boxed them into a corner as the villains of government closings, while the president fought the image of "free-spending Democrats" by concentrating his efforts on issues previously dominated by Republicans: deficit reduction and welfare reform.[13]

The real mystery is why political leaders insist on prolonging bipolar fights, since that route leads so clearly to defeat. Richard E. Cohen and William Schneider of the *National Journal* acknowledged the role of bipolarism and gridlock in the second term of the 103rd Congress as a major factor that led to

the Democratic defeat in 1994. "The votes revealed striking differences between the two parties on most issues and notable regional disparities within
each party," they wrote. "The sharp partisan splits also help to explain why so
little major legislation was enacted."[14]

Another interesting switch from 1994 to 1998 revealed the public's strong
aversion to excessive congressional activity. In its zeal to undo the past forty
years of Democratic rule, the 104th Congress engaged in a frenzy of legislation
under the rubric of the Contract with America. But the Republicans' hostile
position against entitlements—including middle-class entitlements such as
Medicare and Social Security as well as welfare—cost them dearly in the 1996
election and led inexorably to the 105th Congress, which soon became known
for its legislative indolence.

What works in parliamentary systems—clear-cut, programmatic divisions
within and between the two major political parties—apparently has the opposite effect in America. American political parties lack the discipline as well as
the ideological roots of their European counterparts. Moreover, for most of the
past three decades, Americans have been forced to contend with the realities of
what Charles Jones calls "separated government": when two parties share the
executive and legislative branches of government.[15]

Whatever the causes, bipolarism has determined the configuration of politics for years to come, as the long-running budget battle has shown. "When issues are so strong but so polarized, how can we talk to each other?" asked Representative Kaptur. In this environment, leaders learn to move with alacrity to
the north and south poles of issues lest they get left behind in political no-
man's-land. President Clinton and his fellow Democrats successfully positioned themselves as guardians of Medicare, Social Security, and even less popular social programs as the environment and Medicaid, leaving Republicans to
dig their heels in on balancing the budget and curbing welfare.

In fact, once the budget deficit stays down permanently and welfare reform
has receded, what new issues await both sides? As issues such as late-term
abortions have shown, the bipolar politics of the 1990s is here to stay: Whatever the topic, policy positions will most likely be divisive and be forged at the
extremes. The situation is likely to grow even worse as the increasing presence
of television cameras deters compromise and encourages posturing.

## Antigovernment Anger

"The ballot cry is clear," said former one-term Oregon governor Barbara
Roberts, a Democrat. "Citizens don't trust government. The anti-government

attitude is of proportions that threaten our democracy. Citizens are bombarded with stories of government failure. That means they are believing nobody. We're painting all politicians with the same broad brush."[16]

Antigovernment sentiment comes packaged in the wrappings of political anger: apathy, blame, confusion, alienation, anxiety, ignorance, deprivation, and anomie. Poll after poll peels away layers of hostility to government, shedding more light on the individual lives of people than on the nature of public animosity toward government. Belligerence toward government takes many forms; its targets include the president, members of Congress, and civil servants right down to the churlish clerk at the Motor Vehicle Bureau.

Feelings against government are best reflected in polls that measure "confidence in government," which has "declined precipitously and steadily from the mid-1960s on," according to sociologist Seymour Martin Lipset. The results over a thirty-year period are dramatic.

- A poll by Louis Harris showed those expressing a great deal of confidence in government at 41 percent in 1964, compared to 12 percent in 1994.
- A whopping 76 percent responded affirmatively in 1964 to the question posed by Daniel Yankelovich, "How much of the time can you trust the government to do what is right?" compared to 19 percent answering the same question in 1994.[17]
- A riveting series in the *Washington Post* in early 1996 supported these and many other polls, concluding that the public's antigovernment feelings were rooted in feelings of personal alienation, economic distress, and public ignorance. A few of these factors taken separately reveal their intimate relationship to political anger.
- Troubling results from a poll by Peter Hart and Robert Teeter revealed that only 38 percent of Americans believed that government helped them to achieve the American dream. That figure actually rose from 31 percent in 1995.[18]
- The same poll disclosed that 76 percent of the public thought "wasteful government spending is a major cause for the reduced level of confidence in government." Other factors that explained voter mistrust and lack of confidence in government were: crime, poverty, drugs, deeply flawed political leadership, self-interested leaders, the influence of special interests, programs out of step with moral values, partisan politics, low ethical standards among elected officials, and unkept promises.[19]
- A hopeful sign emerged in the fall of 1997, when the Pew Research Council published a report from a series of focus groups and surveys

that showed slight decreases in public criticism of government. Their conclusions: that Americans are still quite critical of government, but not as critical as they were in 1994; 64 percent agreed that government was wasteful and inefficient, down from 69 percent in 1994; and 76 percent agreed that politicians tended to lose touch with the public fairly quickly, a slight decrease from 83 percent in 1994.[20]

- A rather chilling finding from the Pew survey is that the public's view of government is clearly reciprocated: "Government mistrust of the public is striking," said the report. "Only 31 percent of lawmakers . . . said they think Americans know enough about issues facing Congress to form wise opinions. . . . only 13 percent of presidential appointees and 14 percent of SES [Senior Executive Service] members expressed confidence in the public's understanding of the issues. . . . "[21]

- And whom do Americans trust? The military, according to the Pew survey, one of the least democratic of all public institutions. Thirty years ago, the year of the Tet offensive and at the height of the Vietnam War, voters began to lose confidence in the military, a trend that has since been reversed. The public's confidence returned slowly; by the end of the 1990s "a curious picture emerges of a public by and large satisfied and confident in their military and of a military that is increasingly skeptical, critical, and alienated from that public."[22]

## Alienation

Suspicion of government is strongly linked to suspicion of strangers; in fact, the public's "mistrust of each other is a major reason Americans have lost confidence in the federal government and virtually every other major national institution." Every single "generation that has come of age since the 1950s has been more mistrusting of human nature [and] nearly two in three Americans believe that most people can't be trusted." Compare that to data compiled in 1964, when "three in four Americans trusted the federal government all or most of the time."[23]

Anecdotal evidence also supports this theory of growing atomization and alienation among Americans. Nightly film clips during the worst days of the Washington, D.C., blizzard of January 1996 showed people walking miles on main arteries to the Metro while dozens of cars passed them by. Were drivers fearful of crime? Thoughtless? Selfish? Or just immune to the pedestrians struggling through blizzard conditions to get to work? What happened to the old American spirit of barn raising, where whole towns would show up to help their fellow citizens? During the same period Democratic pollster Stan Greenberg surveyed young, married, non-college-educated, blue-collar, white work-ing-class voters, in his words "the people most likely to vote Republican." The message that emerged fortified the theme of alienation, that government made it *harder* to progress economically and the standard of living would rise only through dint of individual self-reliance—which meant taking on second and third jobs.[24]

## Ignorance

The long courtship of ignorance and anger continues; less knowledgeable Americans are more likely to believe that government makes every problem worse. Ironically, the level of political education among voters has remained as low as it was during the 1940s even though the average number of years Amer-icans spend in school has increased from nine to more than twelve. Some hor-rifying specifics: Four in ten of those surveyed didn't know the name of the vice president; two-thirds could not name their congressional representative; and nearly half couldn't name Speaker Newt Gingrich even though he had ap-peared on the cover of *Time Magazine* as its man of the year for 1995. The rigid cynicism that emerged "transcends party identification or political ideology."[25]

It should come as no surprise that ignorance about public issues extends to foreign affairs as well. On the controversial issue of foreign aid nearly six in ten respondents believed that government spent more on foreign aid than on Medicare even though foreign aid, excluding military aid, comes to slightly more than 1 percent of the entire federal budget and Medicare tops out at 13 percent. If the public knew the truth about foreign aid, would they have al-lowed Congress to slash assistance to immunization and agricultural programs destined for Africa, in addition to other international humanitarian pro-grams?[26]

"All you have to do is stop foreign aid for thirty days and you will balance the budget," remarked a Korean War veteran at a town meeting in Freedom Township, Ohio. "Why are we sending $8 million a day to El Salvador? Why $1 billion to Turkey? We're keeping everybody in the world." And from another member of the audience, a furtive question: "What about Israel, while we're talking about it."

From town meetings to factory floors, voters seethe over foreign aid. "We're giving this money away to all these rinky-dink countries," said Harriet Eckel, a worker at Progressive Industries, Inc. "We're never going to get it back. A lot of these countries think we're jerks, anyway."

Representative Kaptur explained patiently that the United States actually gave very little money to assist foreign nations and that, in fact, out of all seventeen industrialized countries, the United States contributed the least in non-military foreign aid. Despite her protestations of fact, however, her constituents remained enraged at government funding for foreign countries, a theme heard everywhere in the district. Perhaps these feelings have become more pronounced as government pleads for individual sacrifice and hard choices while it hacks away at benefits. Indeed, in light of their daily struggle to pay the rising costs of basic dental care, tuition, medical insurance, and transportation just to get to work, no wonder the thought of sending even $12 billion abroad seems excessive to so many Americans.

## Apathy

Falling voter registration numbers also feed into the antigovernment crucible. In the congressional election of 1994, hailed as a huge Republican mandate by the media as well as by the Republicans themselves, only 38 percent of the public voted. Presidential elections draw voter turnouts hovering around the 50 percent mark. And primaries, which can make or break presidential candidates, attract the lowest numbers of all: Voting in the Louisiana primary, which catapulted candidate Pat Buchanan to the status of contender, were only 5 percent of all registered Republican voters in that state; in Iowa, which also elevated Buchanan, the figure was only 17 percent. The election of 1996 was noted for turning out the lowest number of eligible voters (less than 50 percent) since 1924, a conundrum that has mystified political leaders as well as political scientists. Why don't more Americans—who are fortunate enough to live in a free and democratic society—exercise their right to vote?

Several explanations for voter apathy have emerged from the 1996 election cycle. Marcia Smith blamed the lack of media attention, charging that "the mainstream press virtually ignored the turnout debacle, claiming, incredibly, that the poor showing at the polls means the electorate is basically satisfied."[27] Another explanation blames the ubiquitousness of pollsters. Everett Carll Ladd, a renowned scholar of public opinion, noted that it was "likely that pollsters and reporters dampened voters' interest, hence participation, by announcing that the Presidential contest was really no contest at all." During the election season, he continued, no fewer than "300 national polls asked voters one variant or another of the questions: 'How would you vote if the presidential election were being held today?' Polls asked this question only half as often during the 1992 campaign, and only ten times from Labor Day through election even in 1968."[28]

Lack of interest in the candidates has become the most compelling reason for nonvoting, a reason that many interpret as a form of political anger—anger

at the current crop of candidates, anger at government, anger at current policies; take your pick. In fact, some of the 88 million Americans who do not
bother to vote in presidential elections actually make a conscious choice *not* to
vote, even though they might be politically active in other ways, such as can-
vassing voters, distributing campaign literature, and participating in local elections. A recent study on voter apathy concluded that the patterns have not
changed, even though the numbers of nonvoters are rising. Compared to voters, they are apt to be younger and less educated, to have lower household incomes, and they are less likely to follow politics. They are also more likely to
belong to a minority group.[29]

## Anxiety

A great deal of anxiety about the future is leveled at government, with 73 percent
of the public reporting that the country is "on the wrong track." Much of this
anxiety focuses on the economy and how individuals are going to fit into a future
fraught with such unknown variables as globalism and the impact of technology.
The percentage of people "very worried" that they would not be able to afford
health care grew from "50% in March 1994 to 66% in late 1995," accompanied by
uneasiness over "saving enough money to retire, paying for college tuition, losing
a job or taking a pay cut, or being able to afford a home."[30]

Gender differences have also begun to emerge in the anger portfolio, with
women scoring higher on the anxiety and anger scales than men. The explanation: Women are more anxious about the economy, more concerned about the
growing income gap, and more prone to think that government can't be
trusted.[31] As the 1996 presidential and congressional elections drew near, the
specter of a gender gap loomed on the political horizon, forming the image of
women as the newest group on the cutting edge of anger. It was "Working-class
women without college degrees" who threatened to become the "angry white
men of '96 for Democrats," who would clearly benefit in 1996 as the Republicans did in 1994.[32]

In a two-way presidential race, women favored Clinton over Dole by a margin of 52 percent to 34 percent; men were evenly split, according to a *New York
Times–CBS News* poll taken in April 1996. (In the actual election, Clinton
claimed an 11 percent lead among women.) The same poll revealed similar
splits in attitudes toward Congress: Women backed Democratic candidates by
a 16-point margin; men favored Republicans by a 10-point edge. Many women
regarded the Gingrich-led revolution in Congress as having gone too far in efforts to cut back on entitlement programs; they also feared for the future of

programs like Medicare and Social Security.[33] Pro-choice women widened the margins following the Republican debate in South Carolina in March 1996, where virtually all the Republican candidates, even those who considered themselves "moderate," capitulated to the hard right position on abortion when confronted by a young woman in the audience who asked what the candidates would recommend if she were raped by a vicious criminal. Just as the angry white male dominated the 1992 election, "soccer moms" led the postmortem discussions following the 1996 elections. Haley Barbour, then Chairman of the Republican National Committee, admitted that Clinton led Dole by 20 percent among women voters, and he called on his party to figure out how to win women back. The "soccer mom" label never went beyond the phrasemakers to examine the actual components of the women's vote— namely, which issue was more decisive in drawing women into the Democratic fold, entitlements or reproductive choice?

## Corruption

A steady drumbeat of political malfeasance further stokes growing public cynicism. "There has been no administration since Nixon without a scandal," Governor Roberts pointed out. "We all look alike to a disillusioned public. It gets easier and easier to get mad. Americans are given lots of reasons to get mad about government." One reason, according to Roberts, is that "politicians are getting more insular."[34] On the closely related question of corruption, the University of Michigan Survey Research Center found that in 1964, 29 percent of the public believed that government is pretty much run by a few big interests looking out for themselves, compared to 80 percent answering that question affirmatively in 1994.[35]

## Blame and Corruption

The question of political corruption continued to plague voters into the late 1990s. Four in nine Americans (46 percent) identified "low ethical standards" as a major cause of "lowered public confidence in government." What upsets them most is the idea that "politicians pursue their own interests and careers ... *at the expense of serving the people that elect them.*" Moreover, they will "say anything to get elected, then frequently break campaign promises."[36]

It is only natural for people to cast blame when they are angered by corruption, the economy, or gridlock. Blame is the one resource that is flung around generously: Thirty-five percent blame Congress and 27 percent blame themselves. The supreme paradox is that even with such high disapproval ratings for Congress, most voters still plan to reelect their own legislator. The message comes through clearly as "Throw the bums out, but not my bum," concluded Richard Morin, polling director for the *Washington Post*.[37]

Many blame the media, but the media also convey the message of a declining polity. Citizens are assaulted with so many stories of political corruption, bipolarism, incivility, and meanness of spirit that they tend to believe the worst of their leaders. Just take the January 24, 1996, issue of *The Hill* newspaper, tracking just one week's activity on Capitol Hill, where a sampling of headlines uncovered a flurry of anger, ethics violations, the corrupting influences of political money, and conflicts of interest:

- "Gift Ban Angers House Spouses"—about anger and confusion among congressional spouses, particularly working spouses, who can't cope with the confusing new ethics restrictions.
- "House Hands Pink Slip to 113 Postal Workers"—about the new Republican majority's harsh move to fire all but six postal workers to make room for a new privatized service.
- "Hawking Newt at a $125 a Plate Dinner"—about a politics-as-usual fund-raiser for Representative David Funderburk (R–N.C.), using the Speaker's views as bait for campaign funds.
- "Spurned by the Speaker, GOP Frosh Court Armey"—about the division in the ranks of Republican freshmen angered by Gingrich's cancellation of two campaign appearances.
- "Ethics Subcommittee Chairman Porter Goss Faces Potential Conflicts of Interest on GOPAC."[38]

In prior weeks, *The Hill* uncovered the scandalous activities of Representative Enid Waldholtz (R–Utah) and her illegal $1.8 million campaign contribution and Representative Barbara-Rose Collins (D–Mich.) and her financial misconduct involving her campaign, her congressional staff, and her scholarship fund for black underprivileged youth.[39] The following year, *The Hill* newspaper also broke the stories on the aborted Republican coup of Speaker Newt Gingrich, in the summer of 1997, and the questionable business dealings of Representative Earl Hilliard (D–S.C.), who allegedly diverted $100,000 from his campaign coffers to business and nonprofit organizations technically owned or controlled by members of the Hilliard family or by Hilliard himself.

Add to this brew the daily press coverage of Whitewater, focusing on charges from Congress and the special prosecutor leveled against First Lady Hillary Clinton. Did she lie about her role representing the Madison Guaranty Bank in

Arkansas? Was she forthcoming about documents? What made those documents suddenly appear in the family living quarters after two years? And what was her role in the travel office firings?

Soon the focus zoomed in on the president, with relentless attacks forthcoming from Kenneth Starr, the special prosecutor appointed to investigate Whitewater; and a sexual harassment lawsuit brought by a former Arkansas state employee, Paula Jones. A host of scandals riddled the Clinton administration, specifically including:

- The travel office firings: Seven travel office employees in the White House were fired in May 1993, allegedly to make room for Clinton patronage appointees.
- The death of Vincent Foster: Foster's death was officially ruled a suicide, but questions were raised about Foster's involvement in the Whitewater case, the lack of FBI access to his office during the initial investigation of his death, and the suggestion that documents were removed from his office.
- The indictment and conviction of Webster Hubbell: After Hubbell's plea, friends of the president funneled over $700,000 worth of work to Hubbell, raising questions about whether the White House was involved in arranging these payments to ensure his silence. A second indictment for tax evasion against Hubbell, his wife, his accountant, and his tax attorney was handed down in early May 1998, but the charges eventually were dismissed.
- FBI files: Hundreds of FBI background files on prominent Republicans were received by the White House, improperly, aides said. Security Director Craig Livingstone was fired over the matter.
- Billing records: First Lady Hillary Clinton's billing records from the Rose law firm turned up in the White House's private quarters two years after they were subpoenaed by Starr. This led to allegations that the administration was hiding evidence that revealed that Mrs. Clinton had performed legal work for Madison Guaranty Savings and Loan, the failed S&L that figures prominently in the Whitewater investigation.
- Special prosecutors appointed for cabinet members Mike Espy, of the Department of Agriculture, and Henry Cisneros, of the Department of Housing and Urban Development.

The Paula Jones lawsuit eventually was thrown out of court, but her appeal and the suit itself occupied a substantial amount of White House time as well as media attention. Starr's investigation eventually uncovered an entirely new sexual scandal, this time involving taped conversations from a White House intern, Monica Lewinsky, who spoke of her alleged affair with the president. Soon after this scandal broke, Kathleen Willey, a White House volunteer, appeared on *60 Minutes* to describe the president's sexual advances to her in a private meeting at which she was importuning him for a paid position. Charges and countercharges flew between the White House and the special prosecutor. Sources from Starr's office defended the prosecutor on the grounds that he was not interested in the president's private life but focused his investigation on whether the president had exercised improper influence to silence his accusers—in the case of Lewinsky, Clinton was accused of deputizing a friend to find her a job in private industry. Defending the president, White House aides accused their adversaries in Starr's office as well as in the Paula Jones suit of participating in a vast, right-wing conspiracy to unseat the president, impugning the motives of his critics and questioning the sources of their funding. It was no coincidence, they charged, that the Rutherford Institute, the group funding the Paula Jones lawsuit and appeal, was funded by the conservative movement.

The president's problems, together with the escalating number of congressional ethics cases, has created a Washington "culture of scandal," a "multimillion dollar enterprise"—mostly taxpayer funded—that by 1998 employed an army of private investigators, lawyers, congressional staffers, White House aides, and journalists. The business of ferreting out the truth about the president, the White House, or the Democratic Party occupied thirty-one separate investigations in Congress (seven in the Senate, and the rest in House committees). The Republicans are not immune to the highly partisan scandal machine, with the Justice Department investigating the fund-raising activities of Haley Barbour, the former chairman of the Republican National Committee. The cost to the taxpayers has been staggering. Estimates total about $60 million: $50 million to pay for the cost of the five independent counsels investigating past and present members of the Clinton administration, including Kenneth Starr, and $10 million for congressional investigations.[40]

What surprised everyone was the response of the public to this onslaught. People were angrier at the media than they were at the president or the scandals. They were furious at what they considered an unwarranted invasion of the president's privacy; in other words, they regarded the messenger as more of a problem than the message. Indeed, Bill Clinton appeared to be protected with a layer of Teflon thicker than President Reagan's, whose ability to deflect criticism led to the original "Teflon President" label. With each lurid scandal, the president's approval ratings rose steadily, reaching the 68 percent mark in some polls; contributions to the Democratic National Committee also accelerated. The conventional wisdom asserted that as long as the economy hummed along, the president could do no wrong.

Or, as the saying around Washington went: "The People vote Dow Jones, not Paula Jones."

An *NBC–Wall Street Journal* survey explored this apparent dichotomy and came close to producing an explanation: Americans ranked the president low on character and seemed largely indifferent to the recent scandals, but they awarded him a high rating on his job performance. Sixty-six percent of those polled in March 1998 approved of his performance in office, compared with 28 percent who disapproved. The poll, conducted by Democratic pollster Peter Hart and Republican Robert Teeter, also revealed that most people did not believe the president's denials. Of those polled, 34 percent said Clinton's character was average, and 35 percent graded it low or very low; *Washington Post* columnist E. J. Dionne Jr. called this the "amoral majority." Perhaps Americans still find the image of a rogue very appealing: witness the glamorization of Jesse James, a bank robber, and Bonnie and Clyde, notorious gangsters, in popular culture.[41]

Some of the blame gets very personal, as it did in Congress against federal workers. The Republican freshmen in Congress dug in their heels on the budget, guessing that public antagonism toward bureaucrats would carry the day. Epitomizing their view, Rush Limbaugh opened his radio show the day of the first furlough in November 1995, gleefully asking his listeners if they were able to get out of bed, put on their shoes, and make it to work without the help of the federal government. How about an alternative question? When you wake up in the morning can you brush your teeth with tap water, eat unadulterated breakfast foods, and drive safer cars with shatterproof windshields to work? "Yes" to all of the above, thanks to the vigilance of federal government's environmental, food, and auto safety rules.

"Blame the feds" belligerence backfired against the Republicans and to a lesser extent, the Democrats. Two government furloughs meant federal workers weren't paid at Christmas; morale declined precipitously, and the fallout reached many government subcontractors in the private sector. Who could forget the picture of President Clinton and his family boarding a plane for New Year's weekend at Hilton Head smack dab against a picture of a furloughed employee worrying about how he was going to get through the next week without a paycheck? What congressional leaders also failed to realize was that federal furloughs would reach into the far corners of American society and affect many constituents who were not drawing federal paychecks. Not only were the national parks closed, for example; so were the private companies and individuals contracted to run the concessions, prune the trees, and plow the roads. Along with plummeting morale among federal workers, the furloughs also ended up costing millions of tax dollars in lost productivity.

"After all these years, I'm just a number. . . . I'm expendable, just like Willie Loman," said Tim Miles, director of Computer Systems at the International Trade Administration of the Department of Commerce, referring to the character in Arthur Miller's play *Death of a Salesman*. A twenty-year career civil servant, Miles expressed the disillusionment felt by many devoted public officials who were dismayed and angered by being labeled "essential" or "nonessential."

"We took JFK's words to heart when he asked us to do something for our country," he continued. Take the label 'essential': "I went to Tokyo twice recently . . . to negotiate computer procurement agreements. We went two days straight with no sleep. . . . We sat there at MITI (Japan's Ministry of Trade and Industry) and . . . negotiated a computer agreement at 2:30 in the morning. The American public doesn't understand [our] dedication."

Miles maintained that although there was no letdown in productivity, morale was another story. "We are wondering if we're going to be out on the street again. . . . There are a bunch of people on the Hill who are ideologues. They don't care what happens to us because they have an agenda, even if it means they are not going to be reelected."

## Incivility

Although political impertinence has reached new heights today, nothing quite compares with the time in 1765 when an angry mob sacked the house of Massachusetts colonial governor and British loyalist Thomas Hutchinson. The governor and his family barely escaped with their lives as "rioters smashed in the doors with axes, swarmed through the rooms, ripped off the wainscotting and hangings, splintered the furniture, beat down the inner walls, tore up the garden. . . . The determination of the mob was as remarkable as its savagery."[42]

Today, a general meanness of spirit characterizes current political life, recalling more than casually the very reason Congress attempted to ban canes from both chambers after the "brutal caning of Senator Charles Sumner, Republican of Massachusetts," in 1856 by a South Carolina Democrat, Representative Preston S. Brooks. "Covered with blood and barely conscious" from this fierce attack, "Sumner's injuries kept him from the Senate for three years."[43] (Today, in

A group of "nonessential" federal employees protest the government shutdown.
Photo courtesy of *The Hill.*

deference to those with arthritis and other orthopedic problems, canes are allowed on both Senate and House floors.)

Added to the rhetorical bouts and negative campaign ads, actual incidences of fisticuffs have also occurred on Capitol Hill. One scuffle broke out after Representative Randy "Duke" Cunningham, a California Republican and a former fighter pilot, accused Representative James Moran (D–Va.), an amateur boxer, of turning his back on the Gulf War troops. Moran's charge that Republicans were meddling in foreign affairs for purely political gain instigated this melee, which began when Moran shoved Cunningham out of a door leading from the House floor. Robert Dornan (R–Calif.) and George Miller (D–Calif.) soon became embroiled in the scuffle. Other members of Congress broke up the brawl, with Moran quoting Dornan as saying, "Get your Irish ass outta here." Dornan later said "Irish" was a "term of endearment."[44]

In this harsh climate no wonder Representative Gary Ackerman (D–N.Y.) wistfully referred to former House minority leader Robert Michel as "the last Republican gentleman," although his fellow Democrats are no strangers to incendiary language: "It's about retiring that no-account, Georgia-born tax-raising on the middle class, porno-movie-investing, sorry excuse for a senator named Phil Gramm. Our fight is with the turtlenecked turncoat," said Representative Jim Chapman (D–Tex.).[45]

Public nastiness has become such a problem that Republican leaders found it necessary to call a session the day of President Clinton's 1996 State of the Union address just to warn legislators in their party to behave themselves; a few actually called for an invitation to Miss Manners (reporter Judith Martin, who writes a nationally syndicated column under that name) to give lessons in civility. Miss Manners would strongly disapprove of their purely political motivation: Republicans were primarily concerned about their party's image, which took a beating during the 1995–1996 budget battle.

The year after the bruising budget battle some members of Congress attended a retreat on civility in politics. Actually, teaching members of Congress to assuage their anger—or express it in different ways—might not remedy the problems at hand. Acrimony, however unpleasant, brings the issues out in the open; and when public nastiness goes beyond the pale it is refreshing to see how much more powerful public opprobrium is in punishing the offenders than a seminar on niceties.

Old-timers argue that as bad as things seem now, they were far worse in the past, when a few barons—known for their opposition to civil rights, equal rights, and just about anything progressive—ran the Congress. During a debate on the Senate floor in the early 1970s on welfare formulas for New York between Senators Jacob Javits (R–N.Y.) and John McClellan (D–Ark.), McClellan retorted in fury and frustration: "We don't need your kind here," a thinly veiled reference to Javits's religion [Jewish] and ethnicity. It is hard to believe today that men like McClellan were so highly venerated on Capitol Hill; there is even a building named for another staunch opponent of civil rights, Richard Russell (D–Ga.). Thanks to the forces of congressional reform and societal multiculturalism, the bald expressions of racism, anti-Semitism, and gender prejudice that used to be common practice are no longer as prevalent, at least on the surface; and homophobia, an explosive issue since Clinton's attempt to integrate gays into the military, at least seems on the wane thanks to public reaction and pressure.

Where will all this antigovernment sentiment lead? The public appears to blame government more than any other institution for the widening income gap, the rise in violence, and the increase in single-parent homes. Thomas B. Edsall predicts that the antigovernment sentiment reflected in the *Washington Post* polls would be "more damaging to the Democratic Party than to the Republican Party," since the public has become "increasingly sympathetic to the GOP's anti-government themes, and [is] ready to believe that raising taxes to pay for federal programs is a wasteful strategy that may do more harm than good."[46]

## Extremes at Center Stage:
*The Militia, Waco, and Congress*

In this atmosphere, it is not surprising that a critical mass of citizens has reached out to the militia, the Branch Davidians, and other extremist groups for answers. The bombing at Oklahoma City, the siege at Waco, the incident at Ruby Ridge, and the passage of the Brady Bill have emerged as defining events for these groups and have focused public attention on the danger they pose to American society. The Oklahoma bombing, for example, was timed to coincide two years to the day with the FBI attack on the Branch Davidian compound at Waco, during which seventy members of the cult died. Two additional events focus on the obsession with guns and government "plots" to take those guns away from "law-abiding citizens": the shoot-out at Ruby Ridge, Idaho, on August 31, 1992, that left a U.S. marshal and the wife and fourteen-year-old son of white separatist Randy Weaver dead; and President Clinton's signing of the Brady Bill on November 30, 1993, which requires a five-day waiting period for all handgun purchases.

"It doesn't matter to them [members of Congress] that the semi-auto ban gives jack-booted government thugs more power to take away our Constitutional rights, break in our doors, seize our guns, destroy our property, and even injure or kill us," wrote Wayne LaPierre, executive vice president of the National Rifle Association in a May 1995 letter to his constituents. Does he represent the lunatic fringe? Hardly. The NRA remains one of the most powerful interest groups in the country today, striking terror in the hearts of public officials at every level of government who fear the broad reach of its political clout and tactics of political intimidation.

In normal times, groups like the militia would function on the fringes of society. Today, they have moved from the outskirts of politics to the center. Senate hearings on the militia one month after the Oklahoma bombing added new respectability to this movement, offering a legislative platform to a full panel of militia witnesses, one of them in full camouflage regalia. The primary purpose of the hearing, according to its chair, Senator Arlen Specter, was to assess whether the militia presented a threat, especially with "224 militias [operating] in this country," he said, "in 39 states."[47]

The militia witnesses tried to project a reputable image: They were not vigilantes; they considered themselves a "giant neighborhood watch," testified John Trochman of the Montana militia. His goal was simple: to "defend the Constitution . . . against treason from within." To counter charges of racism, the militia introduced an African American from the E Pluribus Unum unit in Ohio. "We're the calm ones," he said. "If our ancestors had been armed, we wouldn't have been slaves."[48]

"I understand anger with government; people have a right to be angry," asserted Senator Max Baucus, Democrat of Montana, a state where the militia have flourished. "But the vast majority of Montanans reject hate. The militia groups are the exception. They create an atmosphere of terror. Since the militia have formed, we have had anti-Semitic incidents all over the state," he continued. "Threats against law enforcement are routine. They have two beliefs: suspicion of government that includes social security and taxes; and a deep strain of anti-Semitism and racism. You can tell from their code words: 'banking elites,' and 'only whites go to heaven.'"[49]

Senator Carl Levin (D–Mich.) offered further evidence of the scary activities of the militia that extend far afield from their rhetoric, namely their "paramilitary training, stalking . . . threatening . . . and surveilling law enforcement personnel . . . and their families . . . and stockpiling munitions." One militia car was stopped in Michigan, he recounted, complete with "loaded guns, armor-piercing bullets, plans, and night vision equipment."[50]

The rage of these groups goes beyond anger. Quotes from the media and from congressional hearings indicate views that fall well outside traditional politics and behavior that borders on paranoia, particularly toward government. They believe in training their troops to combat a secret worldwide order that is seeking to impose a totalitarian system on the United States; the vehicle for this secret order is the United Nations. Some observers, such as James D. Tabor and Eugene V. Gallagher, do not see cults as especially problematical, likening them to religious groups and arguing against government action aimed at stifling them. They may be unorthodox, but after all, Jesus and his early followers shared some of the traits characteristic of cults today, namely, commitment to a leader's interpretation of the Bible; belief that a leader can do no wrong; belief in a revelation that contradicts previous revelations; belief in the coming of the end of the world; a "we-they" mentality; and intense pressure to conform to the dictates of the group.[51]

American politics has long tolerated episodes of paranoia throughout its history; today, once again, economics and cultural clashes have produced evidence of extremism in the mainstream. The "new extremists" have made an "internally consistent case," wrote historian Garry Wills, "for the illegitimacy of federal acts" such as taxation, the jury system, schools, regulations, and police power.[52] But why haven't those views been absorbed by the mainstream? After all, political leaders for more than a decade have been reinforcing this message. Remember Ronald Reagan, who often called government the problem and who won his first presidential campaign promising to "get the government off the backs of the people"?[53]

To offset hearings that were widely criticized for the legitimacy they conferred on the militia, Charles Schumer (D–N.Y.) held a meeting featuring testimony by public officials who had been subjected to militia violence and intimidation. Despite a letter signed by sixty-one Democrats, a majority of Republicans had refused to accede to their request for hearings, forcing them to conduct a "forum" outside the formal hearing process. Led by Schumer, who alliterated his fellow Republicans as "mealy-mouthed mollifiers of militias," witness after witness described harrowing incidences against public officials: city judges, clerk-recorders, and even an attempted shooting of a biologist for the U.S. Forest Service in California. "If we can't beat you at the ballot box, we'll beat you with a bullet," threatened one militia representative.[54]

The hearings investigating the militia, as well as those examining the Branch Davidians, forced the Democrats in the 104th Congress to reverse positions with their Republican colleagues: Instead of their traditional posture upholding civil liberties against police abuse, they found themselves defending law enforcement officials against various groups of zealots holed up in arsenals and claiming violation of their rights. "The Davidians were armed with machine guns," charged Schumer during the Waco hearings. "David Koresh was an armed fanatic who sexually abused children and called it holy. Why are we casting the FBI and the ATF as villains?" What "church buys and sells guns as a business [and] holds people as hostages?" added Representative Gene Taylor (D–Miss.).[55]

"No function of government is beyond scrutiny," thundered Representative Henry Hyde (R–Ill.) on the first day of the hearings. "For more than two years, millions of Americans are still asking why? [They] want answers."[56]

The Waco hearings presaged the course of divided government with Democrats leading off each of the ten days of hearings with requests for subpoena power: the ability to control who testifies and who stays home. They accused the Republicans of "stacking the witness lists"; Republicans replied that they were merely "seeking the truth." Gleeful at possessing a power they hadn't enjoyed in forty years, the Republicans carefully chose witnesses who hammered away at the overzealousness of the ATF and the FBI and repeatedly rebuffed

Democratic entreaties. "What are they complaining about," huffed a Republican aide from the Tennessee delegation. "Their stinking party had this power for forty years, and they never gave anything to us."

Outside the hearing room, others related their individual miseries emanating from the disaster at Waco. Branch Davidian member Gladys Ottman, a slight, gray-haired woman clutching a worn Bible, agonized over whether her daughter would ever be released from jail. The families of dead ATF agents mourned their losses, and FBI agents wondered if they would ever get sufficient public support to do their job.

But ten days of witnesses told a compelling story of political anger and its relationship to government: The lack of coordination among law enforcement agencies, the confusion of roles, and the absence of real leadership from the president and Congress in what was ultimately regarded as one of the worst government mistakes in history. Did the hearings ameliorate or exacerbate the public's anger about Waco? Probably the latter, according to Dr. Bruce Perry, the psychiatrist who treated the Davidian children. "Outlets for anger are good only if the issue comes to constructive fruition," he said. "Otherwise, pure anger by itself can be very destructive."

The incidents at Waco and Ruby Ridge caused much soul-searching and affected the FBI's future treatment of extremist groups. When the Montana Freemen announced they were creating their own government and defied law enforcement officials by holing up in a farmhouse, heavily armed, the FBI patiently waited them out for eighty-one days. Rotating shifts, the armed Freemen stood guard to prevent the FBI from arresting nine wanted federal criminals. Although the FBI's patience was exhausted, the agency's forbearance also evoked public and editorial criticism for wasting taxpayers' money. As the first trial against the Montana Freemen began in March 1998, four of the defendants had to be dragged from the courtroom for screaming obscenities at the judge and threatening U.S. marshals with arrest. Prosecutors argued in their opening statements that they intended to prove that the six defendants were ready and willing to shoot FBI and other law enforcement agents.[57]

Putting extremism at center stage accords added legitimacy to these groups and their views, increases division among the public, and so far has not resolved the major issues of public safety that were ostensibly the purpose of such highly publicized hearings. One wonders why these groups were given such an imprimatur in the first place given that the American people have never displayed any consistent sympathy for their role in political life; on the contrary, they generally ignore fringe groups until tragedies like Oklahoma force them to confront their real dangers. One month after the Oklahoma bombing, a *Washington Post–ABC News* poll showed satisfaction with government up and "anger . . . down" after "seeing the tragic consequences of real rage." Fifty-nine percent of the sample opposed private militia "strongly," 23 percent "opposed them somewhat," and only 2 percent strongly supported them.[58] In view of the polls and the Oklahoma tragedy itself, isn't it surprising that the congressional hearings spent more time on antigovernment diatribes than on the imminent dangers of the militia groups to society?

## Anyone But the Above

With Congress in disarray and the president running scared, an angry electorate has responded by reaching outside the traditional two-party system for answers. The 1992 and 1994 elections proved to be watershed events; public anger drove voters toward Ross Perot and Newt Gingrich, both of whom positioned themselves as "outsiders." In both cases, it is hard to separate the personalities from the parties. Do voters really want a third party or a more right-leaning Republican Party? Or did they just find the iconoclastic ideas of Ross Perot—or the Contract with America—more attractive than "all of the above"?

The 1992 success of Ross Perot drove Republicans to search for ways to bring all the disaffected voters back into the fold for the 1994 election. "Perot voters were the swing voters," said Frank Luntz, whose congressional clients were the chief beneficiaries of this strategy. "Bush was thrown out by angry voters. . . . He had looked the voters in the eye and said, 'Read my lips; no new taxes.' This was his most quoted speech. You don't get a second chance. The real difference between 1992 and 1994 was that in 1992, people took it out on incumbents. In 1994, the reaction was against people in charge." Luntz's polls showed 46 percent of Perot voters "angry" compared with 24 percent of the Bush voters and 28 percent of the Clinton voters. "Perot had a vision," he explained. "Anger needs a place to focus."

Separating party and personality in Perot's case challenged even the most astute political observers. On the day the Perot convention was held in Dallas, August 11, 1995, a CNN–*USA Today* poll showed 62 percent of the voters "expressing a desire for a third party."[59] "For the first time in history, a majority of those interviewed, 53 percent, told Gallup that they would like to see a third major party. . . . Perot [in 1992] secured the highest percentage of the vote ever attained by a third party candidate, with the limited exception of Theodore Roosevelt in 1912."[60]

Perot and his movement, United We Stand, showed the lengths to which voters angry with the system as is were prepared to attach themselves to an unknown candidate and an unknown political infrastructure. The "anyone but the above" pattern persists well into the mid-1990s, from the nation's love affair with Colin Powell in 1995 to those Republican primary voters quick to espouse the candidacy and flat-tax views of publisher Steve Forbes or the social agenda and economic nationalism of Pat Buchanan.

The attraction of Perot, the Republican victory in the 104th Congress, and one-idea candidates do not fit with the pragmatic tenor of American politics. Government furloughs, for example, used to take the form of annual charades: The Washington Monument would close, tourists would complain, and Republicans and Democrats would settle into their traditional comity and emerge with a completed budget. Instead, today everything closes down while Democrats face down Republican members of Congress, who in turn announce their willingness to go down in defeat rather than fail in their mission of reducing government. Even their leader and ideologue-in-chief, Newt Gingrich, finds himself unable to keep them in line.

Once the shock wore off, the Democrats sought an appropriate response to the Republican sweep. After they took the full measure of the "mandate," they finally realized that a 38 percent turnout and a shift of 18,000 votes in all of the congressional districts combined didn't amount to much of a mandate. In fact, in the fourteen closest congressional races, the margins came to a few thousand votes. "Is it an instruction to the politicians?" asked former New York governor Mario Cuomo. "This tiny difference of 6 percent in a total vote of 38 percent? . . . If you asked anybody on Election Day in New York State, 'Where's Cuomo on the Contract With America?' [they'd have said] 'Mario's a good guy; he doesn't make contracts.'"61

Measuring such meager margins gladdened the hearts of Democrats; at last, the prospect of regaining the Congress seemed a distinct possibility. How? By using the same forces of anger that jettisoned them from office in the first place. "We are trying to harness anger against the Republicans," said a Democratic strategist who declined to be quoted on the record. "We have successfully brought them down to our level. If you can't cut Medicare, education, or any other program, what else can you do?" The Democrats harnessed political anger and made it work for presidential elections, but their efforts to organize public ire did not work for congressional elections, which returned a Republican majority in 1996 despite a massive win for the Democratic president. Voters now regard the two-party system in terms of power sharing; they feel comfortable with the Democrats running the executive branch and the Republicans retaining control of the Congress. That is the way checks and balances ought to work. Or is it? People may feel comfortable with separated government, except when it brings gridlock, unalloyed nastiness, and a lot of other baggage along with it. Each party keeps the other on its toes, all right; but the environment becomes increasingly acrimonious as a result.

In the movie *The Candidate,* Robert Redford (starring as the candidate) mounts a herculean effort to get elected. Capturing the authenticity of a real campaign, the film shows how Redford risks his marriage, his family, his ethics, and his friends just to win the prize of political office. In the film's most memorable moment Redford turns to his campaign manager after he has won to ask: "What do we do now?"

The same metaphor applies today. Almost all politicians use the forces of political anger, just as the Democrats figured out how to fight fire with an inferno of their own. Politicians get the voters riled up, promise more than they can deliver, then get elected and can't figure out what to do. The great dilemma is how to both tell the truth and get elected in an acrid political environment. How do you tell voters that the public's attitudes toward raising taxes severely limits the political horizon? And how do you face the dilemma if no one else will join the truth brigade?

Few politicians are as honest with their constituents as Marcy Kaptur, who voted for the Brady Bill despite the animosity of her constituents toward gun control. And despite all the hoopla over "socialized medicine," she's honest enough to face the voters with such statements as "I'm for a unified health program because I don't trust the insurance companies to provide medical care for the elderly." And on the popular tax cuts: "Donald Trump doesn't need a tax cut. My neighbor does. He has epilepsy, four children, and has just started his own business. He told me he didn't need a tax cut; 'just straighten out the country and pay the bills.'" And on the biggest problem of all, putting the lid on political contributions: "Gingrich and Clinton both promised us campaign reform up in New Hampshire. Congress must overturn *Buckley v. Valeo,* the case that said money meant free speech. That's the only answer."

Stymied by harsh political reality and a notable absence of courage, politicians resort to what they do best: campaigning. It is easy to get people angry over Hillary Rodham Clinton's insider trading deals, Speaker Gingrich's GOPAC fund-raising efforts, or the Keating Five's largesse toward corrupt savings and loan institutions. Sadly, at the end no one is left in the ring except those ringing the bell. Will all the congressional hearings, subpoenas, and special prosecutors investigating Mrs. Clinton's legal career lead to improvements in investment ethics? Did the year-long fuss that eventually exonerated

Speaker Gingrich lead to finance reform? And did the troubles of the five senators sucked into the Keating scandal tighten up regulations in the savings and loan industry? A resounding "no" to all of the above.

Without sufficient outlets, public anger will rise and partisan divisions will harden. The bipolar politics so characteristic of the 1990s doesn't begin to address the complex and nuanced issues of our time. No wonder voters are ready to vote for untested candidates, untried third parties, and undercooked ideas.

# 6

..........................................................................................................

# The Vision Thing

## *Competing Angers and Political Change*

There is always an easy solution to every human
problem—neat, plausible and wrong.

— H. L. Mencken[1]

······································································

**T**ODAY, AS AT EVERY TURN in our nation's history, political leaders are
confronted with competing angers. Their responsibility is to try to reconcile
these opposing emotions in a constructive manner. Some people are angered
by inadequate government services; others are incensed by high taxes, bloated
government bureaucracies, unjustifiable costs, and the burgeoning deficit. The
health care debate is fueled by those angered by inadequate health care services
and by those who believe that the government spends far too much on these
services. Gun ownership is strongly opposed by those convinced that weapons
breed violence and supported by those who deem gun ownership necessary for
self-defense, recreational hunting, and personal autonomy. Conflicting view-
points also generate anger over abortion, school prayer, and other social issues,
with many advocates convinced that God is on their side.

George Bush missed the domestic leadership opportunity of his presidency
during the Los Angeles riots, when he had the opportunity to reconcile conflicting angers. While stores and neighborhoods in that tormented city were
being torched and people were suffering physical, economic, and emotional
injuries, a small group of top Republican campaign leaders met for an infor-
mal strategy session about the president's faltering reelection campaign. The
dinner meeting took place on a warm evening in May 1996 in the cozy, wood-
paneled private dining room at the City Club in downtown Washington and
included Frederick Malek, campaign manager of the Bush campaign, several
communications specialists attached to the campaign, and the host, Roy
Goodman, a Republican state senator from New York City. Joining them were
several outsiders, including two journalists and a college professor.

"How can we get George Bush reelected?" asked Malek.

"How about starting right now, during the riots?" offered the professor.
"Tonight's network news shows all showed clips of black and Korean shop-
keepers in tears as they poured out of their blazing liquor stores and groceries.
Everything they had worked for was engulfed in flames, every bit of it unin-
sured. Ask the president to phone his friends in the corporate world and recruit CEOs to each adopt a store and put it back in business. Twenty-five thousand dollars to the president of General Motors for bankrolling a Korean
grocer is like $25 to me. Republicans would be in the enviable position of re-

warding hard work; the GOP could capitalize on its reputation for entrepreneurship; you are rewarding enterprise, not violence; and the president would position himself in the role of leading the city back to racial peace. It is a win-win proposition. No one loses. The companies would get publicity for their good deeds, President Bush would get credit for leadership, and the taxpayer is off the hook because 'big government' doesn't have to spend a dime."

"Wonderful idea," everyone agreed. The following week, President Bush blamed President Lyndon B. Johnson and his Great Society programs for the Los Angeles riots, although LBJ had long been dead and his administration well out of the White House for more than a quarter of a century.

A week later the professor met Fred Malek running for the Washington shuttle at Logan Airport in Boston. "What happened to my idea?" she asked. "Why did the president dig up LBJ?"

"I went in to see George Bush the very next morning with your idea," answered Malek, woefully. "He didn't listen to us on anything."

Politicians lose scores of opportunities, like this one, in their efforts to sort out the options in any given crisis. In the case of Los Angeles, the anger focused on race; but since then, other signs of anger point to a nation in turmoil over cultural values, the economy, and the role of government. Many leaders have ignored public anger at their own peril; in George Bush's case, it cost him the presidency.

Heightened anger was very much part of the elections of 1992, 1994, and 1996, when anger often took the form of apathy and alienation from politics. Indeed, anger has been with us since the founding of the republic. At its best, it is healthy and can lead to positive change. At its worst, it can lead to violence and disaster.

Anger over racial issues has led to violence against Native Americans, African Americans, Latinos, foreign nationals, and immigrants. The nation's history is replete with sordid instances of slaveholder violence, lynchings, police dogs attacking civil rights demonstrators, and other examples of brutality—many of them carried out by the state. Anger at a foreign enemy with a heavy racial undertone led to forcing Japanese Americans into "relocation" camps during World War II, depriving them of their property and all their rights as U.S. citizens. All this savagery also originated with anger, anger on the part of some Americans who acted out their feelings of superiority on a weaker population.

The racial divide fueled the Civil War, which led to the abolition of slavery and the introduction of laws guaranteeing equality. Anger over racism propelled the civil rights movement, which continues to press for equality of opportunity.

The Los Angeles riots showed that the system wasn't working. In our political culture, when anger erupts into violence, it means that other outlets are not functioning. It shows that people on both sides of the racial divide feel totally helpless, that their views are not being heard, and that their votes do not count. Sparked by the Rodney King beating and the acquittal of the club-wielding police officers prosecuted for the offense, the Los Angeles riots exploded into a vivid spectacle of what happens when the political system collapses. Normal outlets for political expression—elections, fair trials, opportunities for responsive government—lacked public confidence, and oversight mechanisms designed to hold the excesses of the Los Angeles Police Department (LAPD) in check were obviously ineffective.

But on the positive side, the reaction to the King beating displayed the nation's anger at its best: universal outrage at an event that could no longer be contained as a local scandal or an isolated incident—white cops in uniform outnumbering, surrounding, and brutally clubbing a defenseless black man. Filmed by an amateur photographer, the event was shown on network television, and clips were repeated over and over again throughout the trial of the white officers. The LAPD was never the same, and the reason was widespread political anger put to good use.

Does that mean the nation is not racist? Not necessarily. Repeated incidents indicate that racism is alive and well: Cheers greeted candidate Pat Buchanan's campaign promises to allow southerners to fly the Confederate flag and sing Dixie, militia and neo-Nazi groups are on the rise, the verdict in the O. J. Simpson trial revealed deep racial divisions that persist long after the trial, and Louis Farrakhan's rhetoric pitting blacks against Jews and other racial and ethnic groups continues to escalate. But when things looked bleakest for race relations in the United States, many white Americans seemed ready, indeed anxious, to nominate a black man, General Colin Powell, for president, apparently finding him vastly preferable to any of the white candidates offered by either party. In his second term President Clinton announced that he would hold a series of town meetings on the subject of race, and appointed a commission headed by the renowned historian John Hope Franklin of Duke University to study the issue. For some reason, Clinton's initiative so far has failed to engage the public's attention.

Public anger forces issues toward the extremes, creating bipolarities in politics that reflect these extremes. The bipolarity, oversimplification, and lack of civility in current politics in turn militate against assuaging anger and encourage the manipulation of it. But people could not be manipulated without a deep well of anger already in existence: Talk show hosts wouldn't find a market without it, Republican pollsters defining the Contract with America wouldn't know which buttons to press, and none-of-the-above primary candidates would be greeted with oblivion instead of the kleig lights. Fearful of a reenactment of 1996, when anger manifested itself partly as alienation and apathy, political leaders today try to whip up the old angers that draw people to the polls and spell electoral victory. Senate Majority Leader Trent Lott (R–Miss.) complained that whenever the Republicans suggested something, Clinton agreed with them, depriving his colleagues of the opportunity to distinguish themselves from their political enemies. Many Democrats agreed with Lott, considering Clinton's policies on welfare, trade, and budget balancing closer in spirit to the Grand Old Party than to the party of Franklin Roosevelt. But ample evidence has emerged indicating that bipolar politics will rise as election cycles approach—even if some of the issues seem trumped up, or frivolous. Indeed, bipolar politics is inevitable as long as separated government—with Republicans in the Congress and Democrats in the White House—dominates the political process.

The early success of the presidential primary campaign of Pat Buchanan was a classic case of political anger, forcing leaders to address issues and opportunities open to them that were rooted in conflicting angers. At its most negative, Buchanan's candidacy recalled the negativism—and racism—of George Wallace, who also forged an alliance between disaffected blue-collar workers and a conservative social agenda.[2] The real lesson of Buchanan, however, is one of denial: The nation's mainstream leaders have ignored all the signs of political anger on the issues of jobs and trade that have appeared so vividly in the 1990s. By ignoring these issues, they have left the field clear for candidates like Buchanan; indeed, if Buchanan hadn't stepped in, another equally eloquent political figure would have filled the void.

"Buchanan is the only one who speaks to their [the voters'] pain," said a highly respected Democratic member of Congress who would otherwise find Buchanan's social agenda anathema. Time and again, leaders have expressed a "let them eat cake" attitude that has dismissed the legitimate concerns of Americans and gulled them into a false sense of security about the economy. Labor issues were relegated to a side agreement in the NAFTA treaty, which meant they were less important than exports and plant sitings. "Let's not deny other countries their comparative advantage," ran another "cake" argument, which meant we winked at such practices as cheap labor, child labor, and prison labor as companies fled to countries where they could hire workers desperate enough to toil for pennies an hour. Boeing workers at the Everett plant in the state of Washington uncrated the same products from China that they had once produced in the Everett plant. Why didn't Boeing keep the work in the Washington factory? Simple: In the United States, aerospace workers make $20 an hour; in China, they make 35 cents an hour.

Locked up in a Cold War mentality long after the Cold War was over, we nevertheless continued to sacrifice our industrial base and all the jobs that went with it for reasons that still defy all logic.[3] Forty-three million jobs were lost in the United States between 1979 and 1996, according to a *New York Times* analysis of Labor Department numbers. Although far more jobs were created than lost during that period, the disappearing positions were those of higher-paid white-collar and blue-collar workers, many at large corporations; those created were part-time and low-end jobs with minimal or nonexistent benefits. Compounding this problem are stagnant wages and an increasingly unequal distribution of wealth, creating "the most acute job insecurity since the Depression."[4] For this reason, despite the peaks and valleys in the business cycle, the issues of jobs and trade will continue to dominate political campaigns well into the new century.

## Anger Validated and Denied

Today's voters have every right to be angry and are crying out for new leaders and new options that will directly address their problems. Their leaders have made a colossal mistake in relegating "populism" to crackpots, since so much of it speaks to many of the real problems facing the vast majority of Americans not fortunate enough to live off trust funds. Those juggling their mounting monthly bills face diminished health and retirement benefits, a yawning wage gap that widens every year, spendable income that has decreased measurably over the past twenty years, the certainty that their children will not do as well as they have done, a roller-coaster stock market that benefited only a small segment of the population, fast disappearing public services, and a growing atmosphere of rancid incivility in the streets paralleled by increasing examples of bigotry and verbal ferocity on the floor of the House of Representatives.

Yet people are told not to worry; after all, inflation is low, the deficit is down, and all the macroeconomic numbers look good. Tell that to the 40,000 workers pounding pavements in their new lives after AT&T. That is not what any of them want to hear from their leaders. They are hearing denial when they need validation, validation that it is *not* wrong to be worried about the future when they see once-stable companies fire tens of thousands of workers right after they have posted record profits, validation that it is *not* wrong to feel genuine distress when Congress threatens to put programs like Medicare, Medicaid, and Social Security at risk, and validation that it is *not* wrong to protest dwindling medical benefits when every other industrialized country—most poorer than our own—is moving in the direction of guaranteed health care.

Politically, anger is good for challengers and bad for incumbents. Thus, American leaders typically lean toward denial of public anger rather than validation in the hope that reinforcing the positive will make good things happen and force bad things to vanish. This strategy makes sense with small problems; but at a certain point, when the problems outgrow their clothes, denial makes them worse.

Denial heightens anger when the nation perceives it is in a state of crisis and when its leaders fail to acknowledge society's pain. In that case, when leaders project a message that neither reflects reality nor a state of crisis, their slogans will boomerang and their ambitions will be dashed. The best example of this dichotomy was Hubert Humphrey's campaign for president in 1968 on a platform that touted the "politics of joy." Joy!—amid the horrors of the Vietnam War, riots in the streets, campus demonstrations, and a brawl at the Chicago Democratic Convention featuring an angry Mayor Richard Daley mouthing obscenities before the cameras and his vengeful police force. Many believed Humphrey would have been elected president and the nation spared the trauma of Watergate had his campaign more honestly addressed the public anger over Vietnam, civil rights, and student unrest.

Clinton has vacillated between a stance of denial toward public anger and a posture of fully validating it. To some extent, he is a prisoner of his role. The role of president means the avoidance of anger simply because his reelection rests on his record of accomplishment; after all, if he has succeeded with the economy, jobs, and foreign relations, why should anyone be angry? No wonder opponents achieve success on the hustings, where it is easier to beat the drums for anger, while the president grapples with the perennial predicament of whether he can win reelection only by basking in the glow of accomplishment—whether it is deserved or not.[5]

In his 1995 State of the Union speech, President Bill Clinton tried to recognize political anger with some of the evangelical fervor of his Baptist roots: "I hear you," he said. "I feel your pain. . . . The rising tide isn't lifting all boats . . . and too many of our people are still working harder and harder for less and less . . . and can't even be sure of having a job next year or even next month."

Then he shifted to the reverse tack, calling for cooling all the angry rhetoric. "We must work together to tear down barriers," he told a meeting of ministers at a White House prayer breakfast. "[We can't do that] unless . . . words become instruments of elevation and liberation."[6] He also urged "more conversation and less combat by politicians . . . to move beyond the vision and the resentment to common ground."[7]

The tragedy in Oklahoma City gave the president the opportunity to express the nation's anger. Clinton denounced the perpetrators and the "loud and angry voices" that encouraged them, urging his fellow citizens to "stand against them. . . . When they talk of hatred we must stand against them. When they talk of violence, we must stand against them. When they say things that are irresponsible, that may have egregious consequences, we must call them on it."[8]

Back in a reelection mode, he told the nation in his 1996 State of the Union address that the economy was "the healthiest it has been in decades." He cited as proof that the stock market had hit eighty-one new highs throughout 1995! Feed those macroeconomic indicators to the fifty-five-year-old machinist looking for work or to the retired grandmother in Toledo raising four children and caring for a disabled husband on her Social Security check.

After easily winning a second term, Clinton abandoned the anger tack and emphasized the positive achievements of his administration. In concrete terms, these were substantial, including his administration's claims of the first balanced budget (FY99) in a generation, after inheriting a $290 billion deficit in 1992; the lowest unemployment rate (from 7.5 percent in 1992 to 4.7 percent in 1998) in a quarter of a century; the creation of 14 million new jobs; tax relief of $500 per child for 27 million families with 45 million children; tax credits for higher education; improved air quality and the elimination of thousands of toxic waste dumps; and the highest home ownership rate (with 6 million new homeowners) in history. He also claimed several foreign policy accomplishments, including the peace settlement in Northern Ireland, the Dayton accords—albeit shaky—in Bosnia, and forcing Saddam Hussein to say he would back down in 1998 from his policy of resisting United Nations arms inspectors, thus avoiding another war for the moment. No doubt the president benefited from good times in the economic cycle and favorable global forces in securing those agreements. But it is also true, unfortunately, that events in those unstable areas of the world have long since undermined the administration's best efforts at world leadership.

While he was trying to convince voters of their nation's economic health, Clinton capitalized on public anger at Republican efforts to scale back benefit programs by successfully positioning himself as the guardian of Social Security and Medicare—actually choosing to close the government down rather than succumb to a controversial budget bill. Moreover, Clinton successfully convinced the public during the 1996 election campaign that it was the Republicans who had actually closed down the government, even though in truth both parties shared the blame. Again, competing angers fought each other: Voters angry over government's excessive spending habits battled other angry groups upset over the threatened cutbacks in entitlements—particularly middle-class entitlements such as student loans, Social Security, and Medicare.

## Anger and the Truth About Government

Easier said than done, especially by politicians who traffic in rhetoric, is the task of confronting the bald lies about government that abound in the public arena. After all, if government is weakened any further, it will become even more incapable of treating real problems than it is today.

A falsehood about government that took on a life of its own involved a story circulated on the floor of the House by Representative David McIntosh, a freshman Republican from Muncie, Indiana, to the effect that "the Consumer Product Safety Commission [issued a] guideline that recommended that . . . every bucket with five gallons or more that could contain water have a hole in the bottom of it." Known as the "leaky bucket" issue, the story added fuel to a bonfire of antiregulatory sentiment on Capitol Hill; after all, why would anyone manufacture a bucket with holes in the bottom? The truth is that the CPSC never issued any such guideline; instead, the agency addressed the issue of the increasing numbers of small children who were drowning in large buckets on construction sites and persuaded the industry to put warning labels on its products.[9]

Some politicians try to replace the "tygers of wrath" with the "horses of instruction," giving government workers credit when they deserve it.[10] Senator Bill Bradley, for example, reminded a crowd of angry citizens that the "Pine Barrens fire would have been worse without Federal firefighters." He added for the benefit of constituents who supported the "unfunded mandates" bill that New Jersey "mandated" that its neighbor New York clean up its toxic dumps, whose fumes wafted across the Hudson River.[11]

Where were all the defenders of government after the Oklahoma bombing, when federal officials once again stepped in to ease the pain and suffering of American citizens? FBI agents arrested Timothy McVeigh within forty-eight hours, federal injury control experts from the Centers for Disease Control and Prevention advised rescue teams, and Social Security and Medicare employees speeded benefits to the survivors.[12]

Leaders should not be telling the voters "what they *want to hear,* . . . but what they *need to know,*" said former Oregon governor Barbara Roberts, who herself got caught in the vise of political anger as soon as she won her "unwinnable" one-term governorship in 1990. "As public anger rose," she recalled, "government became defensive rather than decisive."[13]

Despite all the antigovernment rhetoric flooding the airwaves, the public still turns to government for help when times get tough. In this climate government has become the victim of its own success: The more it has done for people over the years, the more it has been criticized. Many Americans expect public benefits that have cushioned them for half a century to continue to flow unabated, yet they vote for candidates who convince them that government can deliver on the cheap without causing inconvenience or pain. But when Medicare checks fail to arrive on time because there isn't enough money to pay for staff or computers, reality strikes and anger moves in as people reassess what they want government to do.

This does not mean that government should be immune from criticism; on the contrary, political appointees as well as bureaucrats deserve constant scrutiny and oversight. After all, miscreants masquerading as public servants led us straight into Iran-Contra, Watergate, and a series of disasters such as the savings and loan scandals that grew out of banking deregulation. The S&L debacle has already run into hundreds of billions of dollars, which our great-grandchildren will still be paying off well into the next century.

But government has earned our skepticism, not our repudiation. For despite its gross errors in judgment, if we continue to reject government, what is left? Do we really trust all the auto companies to improve safety features without government looking over their shoulders, food companies to purify their products, or chemical companies to search for new ways to clean up the rivers? In fact, the next time Rush Limbaugh and his allies fulminate about how well Americans seem do be doing without government, as they did during the two furloughs of the federal workforce, we should take up a collection, pack their bags, and send them to Kenya, where they could see firsthand what life is like absent the heavy hand of bureaucracy. Call it virtual government: The infrastructure is virtually nonexistent, roads are packed with craters that look like moonscapes, crime is rampant, seven out of eight workers are unemployed, so-called public education comes with fees higher than most people's annual salaries, and no potable drinking water exists anywhere thanks to the absence of onerous legislation like the U.S. Clean Water Act. And what about government's role in what is euphemistically called "redistributive justice"? Don't look for any middle class in between the lush villas circling Nairobi and the corrugated tin shacks that serve as dwellings for the rest of society.[14]

## Anger and the Pollsters

Political leaders take seriously poll findings that confirm voter anxiety as an overwhelming emotion that affects political life. But the polls are ripe for new and fresh interpretation instead of the more typical approach involving what they reveal about politicians' individual ambitions: What are the chances of getting reelected? What opponents can beat them? What positions will attract the most voter approval? Most disturbing, perhaps, is the complacency with which voters view candidates as purely poll-driven, a charge leveled frequently against President Clinton and the strategist who masterminded his reelection campaign, Dick Morris. In this view, politicians read the polls, *then* formulate their ideas. Where does leadership figure into this equation?

Once you take the horse race element out of the polls, they reveal competing angers that express approval as well as disapproval of government. At the same time that people talk about reducing the size and cost of government, for example, polls show support for increased spending when that spending is related to real needs such as schools, anticrime measures, and aid to the poor. Polls also reveal that when pressed, the public also believes that only government can address the issue of corporate heartlessness. The answer to the question of exactly how government can address job losses and other problems stemming from market forces remains elusive: No wonder competing angers manifested by ambivalence and anxiety have taken the place of problem-solving.

As Clinton hails the end of the "era of big government," a conundrum keeps cropping up: increased support for what government *does,* along with public calls for a smaller government. A *New York Times–CBS News* poll investigating the Buchanan phenomenon came to the striking conclusion that 87 percent of respondents thought that government could have a positive impact on their lives! This is an amazing figure in view of the date of the study—February 1996—and the fact that almost no political leader, Democrat or Republican, had said anything positive about the government in years.[15]

## On Welfare

Poll results on public attitudes toward welfare may seem to reveal lack of support for government spending in this area, but much depends on the phrasing of poll questions. There is widespread agreement on the concept that the welfare system is fraught with problems and that the present system may actually have encouraged an increase in illegitimate births. "Aid to the poor," however, is another matter. In 1994, 59 percent of the public favored *increased* spending on "assistance to the poor"; at the same time, 62 percent favored *decreased* spending on "welfare."[16] In other words, Americans truly want to help people in need; they just associate "welfare" with a system that doesn't work, increases their tax burden, and fosters dependence on government.

The strongest anger over welfare comes from those at the lowest end of the pay scale, who doubly resent nonworking recipients who seem to receive higher benefits than those who work. Columnist Ellen Goodman finds the hostility among working women toward welfare mothers especially troubling:

"In the world of working mothers, we have arrived at the point where there is virtually no public support for AFDC," she writes. "Indeed, the women struggling hardest at the lowest-paying jobs are often the most angry at paying taxes for others to stay home. This anger is the real 'mommy war' in America."[17]

## On Increased Spending

Once again, a great deal depends on how you ask the questions. Polls conducted by the National Opinion Research Center in 1994 reveal that 78 percent of the public supports increased spending for "halting the crime rate," 73 percent favors increased funding for "improving the nation's education system," and "increased spending for law enforcement" runs a close third with 65 percent. In other words, the public believes in massive public spending on crime, education, and health—an astonishing finding in view of comparable studies indicating public support for lower taxes, reduction of federal government, and further decentralization.[18]

The issue of medical benefits reveals most dramatically the public's ambivalence toward government. "On the issue of Medicare, Americans accept the idea that the Government should do more, but resist specific proposals that people with higher incomes should pay a greater share of their medical costs." A vast majority of Americans (78 percent) agree, for example, with the Republican proposal that people with higher incomes should pay a greater share of their own medical costs, but when it boils down to specifics they balk: Only 31 percent found the Republican plan to raise Medicare rates (from $46.10 per month to $90 a month) by the year 2002 acceptable.[19]

## On Divisions Between the Public and the Elites

Another tip that political leaders should take from the polls is the wide disparity between the elites and the general public. Elite groups have successfully buried the health care issue, for example, thanks to the Clinton administration's mismanagement of the bill, which included shunning both congressional leaders who might have made a difference and the spectacular lobbying effort against it. Yet polls across the board show a tremendous rise in public anxiety over health care. In 1994, 15 percent listed health care as a major concern; in 1995, 66 percent answered the same question affirmatively. Polls on public attitudes toward government scrutiny of big business exposed the same disparity: Twenty-four percent wanted greater scrutiny of merger activity in 1994; in late 1995 the figure rose to 78 percent.[20]

One of the best examples of competing angers has emerged in the area of health care. After Clinton's failure to bring closure to the dilemma of health insurance, health maintenance organizations (HMOs) moved in to fill the vacuum and dominate the system. Because their emphasis on the bottom line has often been at the expense of the kind of quality health care Americans have grown to expect, calls for their regulation have increased. In fact, in the absence of federal involvement and faced with intense public pressure, almost all the states have moved to regulate these new entities. Here, too, the polls are confusing. Surveys show widespread support for halting the abuses of HMOs, yet the data also show scant support for increased government regulation. On the one hand, the public is crying out for more government control; on the other, people balk at the word "regulation." Meanwhile, public policy grinds to a halt.[21]

Trade has emerged as the most divisive issue of all in terms of the gap between the elites and the electorate. Republican leaders pride themselves on their free-trade stance, yet polls show Republican primary voters favored candidate Pat Buchanan's economic nationalism by huge margins: Sixty-nine percent, for example, supported his call for tariffs on products from countries running trade deficits with the United States. "Voters seem ready to embargo ideas promoted by free traders," said Ed Sarpolus, vice president of EPIC/MRA, the polling firm that conducted the poll. Also, more than half supported Buchanan's proposal for a tariff on imports from countries that paid their workers low wages, and 37 percent blamed trade for stagnating industrial wages in the United States.[22] Yet trade has not become a truly national issue: it was not a factor in the 1996 presidential election; it is rarely part of congressional campaigns, and except for President Clinton's failure to pass "fast-track" legislation in 1997, it appears at this point to have slid totally off the public's radar screen. When trade becomes clearly part of the pocketbook issue, American insularity fades quickly, as it did during the Asian financial crisis and when the issue of payments to the United Nations and the IMF came under discussion in Congress.

## Anger and Blame

The pope and President Clinton went fishing one day, according to a popular story making the rounds in Washington in 1994, when a sudden gust of wind blew the pontiff's hat off his head and into the water. In a flash, Clinton climbed overboard and walked straight out on the water. Plucking the hat from the briny deep, he strode back to the boat atop the waves and presented it to His Holiness. The next day, the headlines read: "President Clinton Can't Swim."

Just as President Reagan was labeled the Teflon president for his ability to deflect even well-deserved criticism, President Clinton was branded the Velcro president because of his propensity to attract blame. He was blamed for everything: the economy, Somali warlords, the weather. Part of the problem was Clinton himself; he agonized openly about problems and betrayed his insecurities to a public that preferred more self-confidence in its leaders. But most of the problem focused on anger, with blame flung about indiscriminately as people searched for solutions to their problems.

The legislation that emerged from the 104th Congress was replete with blame and characterized by the moralistic, punitive, and antigovernment language that reflected public anger—as well as the Republican leadership's interpretation of how to respond to that anger. Welfare reform, in particular, was a good example of this trend; the House of Representatives version denied funds to unwed teenage mothers and to children born to welfare recipients; the Senate version would leave it up to the states. An unfortunate racial undertone accompanied the national debate over welfare. The assumption was that the three-generation welfare family was typically African American and lived in an urban ghetto, despite the fact that the majority of welfare recipients nationally were white. An article by Sid Blumenthal in the *New Yorker* divulged the startling fact that 44 percent of the live births in Idaho were funded by Medicaid.[23]

## Anger and the Limits of Government

"People are not directing their anger at what is screwing them," complained Ambassador Jim Sasser. "[It is] the corporations. Downsizing is a euphemism for depriving people of benefits. It is economic heartlessness, yet people are *conditioned* to view government as solving their problems. Corporations are the ones doing the downsizing."

Indeed, what can today's political leaders do about the "corporate killers" who are winning huge bonuses for themselves for firing hundreds of thousands of American workers? Today's leaders are so anxious to please Wall Street that the only policies affecting the private sector open for debate seem to involve further cuts in the capital gains tax, elimination of the corporate tax, and new and improved ways to free companies from government regulation.

"We need a leader with respect," said Sasser. "Someone who commands the attention of the media. Someone to articulate economic populism. The Re-

publicans were savvy enough to tap into this. In their case, it was phony populism. I ran a populist economic campaign in 1976 against the oil companies.
No one is articulating this. Political people are not saying these things because
of the PACs. And because of the high cost of running for public office."

Sasser recalled Franklin D. Roosevelt as a leader who responded to public
anger, denouncing the nation's "economic royalists" who, he felt, blocked his
programs and impeded his efforts to overcome the devastation of the depression. "We have not come this far without a struggle," Roosevelt warned. "We
had to struggle with the old enemies of . . . financial monopoly, speculation,
reckless banking, class antagonism, sectionalism, war profiteering. They had
begun to consider the Government of the United States as a mere appendage
to their own affairs. . . . never before in all our history have these forces been so
united against one candidate as they stand today. They are unanimous in their
hate for me—and I welcome their hatred."[24]

As in Roosevelt's case, blame can serve as an effective and constructive tool if
directed at the right source. Used indiscriminately, it backfires, as it did when
Bush blamed LBJ for the Los Angeles riots or when candidates everywhere
blame the welfare state or poor people for all of society's sins. "How can it be
that if you put more money in a rich person's pocket it is good for the economy,
but if it is in a poor person's pocket, it hurts the economy?" remarked Sherrie
Voyles, an attorney with the International Brotherhood of Electrical Workers.

Negative advertising, a staple of political campaigns, capitalizes most successfully on the blame component of public anger. Of course, candidates have
always won elections by painting their opponents in the worst possible colors:
"Martin Van Buren was called a transvestite; Lincoln a baboon; Cleveland a
wife beater; Theodore Roosevelt a drug addict."[25] But in today's atmosphere of
heightened awareness and competing angers, candidates are being taken to
task for some of their more blatant falsehoods. Two nights before the 1996
New Hampshire primary, for example, all three major networks and CNN ran
stories criticizing Dole for lying about former Tennessee governor Lamar
Alexander's tax record. Dole's ads charged Alexander had raised taxes many
times more than he actually had and that he had added a host of new taxes as
well. The truth is that Dole was counting license fees of several dollars and user
charges to create a false picture of Alexander.

Clinton quickly learned the lessons of anger and blame, and he spent the
first half of his second term accentuating the positive: the economy, the absence of war, and his administration's focus on children. His campaign stood
him in good stead with voters who wanted to hear only good news and an optimistic message. At the height of the Whitewater investigation and the Monica

Lewinsky scandal, Clinton's polls rose to new heights: A month after his State of the Union message in late January 1998, his job approval rating rose twelve points to 68 percent among all demographic groups—the highest of his presidency. Significantly, polls showed the public's willingness to separate Clinton's personal problems from his performance as president, with a resounding 84 percent agreeing with the idea that "someone can still be a good President even if they do things in their personal life that you disapprove of." Clinton's focus on the health of the economy clearly paid off, as the poll indicated that 88 percent of the public considered the economy the key source of the president's popularity, while three-fourths—the highest proportion ever recorded since 1971—considered themselves pleased with Clinton's handling of the economy. Whether this is a long-term trend, a cyclical phenomenon, or a temporary respite remains anyone's guess, particularly in view of the president's problems with the unfolding Monica Lewinsky scandal and the Starr investigation.[26]

## Anger on the High Road

Voters are crying out for new ideas and new options, particularly in relation to jobs. Republicans have tried to show that their methods—slashing government, ignoring antitrust enforcement while corporations frantically merge with each other, and balancing the budget—will lead to growth and jobs, but so far they have not shown any direct link between deficit cutting and economic security. In fact, the reverse may be true as voters rebel against congressional attempts to scale back benefits.

Politics abhors a vacuum, leaving the high road open to a group of congressional Democrats who believe they have the answer: tax breaks for corporations who show good citizenship. Corporations that offer decent pensions and health care for their workers, research and development conducted in the United States, employee training, and some effort to curb corporate compensation would be designated in a special category, A-Corps, and taxed at a lower rate than other companies.[27] The philosophy of rewarding companies for progressive policies emerges as a creative alternative to our current posture of laissez-faire; whether it can work politically in the deregulatory, privatizing, buccaneer environment that has taken hold of capitalism today is another matter. It all depends on the heights public anger reaches over economic issues and whether that anger will extend to the ballot box.

The biggest surprise on the anger agenda was the absence of support for campaign finance reform. When the McCain-Feingold bill—which would have banned "soft money" contributions from labor unions, corporations, and individuals to national political parties—came up in the 105th Congress, very little public support backed the measure. Members of Congress reported very little constituent pressure on the issue, and a successful Republican filibuster left the legislation by the wayside for the foreseeable future. (The bill was proposed by Senators John McCain [R–Ariz.] and Russell D. Feingold [D–Wisc.].)

Creative leadership can channel anger into political power and provide the vehicle for turning anger into a force for justice. In Blakely, Georgia, for example, black leaders complained to the mayor when several homes in their community were burned to the ground while the fire chief, who happened to be a member of the Ku Klux Klan, refused to help. Getting nowhere with the mayor, the leaders spent their time registering voters and gaining two seats on the city council, where they were able to dismiss the fire chief.

Leaders need to remain positive about solutions to political anger; in fact, politicians not deft enough to switch from pit bull to leader will find their popularity quickly sinking, the experience of Speaker Gingrich, widely regarded—at least before Buchanan—as the most effective practitioner in recent memory of the anger craft. He can still bring audiences of the Republican faithful to their feet but finds larger constituencies unsettled by his views. And candidates for the Republican primaries in 1995 and 1996 have been notably silent on the Contract with America, almost embarrassed by a program that was so wildly successful politically in 1994 that it threw the Democrats into a temporary state of paralysis and denial. But Gingrich was a fast learner. He moderated his anger pitch for a wider audience; survived a coup attempt by his lieutenants in 1997; and set his sights to run for president in the year 2000.

In a volatile era such as our own, quick-fix solutions are more tempting than ever. In fact, before they take out the snake oil, desperate politicians ought to heed H. L. Mencken's admonition: "There is always an easy solution to every human problem—neat, plausible and wrong."

Unfortunately, for many problems there is no solution, at least no short-term solution. How can you cut the budget deficit without touching entitlements or the defense budget? How can you cut the trade deficit and remain "free-traders?" How can you produce corruption-free political leadership without getting serious about campaign finance? And how do you heal the nation's growing cultural divisions, a problem that does not lend itself to facile solutions.

Many solutions that are readily at hand spell potential disaster, for example, tax reductions that cut vital services such as education and the unraveling of hard-won environmental, worker safety, and consumer protections. Americans are uncomfortable with uncertainty and ambiguity, which is why they are angry. Perhaps the new message of the millennium is that we must live with a certain amount of confusion and evolve solutions that will live into the future, lest we find ourselves boxed into a past more reminiscent of the nineteenth century than the twenty-first.

"See your own hatred and live," an angry husband cautioned his wife in Arthur Miller's play *After the Fall*.[28] The message that could just as easily be applied to politics as marriage is that close attention to strong emotions such as anger will lead to enhanced understanding and the freedom from being crippled by them.

Today's leaders need to fully recognize the existence of political anger and guide it to a higher path. That means sorting out genuine issues from false ones, then mustering the courage to follow through with solutions that reflect the art of the possible. For only authoritarian cultures suppress anger, to their ultimate regret. Democracies do better when they recognize anger, deal with the problems generating it, and fight to keep the outlets for expressing anger open and free from restraint.

# Discussion Questions

## Chapter 1

1. How did political anger affect the 1992, 1994, and 1996 elections? Can you differentiate between anger in the mainstream and anger that gives rise to extremist groups, new political party movements, or changes in the laws?

2. What are the roots of antigovernment anger? Is this form of anger justified, and if so, why? What do the polls reflect about the voters' views of politics and government? Has government become less legitimate in the eyes of the public, and if so, why?

3. Can you track the impact of political anger on current legislative issues? Why have the issues become more bipolar in nature than ever before, and how does this affect democracy?

4. Do Americans need an external threat to keep their political system intact? What societal resources remain constant?

## Chapter 2

1. What are the key components of the psychology of political anger? How do they relate to politics?

2. How does the glorification of violence in popular culture contribute to anger in politics? Why do U.S. citizens bear a legacy of distrust toward their government?

3. Trace the parallels between the Populism of the 1890s and the current waves of populist sentiment in the 1990s.

4. Of all the industrialized nations, the United States still has the lowest taxes as well as the lowest level of social benefits. Why, then, have the campaigns against entitlements and taxes created so much political anger? Why have these campaigns achieved so much success for their proponents?

## Chapter 3

1. What are the economic indicators that *count* when it comes to winning elections and sustaining political support?

2. Have the repeated downsizings of corporations had any impact on politics?

3. Discuss the impact of globalism on campaigns at the state and national level.

4. The conventional wisdom supports the view that when the economy is good, incumbents are invulnerable. Do you agree?

## Chapter 4

1. Widespread disagreement over values has fostered the creation of political movements, such as the Christian Coalition, that have organized open challenges to the media. What are the bases for these challenges, how have they manifested themselves, and how have political leaders entered the fray?

2. How have the battles over values impinged on America's traditional belief system, which relies on tolerance and unity? What are the values causing the most divisiveness?

3. What is the role of the media in aggravating the more negative elements of political anger? Which media outlets have the most influence on political life today? Does the media reflect or manipulate political anger?

4. What is the relationship of hate language to public policy?

## Chapter 5

1. What has happened to the center in American politics?

2. What have the polls revealed over time about the key elements of antigovernment anger?

3. What roles do apathy, blame, corruption, and voter anxiety play in perpetuating political anger?

## Chapter 6

1. Analyze the positive features of political anger, including its contributions to political change.

2. Is anger toward government justified? Has this anger led to the downsizing of government?

3. How have the polls distorted some of the issues?

4. What are the limits and possibilities of government?

5. How can our leaders channel anger into political power as a force for constructive change?

# Glossary

**Alienation,** the act of withdrawal from political life—from voting, from participating in community activities, and from involvement in keeping informed through attention to media reports.

**Anger-repository theory,** the view that although an issue may be quiescent for a certain period of time, the public has stored up anger that is released when the topic reaches the airwaves.

**Apathy,** an indifference to politics, manifested in nonvoting or in low voting rates at the polls. Analysts were especially concerned after the 1996 presidential election, when barely 50 percent of the eligible voters turned out to vote for the leader of the world's largest democracy.

**Bipolarism, or bipolarity,** the tendency to move to the extremes on issues and forgo compromise.

**Communitarian movement,** founded by sociologist Amitai Etzioni in 1991, the communitarian movement seeks to find a common ground on current salient issues by balancing societal values and individual rights.

**Civility movement,** a reaction to the political anger of the 1990s, the civility movement emphasizes the importance of rational dialogue in political life.

**Downsizing,** the increasingly common strategy of corporations to fire thousands of employees in order, argue its defenders, to improve efficiency.

**Entitlement,** a guaranteed government stipend awarded by law to all individuals who qualify in a specific category—such as veterans, for veterans benefits, or senior citizens, who are eligible to received Medicare, which ensures a specific level of health care.

**Freedom of Information Act,** the law that guarantees public access to all government information not protected by national security or proprietary rights.

**General Agreement on Tariffs and Trade (GATT),** a world trade agreement that preceded the World Trade Organization (WTO).

**Globalization,** the fast-moving trend toward erasing borders and national sovereignty on trade issues involving the manufacture, import, investment, and export of products and services.

**Gridlock (congressional),** a state of affairs in which Congress comes to a standstill when Democratic and Republican lawmakers prefer to face each other off and do nothing rather than move ahead on issues over which they disagree. The now infamous government shutdowns in the winter of 1995–1996 resulted from gridlock over the budget.

*Habeas corpus,* literally means "you should have the body." The legal requirement of producing the "body" before the court (theoretically, at least) protects citizens from illegal arrest and imprisonment.

**Militia movement,** a network of paramilitary groups organized on the state level that traces its roots back to the Revolutionary War period. Dedicated to antigovernment views and to private military exercises for its members, the militia movement began to draw public attention in 1995.

**North American Free Trade Agreement (NAFTA),** a trade agreement between Canada, the United States, and Mexico to suspend most tariffs among the three nations in order to create a free trade zone.

**Negative campaigning,** manifested mostly in negative advertising, a form of communication best known for capitalizing on the blame component of political anger by depicting opponents in an adverse, exaggerated, and often untrue light.

**Paradigm,** a model that helps scholars make sense of new patterns and trends in social science.

**Pluralism,** a mélange of diverse ethnic, racial, religious, and social groups that coexist in relative peace in society. The ability to absorb so many groups at different times in the nation's history has characterized American democracy since the birth of the Republic.

**Populist movement (populism),** a period of intense reform activity during the 1890s that was rooted in widespread public discontent with the economic and social changes wrought by industrialization.

*Quid pro quo,* a tangible service or product that is given in exchange for something else. Used in contract language, but also in politics to convey the real "price" of an agreement.

**Sunshine laws,** laws requiring that hearings held by designated regulatory agencies to be open to the public; passed first by many states, and then by the federal government on a selective basis.

**Takings legislation,** mandates that government compensate private companies or citizens for financial losses stemming from regulatory action. No version of takings legislation has yet passed the U.S. Congress.

**Unfunded mandates,** a popular political issue that criticizes the federal government for requiring that states, localities, companies, and private citizens pay the price of enforcing often costly federal laws and regulations.

**Wetlands legislation,** designates land containing excess moisture, such as swamps or tidal flats, for government protection in order to safeguard migratory fowl and delicate ecosystems from extinction. This may involve expropriating the land from its owners, an issue that has given rise to opposition from groups of individuals affected by these laws, such as farmers, resort owners, and other businesses.

# Notes

## Chapter 1

1. Henry Adams, *The Education of Henry Adams: An Autobiography* (Boston and New York: Houghton Mifflin, 1918), p. 7.

2. Monica Maples, speech at the National Capital Area Political Science Association (NCAPSA) annual convention, March 25, 1995, Washington, D.C. A substantial part of this book is based on interview material or is from material that comes directly from hearings or speeches (as the aforementioned speech at the NCAPSA) attended by the author. All direct quotes in the text that are not cited in the notes are drawn from these interviews, hearings, or speeches. Respondents are noted in the Preface and Acknowledgments.

3. Public Affairs Research Institute, "Record Number of Citizen-Initiated Questions Slated for November Ballots in 20 States," Princeton, N.J., October 8, 1996.

4. Statement from Nebraska U.S. Senator J. James Exon that he would not seek reelection, March 17, 1995.

5. Helen Dewar, "New Jersey: Only Mention of Contract Was Made by a Democrat," *Washington Post,* April 24, 1995, p. A6.

6. *Congressional Record—House,* March 29, 1995, H3905.

7. *Gallup Poll Monthly,* May 1992, p. 2.

8. Clyde Wilcox, *Onward Christian Soldiers? The Religious Right in American Politics* (Boulder: Westview Press, 1996).

9. John Harwood, "Maryland May Be Exception in Year of the Incumbent," *Wall Street Journal,* March 10, 1998, p. A24.

10. *Washington Post,* February 2, 1995.

11. Compiled from poll data from the *Gallup Poll Monthly,* the Times Mirror Center for the People and the Press, and the *Harris Survey.* See also Joseph S. Nye Jr., Philip D. Zelikow, and David C. King, *Why People Don't Trust Government* (Cambridge: Harvard University Press, 1997).

12. Statement from Douglas Duncan, county executive, Montgomery County, Maryland. Originally mentioned in Maureen Dowd, "Identity Crisis City," *New York Times,* October 29, 1995, p. E13. Attempts to get the original document were met by embarrassment from county officials, who admitted the existence of the document but failed to produce it.

13. For further material on term limits, see "Congressional Term Limits," *Congressional Digest* 74, no. 4, April 1995. See also *U.S. Term Limits Inc. v. Thornton,* U.S. Supreme Court, nos. 93-1456 and 93-1828. The voters of Mississippi rejected term lim-

its for legislators and many state and local officials by a 54–46 percent margin on November 7, 1995. Mississippi was the only state to turn down such an initiative in the 1995 elections. The law would not have applied to members of Congress because the Supreme Court has already ruled that unconstitutional. The group U.S. Term Limits pumped $220,000 into the effort. Mississippi has already imposed two-term limits on the offices of governor and lieutenant governor. See "Term Limits Bid Heads to Defeat," *Commercial Appeal* (Memphis), November 8, 1995, p. 9A.

14. *Gallup Poll Monthly,* April 1995, p. 25.

15. Larry Hugick and Leslie McAneny, "A Gloomy America Sees a Nation in Decline, No Easy Solutions Ahead," *Gallup Satisfaction Index,* special issue of *Gallup Poll Monthly,* September 1992, p. 2.

16. Times Mirror Center for the People and the Press, *The People, the Press and Politics: The Political Landscape* (Washington, D.C., October 1994), pp. 23–24.

17. "Confidence in Political Institutions 1967–1995, *Harris Survey,* 1995, pp. 1–4.

18. "Findings from a Research Project About Attitudes Toward Government," sponsored by the Council for Excellence in Government, February and March 1997, p. 3. See also Pew Research Center for The People and the Press, *Deconstructing Distrust: How Americans View Government,* 1998.

19. Joe Klein, "Why Moderate Democrats like Dave McCurdy Are in Trouble This Year," *Newsweek,* October 31, 1994, p. 33.

20. Theodore Lowi, *The End of Liberalism: Ideology, Policy, and the Crisis of Public Authority* (New York: W. W. Norton, 1969), p. 291.

21. Several monographs published by the Western States Center and affiliated groups include Mark McAllister and Jeff Fox, *The Wise Use Movement in Utah* (Portland, Ore., and Helena, Mont.: Western States Center and Montana AFL/CIO, 1994); and *The Wise Use Movement: Strategic Analysis and Fifty State Review* (Washington, D.C.: Clearinghouse on Environmental Advocacy and Research, 1993, 3d printing).

22. For an account of the Oklahoma tragedy, see Joel Dyer, *Harvest of Rage: Why Oklahoma City Is Only the Beginning* (Boulder: Westview Press, 1997).

23. Marc Cooper, "Montana's Mother of All Militias," *Nation* 260, no. 20, May 22, 1995, p. 714.

24. Tim Curran and Benjamin Sheffner, "Three Members Tied to Militias," *Roll Call* (Washington, D.C., April 27, 1995).

25. The Anti-Defamation League, a national organization with twenty-eight regional offices, monitored the militia movement long before the Oklahoma crisis. Its research indicates that there are "militias operating in at least 40 states, with membership reaching some 15,000." The California militia movement, for example, has thirty-five units and is growing rapidly. See "The Militia Movement in America," in *ADL Special Report* (Washington, D.C., 1995).

26. Southern Poverty Law Center website, http://www.splcenter.com/klanwatch .html, March 1998.

27. Howard Kurtz, "Gordon Liddy on Shooting from the Lip: Radio Host Denies Fueling the Lunatic Fringe," *Washington Post,* April 26, 1995, p. C1.

28. Diane Rehm, "Hot Mouths, Hot Buttons, and the Danger to Public Dialogue," *Washington Post,* "Outlook," February 18, 1996, p. C3.

29. Aristotle, *Nichomachean Ethics,* trans. Martin Ostwald (Indianapolis: Bobbs-Merrill, 1962), vol. 4, p. 11. Also cited in Solomon Schimmel, *The Seven Deadly Sins* (New York: Free Press, 1992), p. 89; and in Eugene Kennedy, *New York Times Book Review,* September 9, 1995, pp. 1–4.

30. H. G. Wells, *The Invisible Man and the War of the Worlds* (New York: Washington Square Press, 1962).

31. Ralph Ellison, *Invisible Man* (New York: Modern Library, 1952).

32. Amitai Etzioni, ed., *New Communitarian Thinking: Persons, Virtues, Institutions, and Communities* (Charlottesville: University of Virginia Press, 1995).

## Chapter 2

1. Eleanor Clift and Evan Thomas with Tara Sonenshine, "Why the General's Wife Is a Reluctant Warrior," and Howard Fineman, "Powell on the Brink," *Newsweek,* November 6, 1995, pp. 39 and 37, respectively.

2. Colin Powell with Joseph Persico, *My American Journey* (New York: Random House, 1995), p. 43.

3. Carol Green Wilson, *Herbert Hoover: A Challenge for Today* (New York: Evans, 1968), p. 231. An exhibition of political cartoons from the 1860s to the 1890s on display at the Smithsonian Institution in Washington, D.C., sported the title *Savage Glee,* so termed for its depiction of politicians (and immigrants) as subhuman.

4. Willard Gaylin, *The Rage Within: Anger in Modern Life* (New York: Simon & Schuster, 1984), p. 37.

5. Max Scheler, *Ressentiment* (New York: Free Press of Glencoe, 1961). Cited in Gaylin, *op. cit.,* p. 143.

6. Gaylin, *op. cit.,* p. 143.

7. Carol Tavris, *Anger: The Misunderstood Emotion* (New York: Touchstone, 1982). See also Harriet Lerner, *The Dance of Anger* (New York: Perennial Library, 1985).

8. Gaylin, *op. cit.,* p. 143.

9. At least ten bills were introduced in the 104th Congress involving the "takings" issue, portrayed as a Fifth Amendment right to own property free of government ex-appropriation or even just compensation. Takings bills in the same year were pending in at least two dozen states. Appealing on the surface to a public intent on reducing regulatory burdens on small business or property owners, "takings" bills could also be subject to considerable abuse by land speculators and others seeking to make a quick profit from the government till. See Kenneth Green and George Abney, "Commentary . . . on 'Takings,'" *Public Administration Times* 18, no. 11 (November 1, 1995), p. 10.

10. *New York Times Book Review,* September 9, 1995, p. 3.

11. Christian Coalition website, http://www.cc.org/publications/ccnews, February 10, 1998.

12. Franz Neumann, "Anxiety and Politics," in Maurice R. Stein, Arthur J. Vidich, and David Manning White, eds., *Identity and Anxiety* (Glencoe, Ill.: Free Press, 1960), p. 284.

13. David J. Finlay, Ole R. Holsti, and Richard B. Fagen, *Enemies in Politics* (Chicago: Rand, McNally, 1967), p. 8.

14. Finlay, Holsti, Fagen, *op. cit.*, p. 19, quoting Quincy Wright.

15. Redford and Virginia Williams, *Anger Kills: Seventeen Strategies for Controlling the Hostility that Can Harm Your Health* (New York: HarperCollins, 1994).

16. Jeffrey Birnbaum, "The Pat Solution: Who's Really to Blame?" *Time,* November 6, 1995, p. 30.

17. Judith Shklar, *Ordinary Vices* (Cambridge: Belknap Press of Harvard University, 1984), p. 177.

18. Robert Jay Lifton, *The Protean Self: Human Resilience in an Age of Fragmentation* (New York: Basic Books, 1993).

19. Such political upheavals also release creativity. Witness the "angry young men" in postwar Great Britain in the 1950s; Berthold Brecht's "long anger" at his native Germany between the wars, which informed his plays; and William Shakespeare, whose plays have been interpreted as a reaction to an era of great confusion, upheaval, and anger in Elizabethan England.

20. See Tavris, *op cit.*, and Lerner, *op. cit.*

21. Harriet Zisowitz Stearns and Peter Stearns, *Anger: The Struggle for Emotional Control in America's History* (Chicago: University of Chicago Press, 1986).

22. Richard Hofstadter, *The Age of Reform* (New York: Alfred A. Knopf, 1956), pp. 78–79. See also Michael Kazin, *The Populist Persuasion: An American History* (New York: Basic Books, 1995).

23. For a new and fresh interpretation of the Progressive period and the relationship it bears to our own, see E. J. Dionne Jr., *They Only Look Dead: Why Progressives Will Dominate the Next Political Era* (New York: Simon & Schuster, 1996).

24. Hofstadter, *op. cit.*, pp. 78–79.

25. Eric Hobsbawm, *The Age of Extremes: A History of the World, 1914–1991* (New York: Pantheon Books, 1994).

26. Robert McNamara, *In Retrospect* (New York: Times Books/Random House, 1995).

27. An excellent book on lying in public life is Sissela Bok's *Lying: Moral Choice in Public and Private Life* (New York: Pantheon Books, 1978).

28. Gary Lee, "One Quarter of Participants in Federal Medical Research Take Part Unwittingly," *Washington Post,* June 23, 1995, p. A11.

29. Richard Morin and Sharon Warden, "Americans Vent Anger at Affirmative Action," *Washington Post,* March 24, 1995, pp. A1, A4. For an excellent study of race in American politics, see Paula D. McClain and Joseph Stewart Jr., *Can We All Get Along? Racial and Ethnic Minorities in American Politics, Second Edition* (Boulder: Westview Press, 1998).

30. "Entitlements: The Untouchable May Become Unavoidable," *Congressional Quarterly Weekly Report,* January 2, 1993, pp. 108–116.

31. Ellis Cose, *Rage of a Privileged Class* (New York: HarperCollins, 1993).

32. Dick Armey, "IRS Code Revisions," statement before the Senate Budget Committee, February 22, 1995.

33. Allan Nevins and Henry Steele Commager, *A Short History of the United States* (New York: Random House, 1945), pp. 119–120, 150–151.

34. Kevin Phillips, *Boiling Point* (New York: Random House, 1993), p. 212.

35. Marc Robichaux, "Viacom May Face Congressional Hitch in Cable-System Sale to Minority Buyer," *Wall Street Journal,* January 18, 1995, p. B2.

36. Ted Robert Gurr, *Why Men Rebel* (Princeton: Princeton University Press, 1970), pp. 355–356; Ted Robert Gurr, Ivo K. Feierabend, and Rosalind L. Feierabend, eds., *Anger, Violence, and Politics: Theories and Research* (Englewood Cliffs, N.J.: Prentice-Hall, 1972).

37. Solomon Schimmel, *The Seven Deadly Sins* (New York: Free Press, 1992), p. 105.

38. Ibid., p. 109.

39. Unscrupulous colonists also found it handy to designate propertied women as "witches" in order to grab their land, according to recent scholars.

40. Seneca, "On Anger," in *Moral Essays,* vol. 1 (Cambridge: Harvard University Press, 1928), cited in Schimmel, *op. cit.,* p. 105; and Plutarch, "On the Control of Anger," in *Moralia,* vol. 6 (Cambridge: Harvard University Press, 1939), cited in Schimmel, *op. cit.,* p. 105.

41. St. Thomas Aquinas, *Summa Theologica.* . . . (Blackfriars: McGraw-Hill, 1964), cited in Gaylin, *op. cit.,* pp. 77–78.

42. Schimmel, *op. cit.,* pp. 105, 109.

43. Jamie Stiehm, "Restrictions on Habeas Corpus Spark a Constitutional Debate," *The Hill,* November 22, 1995, p. 4. *Habeas corpus* provisions, attached to the 1995 debt ceiling bill and approved by the House and the Senate, would restrict the intervention of federal courts in state cases. The original meaning of *habeas corpus,* as guaranteed by the U.S. Constitution, involves the rights of citizens to be protected against illegal detention by the government.

44. Charles S. Maier, "Democracy and Its Discontents," *Foreign Affairs* 73, no. 4 (July/August, l994), pp. 48–64.

45. Harry Eckstein, "On the Etiology of Internal Wars," in Gurr, Feierabend, and Feierabend, eds., *Anger, Violence, and Politics,* pp. 13–14.

46. Murray Edelman, *The Symbolic Uses of Politics* (Urbana: University of Illinois Press, 1967), p. 8. See also Murray Edelman, *Politics as Symbolic Action: Mass Arousal and Quiescence* (Chicago: Markham, 1971), pp. 57–62.

47. Eric Hoffer, *The True Believer* (New York: Harper & Row, 1951), pp. 17 and 85.

48. Paul R. Abramson and Ronald Inglehart, *Value Change in Global Perspective* (Ann Arbor: University of Michigan Press, 1995), p. 9.

## Chapter 3

1. "Why Are You So Angry?" *U.S. News & World Report,* November 7, 1994.

2. Ibid.

3. Dennis Farney, "Have Liberals Ignored 'Have-Less Whites' at Their Own Peril?" *Wall Street Journal,* December 14, 1995, pp. A1, A8.

4. Linda Cashdan, "Telecommunications Turmoil," *Spotlight on Business and Finance, Voice of America,* October 13, 1995.

5. Michele Galen and Mark Vamos, "Portrait of an Anxious Public," *Business Week,* March 13, 1995, p. 80.

6. Reprinted as *The Downsizing of America* (New York: Times Books, 1996).

7. Jeffrey Madrick, *The End of Affluence: The Causes and Consequences of America's Economic Dilemma* (New York: Random House, 1995), pp. 160–161.

8. Isabel V. Sawhill, "Opportunity in America," paper presented to the Aspen Institute's Domestic Strategy Group, August 20, 1995, Aspen, Colorado. See also Urban Institute, "Is U.S. Income Inequality Really Growing? Sorting Out the Fairness Question," *Policy Bites,* no. 13, June 1992.

9. "Changes in Family Finances from 1989–1992," *Federal Reserve Bulletin,* October 1994, pp. 861–882. This report correlates macroeconomic trends—the expansion of the U.S. economy and the decline of blue-collar jobs—with stagnant earning power.

10. Keith Bradsher, "Gap in Wealth in U.S. Called Widest in West," *New York Times,* April 17, 1995, pp. A1, D4.

11. Bradsher has written extensively on this subject. See also "America's Opportunity Gap," *New York Times* "Week in Review," June 4, 1995, p. E4.

12. Sam Roberts, "Gap Between Rich and Poor in New York City Grows Wider," *New York Times,* December 25, 1994, pp. 33–34. "The top fifth of Manhattan households made 32 times as much as the bottom fifth, an average of $174,486 compared with $5,435."

13. Louis Uchitelle, "Lacking Child Care, Parents Take Their Children to Work," *New York Times,* December 23, 1994, pp. A1, D2.

14. Steven Pearlstein, "Widening the Income Gap," *Washington Post,* May 29, 1995, pp. A1, A12. See also Rochelle L. Stanfield, "Rutsville," *National Journal,* December 3, 1994, pp. 2835–2839.

15. Robert J. Samuelson, *The Good Life and Its Discontents: The American Dream in the Age of Entitlement, 1945–1955* (New York: Times Books, 1996).

16. Michael Lind, *The Next American Nation: The New Nationalism and the Fourth American Revolution* (New York: Free Press, 1995).

17. Lerman added that "between 1970 and 1991, the proportion of children in one-parent families jumped from 15% to 28%. The share of children in families headed by never-married mothers—the group with the highest rates of poverty—jumped from 1% to 8% [and] the married proportion of the 25–29 year-old men dropped form 81% to 53%." Robert I. Lerman, "The Impact of the Changing U.S. Family Structure on

Child Poverty and Income Inequality," paper presented to the Urban Institute, Washington, D.C., 1995.

18. Ann Gerhart and Annie Groer, "Whoopi Makes Waves over Welfare," *Washington Post,* December 6, 1995, p. C3.

19. The Luxembourg Income Study, referred to in Keith Bradsher, "Low Ranking for Poor American Children," *New York Times,* August 14, 1995, p. A9.

20. Robert B. Reich, "Frayed-Collar Workers in Gold-Plated Times: The State of the American Workforce 1995," speech at the Center for National Policy, Washington, D.C., August 31, 1995, pp. 1–6.

21. Executive Pay Watch, "Runaway CEO Pay," http://paywatch.org/problem/index. html, April 24, 1998.

22. Although according to Graef S. Crystal, who studies corporate compensation, the average CEO made 35 times what his average worker made in 1974, the multiple for today's CEO looks more like 120 times. Steven Pearlstein, "Reshaped Economy Exacts mTough Toll," *Washington Post,* September 12, 1995, pp. A1, A14.

23. Charles McMillion, "The Clinton Record of Net New Jobs," MGB Information Services, April 20, 1998.

24. Robert H. Frank and Philip J. Cook, *Winner-Take-All Society: How More and More Americans Compete for Ever Fewer and Bigger Prizes, Encouraging Economic Waste, Income Inequality, and an Impoverished Cultural Life* (New York: Martin Kessler/Free Press, 1995).

25. Robert Kuttner, *The End of Laissez-Faire* (New York: Alfred A. Knopf, 1991); Robert Kuttner, "Where Have All the Good Jobs Gone?" *Business Week,* August 29, 1994, p. 16. See also Robert Kuttner, "Fewer Fruits for Our Labors," *Washington Post,* September 4, 1995, p. A25.

26. David Greising, Michael Oneal, and Ronald Grover, "Wow! That's Some Bank," *Business Week,* September 11, 1995, p. 38; and Michael J. Mandel, Christopher Farrell, and Catherine Yang, "Land of the Giants," *Business Week,* September 11, 1995, pp. 34–41.

27. Kirstin Downey Grimsley, "The Ax That Cuts Both Ways," *Washington Post,* November 5, 1995, p. H1.

28. Brahm Resnick, "Kodak Job Cuts Climb to 19,900," *Rochester Democrat and Chronicle,* December 19, 1997, http://www.rochesterdandc.com/extras/kodak/ ek7352c. html.

29. Timothy L. O'Brien, "2,250 Layoffs Set at Chase, or 3% of Staff," *New York Times,* March 18, 1998, pp. D1 and D2.

30. Alan Sloan, "The Hit Men," *Newsweek,* February 26, 1996, pp. 44–48.

31. Grimsley, *op. cit.*

32. James Sterngold, "NAFTA Trade-Off: Some Jobs Lost, Others Gained," *New York Times,* October 9, 1995, p. A1. See also Peter Cooper and Lori Wallach, *NAFTA's Broken Promises: Job Creation Under NAFTA* (Washington, D.C.: Public Citizen, September 1995).

33. A. M. Rosenthal, "What Dole Owes Us," *New York Times*, February 23, 1996, p. A31.

34. Bob Davis, "Brimstone Conservative or Working-Class Hero? Buchanan Followers Can Only Answer, It's Pat," *Wall Street Journal*, December 1, 1995, p. A16 (EPIC poll).

35. Barnaby Feder, "Citing Trade Treaties, Fruit of the Loom Will Close Six U.S. Plants, *New York Times*, October 31, 1995, p. D5.

36. Thomas B. Edsall, "Organized Labor Flexes Muscle with Democrats," *Washington Post*, November 16, 1997, p. A10.

37. Randy Barber and Robert E. Scott, *Jobs on the Wing: Trading Away the Future of the Aerospace Industry* (Washington, D.C.: Economic Policy Institute, 1995), p. A47.

38. For a discussion of international trade and technology transfer, see Martin Tolchin and Susan Tolchin, *Selling Our Security: The Erosion of America's Assets* (New York: Alfred A. Knopf, 1992).

39. International Association of Machinists and Aerospace Workers, *Confidential Briefing Book* (Upper Marlboro, Md., 1995).

40. An excellent synopsis of what works and what doesn't is Jodie T. Allen's "Why Retooling Workers Is No Quick Fix for Anxious America," *Washington Post*, "Outlook," January 22, 1995, p. C3. Allen concludes that programs can work if the goals are reasonable and that "there are important economic and social gains to be made through a sensible restructuring of employment programs." Other literature corroborates this view. See U.S. Department of Labor, Office of the Chief Economist, *What's Working and What's Not: A Summary of Research on the Economic Impacts of Employment and Training Programs* (Washington, D.C.: Government Printing Office, January 1995); and Christina Del Valle, "Doing a Job on the Job Corps," *Business Week*, January 16, 1995, p.

41. Aaron Wildavsky and Jeffrey L. Pressman's original conclusion in their classic work on Oakland, California, was that waste, poor planning, and the difficulties of administering programs locally with central direction from Washington might still hold true today, especially given the political criticism and sparse resources. Aaron Wildavsky and Jeffrey L. Pressman, *Implementation: How Great Expectations in Washington Are Dashed in Oakland; or, Why It's Amazing That Federal Programs Work at All* (Berkeley: University of California Press, 1973). This is a saga of the Economic Development Administration as told by two sympathetic observers who seek to build morals on a foundation of ruined hopes.

41. Thomas Byrne Edsall, *The New Politics of Inequality* (New York: W. W. Norton, 1984), p. 179.

42. Marianne Means, "Ignoring the Gap," *King Features*, May 10, 1995.

43. Marianne Means, "Zig or Zag," *King Features*, June 16, 1995.

44. Martin Tolchin and Susan Tolchin, *Buying Into America: How Foreign Money Is Changing the Face of Our Nation* (New York: Times Books/Random House, 1988).

45. James Fallows, *Breaking the News: How the Media Undermine American Democracy* (New York: Pantheon Books, 1996).

46. James Risen, "Opposition to Rescue Erodes U.S. Credibility," *Los Angeles Times,* February 1, 1995, p. A1.

47. Aaron Bernstein, "The Wage Squeeze," *Business Week,* July 17, 1995, p. 56.

48. Steven Pearlstein, "Income Gap Is Issue No. 1, Debaters Agree," *Washington Post,* December 7, 1995, p. B11.

49. Pat Choate is the author of *Agents of Influence* (New York: Alfred A. Knopf, 1990).

50. Timothy J. Penny and Steven E. Schier, *Payment Due: A Nation in Debt, A Generation in Trouble* (Boulder: Westview Press, 1996); and G. Calvin Mackenzie and Saranna Thornton, *Bucking the Deficit: Economic Policymaking in America* (Boulder: Westview Press, 1996).

51. Department of Labor website, www.dol.gov/dol/public/media/main.htm. March 25, 1998.

52. Louis Uchitelle, "The Dark Side of Optimism," *New York Times,* March 8, 1998, "News of the Week in Review," p. 4.

## Chapter 4

1. William Blake, "The Proverbs of Hell," in *The Marriage of Heaven and Hell* (New York and Paris: Oxford University Press in association with Trianon Press, 1975). (Original work completed in 1790.)

2. Dan Quayle, "Restoring Basic Values," *Vital Speeches of the Day* 58 (June 15, 1992), p. 519. See also John E. Yang, "Quayle Decries 'Poverty of Values,'" *Washington Post,* May 19, 1992, p. A1.

3. The strong correlation between single parenting and the increase in child poverty showed up in the Census Bureau's statistic for 1994, which cited the median income for a married couple with children at $47,244, compared with $14,902, the median income for a single mother.

4. Yang, *op. cit.,* p. A1.

5. Empower America, news release, October 26, 1995. See also William J. Bennett, ed. with commentary, *The Book of Virtues: A Treasury of Great Moral Stories* (New York: Simon & Schuster, 1993).

6. Marc Fisher, "Kinsey Report, Fast and Loose," *Washington Post,* December 8, 1995, pp. F1, F4.

7. For an excellent exposition of the agenda of the Christian Coalition, see *Contract with the American Family,* a bold plan by Christian Coalition to strengthen the family and restore common sense values. Introduction by Ralph Reed (Nashville, Tenn.: Moorings/Ballantine/Random House, 1995). For a historical treatment of the role of religions in American history, see Patricia U. Bonomi, *Under the Cope of Heaven: Religion, Society, and Politics in Colonial America* (New York: Oxford University Press, 1986); Garry Wills, *Under God: Religion and American Politics* (New York: Simon & Schuster, 1990); and Leo Ribuffo, "God and Contemporary Politics," *Journal of American History* 79, no. 4 (March 1993), pp. 1515–1533.

8. Gustave Neibuhr, "Advice for Parents and for Politicians," *New York Times*, May 30, 1995, p. A12. The reverse approach to the "discipline" question correlates negative anger to behavior problems in children. See Lizzette Peterson, Bernard Ewigman, and Trish Vandiver, "The Role of Parental Anger in Low-Income Women: Discipline Strategy, Perceptions of Behavior Problems, and the Need for Control," *Journal of Clinical Child Psychology* 23 (December 1994), pp. 435–436, 442.

9. Handgun Control, Inc. (chaired by former Reagan press secretary Jim Brady), from data culled in 1992.

10. Lisa Frazier, "Oxon Hill Principal Removed in Wake of Student's Slaying," *Washington Post*, January 2, 1996, pp. A1, A12.

11. The White House Conference on Hate Crimes, November 10, 1997, p. 1.

12. "Home Schooling Movement Gives House a Lesson," *Congressional Quarterly Weekly Report*, February 26, 1994, p. 51.

13. Susan J. Tolchin, "What's Being Taken Away from Us," *Earth Times*, May 15–30, 1995. See also Susan J. Tolchin and Martin Tolchin, *Dismantling America: The Rush to Deregulate* (Boston: Houghton Mifflin, 1983).

14. A popular antiregulation book that spent a fair amount of time on the best-seller list used this term. See Philip Howard, *The Death of Common Sense: How Law Is Suffocating America* (New York: Random House, 1994).

15. For an excellent treatment of modern media and their role in politics, see Matthew Robert Kerbel, *Remote and Controlled: Media Politics in a Cynical Age* (Boulder: Westview Press, 1995). See also Stephen Ansolabehere and Shanto Iyengar, *Going Negative: How Attack Ads Shrink and Polarize the Electorate* (New York: Free Press, 1995).

16. Larry J. Sabato, *Feeding Frenzy: How Attack Journalism Has Transformed American Politics* (New York: The Free Press, 1991).

17. Center for People and the Press, National Social Trust Survey, "Press, 'Unfair,' Inaccurate, and Pushy," March, 21, 1997, http://www.people-press.org/97medrpt.html.

18. Scott Keeter, "Origins of the Disjuncture of Perception and Reality: The Cases of Racial Equality and Environmental Protection," unpublished paper prepared for the American Political Science Association annual meeting, September 1996.

19. On secrecy in government, see Sissela Bok, *Secrets: On the Ethics of Concealment and Revelation* (New York: Pantheon Books, 1982).

20. "Conflict v. Context in Covering . . . Clinton's Health Care Proposal," *National Journal*, November 19, 1994, p. 2739.

21. "Talk-Radio Hosts Decide to Go off the Air and on the Ballot," *Congressional Quarterly Weekly Report*, April 9, 1994, pp. 48–49.

22. Doug Obey, "Red Hot Rhetoric," *The Hill*, April 26, 1995, p. 8.

23. Joe Klein, "Stalking the Radical Middle," *Newsweek*, September 25, 1995, pp. 32–36.

24. Robert Putnam with Robert Leonardi and Raffaella Y. Nanetti, *Making Democracy Work: Civic Tradition and Modern Italy* (Princeton: Princeton University Press, 1993).

25. Robert Putnam, "Bowling Alone: America's Declining Social Capital," *Journal of Democracy* 6, no. 1 (January 1995), pp. 65, 76.

26. Even the "violent millenarian frenzies of medieval Europe on the part of un-skilled workers and landless peasants" looked for roots in the disintegration of traditional groups, which offered "material and emotional support" as well as "institutional-ized methods of voicing their grievances or pressing their claims." Ted Robert Gurr, "Psychological Factors in Civil Violence," in Ted Robert Gurr, Ivo K. Feierabend, and Rosalind L. Feierabend, eds., *Anger, Violence, and Politics: Theories and Research* (Engle-wood Cliffs, N.J.: Prentice-Hall, 1972), p. 45. See also Norman Cohn, *The Pursuit of the Millennium: Revolutionary Millenarians and Mystical Anarchists of the Middle Ages* (New York: Oxford University Press, 1957); Mike Freeman, "Clinton Bypasses Nets for Town Hall," *Broadcasting* 123 (February 8, 1993), p. 10; Joel Harmon, Joy A. Schneer, and L. Richard Hoffman, "Electronic Meetings and Established Decision Groups: Au-dioconferencing Effects on Performance and Structural Society," *Organizational Behav-ior and Human Decision Processes* 61 (February 1995), pp. 138–140.

27. Murray Edelman, *Politics as Symbolic Action: Mass Arousal and Quiescence* (Chicago: Markham, 1971), p. 57.

28. Eamon Javers, "Waxman Assails Burton for Calling Clinton a 'Scumbag,'" *The Hill,* April 22, 1998, pp. 1 and 48.

29. Dick Armey, letter to the editor, *New York Times,* January 30, 1995, p. A18.

30. John Leo, "Just Too Much Rage," *U.S. News & World Report,* May 8, 1995, p. 22.

31. Katharine Q. Seelye, "Adviser to Dole Campaign Uses Slur for Two Jewish Con-gressmen," *New York Times,* May 20, 1995, p. 24.

32. Remarks by House Democratic leader Richard A. Gephardt, National Association of Radio Talk Show Hosts, seventh annual conference, June 24, 1995, Houston, Texas. See also Howard Kurtz, "Gordon Liddy on Shooting from the Lip," *Washington Post,* April 26, 1995, p. C1.

33. Dwayne Yancey, "Loud and Angry Voices," *Roanoke Times & World News,* May 7, 1995, p. 1.

34. Esther Iverem, "Marching to a Different Beat," *Washington Post,* December 12, 1995, pp. C1, C11.

35. Bill Johnson, "Women: Revolt Against What Gangsta Rap Represents," *Detroit News,* July 7, 1995.

36. C. Delores Tucker and William Bennett, "Lyrics from the Gutter," *New York Times,* June 2, 1995, p. A29.

37. Empower America, *op. cit.*

38. "The War on Time Warner," *George,* Fall 1995, pp. 160–165.

39. Arlene Vigoda, "'Too Hot' Video Bares 'Springer' Appeal," *USA Today,* February 4, 1998.

40. Lawrie Mifflin, "TV Stretches Limit of Taste, to Little Outcry," *New York Times,* April 6, 1998, p. A1.

41. Willard Gaylin, *The Rage Within: Anger in Modern Life* (New York: Simon & Schuster, 1984), p. 117.

42. Blake, *op. cit.*

43. Gaylin, *op. cit.*, p. 116.

44. Homi K. Bhabha, ed., *Nation and Narration* (New York and London: Routledge, 1990).

45. Dirk Johnson, "Civility in Politics: Going, Going, Gone," *New York Times*, December 10, 1997, p. A20.


## Chapter 5

1. For an excellent synopsis of Ohio, its politics, and the Ninth Congressional District, see Michael Barone and Grant Ujifusa, *The Almanac of American Politics 1996* (Washington, D.C.: National Journal Inc., 1995), pp. 1028–1081.

2. Grandparents raising grandchildren is an increasing societal problem. For more on the subject see Nancy K. Schlossberg, "An Intergenerational Challenge for Employers: Grandparents Raising Grandchildren," paper presented to the American Psychological Association, New York, August 11, 1995.

3. Southern Poverty Law Center website, http://www.splcenter.com/klanwatch.html. See also Jonathan Karl, *The Right to Bear Arms: The Rise of America's New Militias* (New York: HarperPaperbacks, 1995). Karl argues that the militia movement is a small one, estimating that membership fluctuates between 15,000 and 100,000; there is no significant national organization in charge of the militia; and their rhetoric is more belligerent and extreme than its members. "The overwhelming majority of militia members, he contends, are "harmless . . . often angry and disillusioned, but . . . dedicated to self-defense" (p. 157).

4. David Beiler, "Surgical Precision: How Senate Power Jim Sasser Was Stomped by a Political Novice in Tennessee," *Campaigns and Elections,* April 1995.

5. The thirteen senators who had announced by January 1996 were William Cohen (R–Maine.), Alan Simpson (R–Wyo.), James Exon (D–Neb.), Bill Bradley (D–N.J.), Howell Heflin (D–Ala.), Bennett Johnston (D–La.), Nancy Kassebaum (R–Kans.), Sam Nunn (D–Ga.), Paul Simon (D–Ill.), Hank Brown (R–Colo.), Mark O. Hatfield (R–Ore.), Claiborne Pell (D–R.I.), and David Pryor (D–Ark.).

6. *Nightline,* March 29, 1995. For an excellent critique of term limits, see Victor Kamber, *Giving Up on Democracy: Why Term Limits Are Bad for America* (Washington, D.C.: Regnery, 1995).

7. See http://allpolitics.com/1998/02/25/paxon.

8. *National Journal's CongressDaily/A.M.*, April 20, 1998, p. 6.

9. A. B. Stoddard, "Simpson Leaves with Blast at Media," *The Hill,* December 6, 1995, p. 22.

10. Marcia Gelbart, "Cohen Makes 13 Unlucky Number As Senate Retirees Break Record," *The Hill,* January 17, 1996, p. 12.

11. David E. Rosenbaum, "In with the Ideologues, on with Deadlock," *New York Times*, "News of the Week in Review," January 21, 1996, p. E5.

12. Richard Morin, "Poll Shows a Divided America," *Washington Post*, July 19, 1995, pp. A1, A12.

13. The new welfare reform bill requires welfare recipients to work twenty hours per week or be in a state-approved job training program after two years of aid. Among other provisions, the bill cuts food stamps by 13 percent, puts a lifetime limit of five years on families, forces states to enforce laws against deadbeat parents, and bars aid to illegal immigrants. *The Personal Responsibility and Work Opportunity Reconciliation Act of 1996*, Public Law #104-193.

14. Richard E. Cohen and William Schneider, "Epitaph for an Era," *National Journal*, January 14, 1995, pp. 83–105.

15. Charles O. Jones, *The Presidency in a Separated System* (Washington, D.C.: Brookings Institution, 1994).

16. Barbara Roberts, speech delivered to the semiannual convention of the National Academy of Public Administration, Savannah, Georgia, June 9, 1995. Official publication: "Barbara Roberts on Federalism," Elmer B. Staats Lecture, Academy Spring Meeting, June 9, 1995.

17. Seymour Martin Lipset, "American Democracy in Comparative Perspective," unpublished paper, 1995, p. 6. The paper is discussed in Lipset's *American Exceptionalism: A Double-Edged Sword* (New York: W. W. Norton, 1996).

18. "Findings from a Research Project About Attitudes Toward Government," sponsored by the Council for Excellence in Government, February and March 1997, p. 3.

19. Ibid., p. 8.

20. Pew Research Center for the People and the Press, "Deconstructing Distrust: How Americans View Government," 1998, p. 4.

21. Alexis Simendinger, "Of the People, For the People," *National Journal*, April 18, 1998, p. 852.

22. Zachary Karabell and David King, "An American Anomaly: The Evolution of Public Trust in the Military from Tet to Today," monograph for the Pew Charitable Trusts, April 1998.

23. Richard Morin and Dan Balz, "Americans Losing Trust in Each Other and Institutions," *Washington Post*, January 28, 1996, pp. A1, A6–A7.

24. Stanley Greenberg, survey reported in February 1996. See also Stanley Greenberg, *Middle Class Dreams* (New York: Times Books/Random House, 1995).

25. Richard Morin, "Who's in Control? Many Don't Know or Care," *Washington Post*, January 29, 1996, pp. A1, A6.

26. Ibid. See also Susan J. Tolchin, "Short-sightedness in Foreign Affairs," *Earth Times*, May 31–June 14, 1995.

27. Marcia Smith, "Alone at the Polls: A National Embarrassment," *Social Policy* 27, no. 1 (Fall 1996), p. 5.

28. Everett Carll Ladd, "The Election Polls," *Current,* no. 390 (February 1998), pp. 26–28.

29. Campaign Study Group, "No-Show '96: Americans Who Don't Vote: A Study of Likely Nonvoters for the Medill News Service and WTTW Television," monograph, 1996.

30. Times Mirror Center for the People and the Press, "Voter Anxiety Dividing GOP; Energized Democrats Backing Clinton," news release, November 14, 1995.

31. Steven Pearlstein, "Angry Female Voters a Growing Force," *Washington Post,* January 31, 1996, pp. A1, A5.

32. Hilary Stout, "Working-Class Women Without College Degrees Become Angry White Men of '96 for Democrats," *Wall Street Journal,* April 8, 1996, p. A20.

33. Robin Toner, "With G.O.P. Congress the Issue, 'Gender Gap' Is Growing Wider," *New York Times,* April 21, 1996, pp. 1, 26.

34. Roberts, *op. cit.*

35. Lipset, *op. cit.*

36. Council for Excellence, *op. cit.,* p. 11.

37. Gannett News Service, November 6, 1994.

38. *The Hill,* January 24, 1996, by reporters Marcia Gelbart, A. B. Stoddard, Craig Karmin, and Sarah Pekkanen.

39. Stories by reporters Sarah Pekkanen, Jennifer Senior, and editor Albert Eisele, *The Hill,* January 24, 1996.

40. Jill Abramson, "Washington's Culture of Scandal Is Turning Inquiry into an Industry," *New York Times,* April 26, 1998, pp. A1 and A22.

41. Bobbi Nodell, "Clinton Gets Low Marks on Character," March 8, 1998, http://www.msnbc.com/news/14810.asp. See also Ron Suskind, "What's Sex Got to Do with It? In the World of Politics, Quite a Bit," *Wall Street Journal,* March 24, 2998, p. A1 and A9; and E. J. Dionne Jr., "An Amoral Majority," *Washington Post,* February 4, 1998, p. A17.

42. Bernard Bailyn, *The Ordeal of Thomas Hutchinson* (Cambridge: Belknap Press of Harvard University, 1974), p. 35.

43. Donald C. Bacon, Roger H. Davidson, and Morton Keller, eds., *The Encyclopedia of the United States Congress,* vol. 4 (New York: Simon & Schuster, 1995), p. 2065.

44. Garnered from the following sources: *Washington Times,* November 18, 1995; *Commercial Appeal* (Memphis), November 18, 1995; and Jim Adams, "House Votes Bosnia Restriction Despite Peace Hopes," *Reuters* and *United Press International,* November 18, 1995.

45. Eamon Javers, "Red Hot Rhetoric," *The Hill,* January 24, 1996, p. 9.

46. Thomas B. Edsall, "Public Grows More Receptive to Anti-Government Message," *Washington Post,* January 31, 1996, pp. A1, A5.

47. Hearings of the Subcommittee on Terrorism of the Committee on the Judiciary, C-SPAN, June 15, 1995.

48. Ibid.

49. Ibid.

50. Ibid.

51. James D. Tabor and Eugene V. Gallagher, *Why Waco? Cults and the Battle for Religious Freedom in America* (Berkeley: University of California Press, 1995).

52. Garry Wills, "The New Revolutionaries," *New York Review of Books,* September 10, 1995, p. 49. See also Richard Hofstadter's classic work *The Paranoid Style in American Politics and Other Essays* (New York: Vintage Books, 1967); and Michael Kelly, "The Road to Paranoia," *New Yorker,* June 19, 1995, pp. 60–75.

53. Susan Tolchin and Martin Tolchin, *Dismantling America: The Rush to Deregulate* (Boston: Houghton Mifflin, 1983), chapters 3, 4.

54. Serge Kovaleski, "Officials at Forum Describe Alleged Militia Threats," *Washington Post,* July 12, 1995, p. A8.

55. Hearings, House Committee on the Judiciary, July 18, 1995.

56. Ibid.

57. "Prosecutor: Freemen planned to shoot FBI agents," CNN.Com/ USs9803/17/freemen.trial/index/html, March 17, 1998.

58. Richard Morin, "Anger at Washington Cools in Aftermath of Bombing," *Washington Post,* May 18, 1995, pp. A1, A12.

59. Joe Klein, "Who Are These People?" *Newsweek,* August 21, 1995, p. 31.

60. Lipset, *op. cit.,* p. 7. Also discussed in Seymour Martin Lipset and William Schneider, *The Confidence Gap: Business, Labor, and Government in the Public Mind* (Baltimore: Johns Hopkins University Press, 1987).

61. Todd Purdum, "What, Us Worry?" *New York Times Magazine,* March 19, 1996, p. 41.

## Chapter 6

1. H. L. Mencken, "The Divine Afflatus," in *A Mencken Chrestomathy* (New York: Vintage Books, 1982), p. 443.

2. An excellent study of George Wallace that relates public anger to his candidacy is Dan T. Carter, *The Politics of Rage: George Wallace, the Origins of the New Conservatism, and the Transformation of American Politics* (New York: Simon & Schuster, 1995).

3. For a more detailed examination of the erosion of the industrial and technological base, particularly as it related to trade policy during the Reagan and Bush years, see Martin Tolchin and Susan Tolchin, *Selling Our Security: The Erosion of America's Assets* (New York: Alfred A. Knopf, 1992).

4. Louis Uchitelle and N. R. Kleinfield, "On the Battlefields of Business, Millions of Casualties," *New York Times,* March 3, 1996, p. 1.

5. One of the problems Clinton suffers from is his insecurity about winning office as a minority president with only 43 percent of the popular vote. How can he claim a mandate to govern with only a minority of the people behind him? How can he admit to the failures of the economy—many of those failures not even within his jurisdiction—after running on a platform that featured the slogan "It's the economy, stupid"? Do these factors constitute an excuse not to lead or not to validate public distress? Actually, a glance backward would show that he does not stand alone in the category of mi-

nority presidents; many presidents elected in the past hundred years took office without the comfort of a majority of the popular vote: Abraham Lincoln (took office with 39 percent of the popular vote); Woodrow Wilson (41.8 percent in 1914 and 49.2 percent in 1916—at the peak of World War I); Harry S. Truman (49.5 percent); John F. Kennedy (49.8 percent); and even Richard Nixon, in 1968, who came close to Clinton's tally with 42.3 percent. Thanks to the vagaries of the electoral college, even the popular Ronald Reagan received only a bare popular majority (50.7 percent in 1980).

6. The White House, Office of the Press Secretary, February 2, 1995.

7. Alison Mitchell, "Clinton Urges 'Less Combat' by Politicians," *New York Times*, July 7, 1995, pp. A1, A14.

8. Dan Balz and Howard Kurtz, "Clinton Assails Spread of Hate Through Media," *Washington Post*, April 25, 1995, p. A1.

9. *Congressional Record*, February 23, 1994, p. H2906.

10. Referring to the line by William Blake: "The tygers of hell are stronger than the horses of instruction" in "The Proverbs of Hell," in *The Marriage of Heaven and Hell* (New York and Paris: Oxford University Press in association with Trianon Press, 1975). (Original work completed in 1790.) See Chapter 4.

11. Helen Dewar, "New Jersey: Only Mention of Contract Was Made by a Democrat," *Washington Post*, April 24, 1995, p. A6.

12. Advocacy Institute, "Talking Back Advisory #3: Speaking of Oklahoma City," Washington, D.C., July 4, 1995, p. 3.

13. Barbara Roberts, speech delivered to the semiannual convention of the National Academy of Public Administration, Savannah, Georgia, June 9, 1995. Official publication: "Barbara Roberts on Federalism," Elmer B. Staats Lecture, Academy Spring Meeting, June 9, 1995.

14. Susan J. Tolchin, "Once Africa's 'Paradise,' Now a Maelstrom of Violence," *Earth Times*, January 31–February 14, 1996, p. 23.

15. R. W. Apple, "Social Issues Give Buchanan Boost," *New York Times*, February 27, 1996, pp. A1, A19. The poll revealed that although Buchanan supporters were attracted to his candidacy primarily for his social agenda, there appeared to be a significant convergence with Buchanan's views, particularly on trade, with 57 percent of the public agreeing that trade restrictions are needed to protect domestic industries.

16. Tom Smith, "Public Support for Spending, 1973–1994," *Public Perspective* 6, no. 3 (April–May 1995), pp. 1–3.

17. Ellen Goodman, "The End of Motherhood As We Knew It," *Washington Post*, September 16, 1995, p. A17.

18. Smith, *op. cit.*

19. Richard I. Berke, "Clinton's Ratings over 50% in Poll As G.O.P. Declines," *New York Times*, December 13, 1995, p. B17.

20. Times Mirror Center for the People and the Press, "Voter Anxiety Dividing GOP, Energized Dems Backing Clinton," news release, November 14, 1995.

21. "HMOs Legislation Likely to Continue," Reuters, www.pathfinder.com/living/latest/RB/1998Mar09/719.html.

22. *National Journal's Congress Daily,* November 14, 1995, p. 7. See also Alfred Eckes, *Opening America's Market: United States Trade Policy Since 1776* (Chapel Hill: University of North Carolina Press, 1995), for a discussion of the history of tariffs in the United States since the Revolutionary War. It is Eckes's contention that Republicans have always supported tariffs against the "free trade" Democrats and that tariffs until World War II were traditionally associated with rising wages, industrialization, and economic prosperity, whereas the reverse—the suspension of tariffs—was linked to declining wages.

23. Sid Blumenthal, "Her Own Private Idaho," *New Yorker,* July 10, 1995, p. 32.

24. Patrick J. Maney, *The Roosevelt Presence: A Biography of Franklin Delano Roosevelt* (New York: Twayne, 1992), pp. 85–86.

25. Edwin Diamond, "Who Says Negative TV Ads Are Bad?" *The Hill,* February 21, 1996. See also the book by two political scientists, Stephen Ansolabehere and Shanto Iyengar, *Going Negative: How Attack Ads Shrink and Polarize the Electorate* (New York: Free Press, 1995).

26. From a *New York Times–CBS News* Poll, cited in James Bennet and Janet Elder, "Despite Intern, President Stays in Good Graces," *New York Times,* February 24, 1998, pp. A1 and A14.

27. They consider curbing corporate compensation as giving the highest-paid employee no more than fifty times the salary of the lowest-paid full-time worker; in Japan, corporate chiefs draw salaries about six times those of the lowest-paid employees. The Democratic leaders promoting this program were Senate Minority Leader Thomas A. Daschle (S.D.) and Senator Jeff Bingaman (N.M.).

28. Arthur Miller, *After the Fall, a Play* (New York: Viking Press, 1964), p. 108.

# References

Abramson, Paul R. *Change and Continuity in the 1992 Elections.* Washington, D.C.: Congressional Quarterly Press, 1995.

Abramson, Paul R., and Ronald Inglehart. *Value Change in Global Perspective.* Ann Arbor: University of Michigan Press, 1995.

Adams, Henry. *The Education of Henry Adams: An Autobiography.* Boston and New York: Houghton Mifflin, 1918.

Ansolabehere, Stephen, and Shanto Iyengar. *Going Negative: How Attack Ads Shrink and Polarize the Electorate.* New York: Free Press, 1995.

Aristotle. *Nichomachean Ethics.* Translated, with introduction and notes, by Martin Ostwald. Indianapolis: Bobbs-Merrill, 1962.

Averill, James R. *Anger and Aggression: An Essay on Emotion.* New York: Springer-Verlag, 1982.

Bacon, Donald C., Roger H. Davidson, and Morton Keller, eds. *The Encyclopedia of the United States Congress.* New York: Simon & Schuster, 1995.

Bailyn, Bernard. *The Ordeal of Thomas Hutchinson.* Cambridge: Belknap Press of Harvard University, 1974.

Baldwin, James. *The Fire Next Time.* New York: Dell, 1964.

Balz, Dan, and Ronald Brownstein. *Storming the Gates: Protest Politics and the Republican Revival.* Boston: Little, Brown, 1996.

Barber, Randy, and Robert E. Scott. *Jobs on the Wing: Trading Away the Future of the Aerospace Industry.* Washington, D.C.: Economic Policy Institute, 1995.

Barkun, Michael. *Religion and the Racist Right: The Origins of the Christian Identity Movement.* Chapel Hill: University of North Carolina Press, 1994.

Barone, Michael, and Grant Ujifusa, *The Almanac of American Politics 1996.* Washington, D.C.: National Journal, 1996.

Bergmann, Barbara R. *In Defense of Affirmative Action.* New York: Basic Books/HarperCollins, 1996.

Berkowitz, Leonard. *Aggression: A Social Psychological Analysis.* New York: McGraw-Hill, 1962.

Bhabha, Homi K., ed. *Nation and Narration.* New York and London: Routledge, 1990.

Blake, William. *The Marriage of Heaven and Hell.* New York and Paris: Oxford University Press in association with Trianon Press, 1975. (Original work completed in 1790.)

Bok, Sissela. *Lying: Moral Choice in Public and Private Life.* New York: Pantheon Books, 1978.

_____. *Secrets: On the Ethics of Concealment and Revelation.* New York: Pantheon Books, 1982.

Bonomi, Patricia U. *Under the Cope of Heaven: Religion, Society and Politics in Colonial America.* New York: Oxford University Press, 1986.

Brody, Richard A. *Addressing the President: The Media, Elite Opinion, and Public Support.* Stanford: Stanford University Press, 1991.

Carter, Dan C. *The Politics of Rage: George Wallace, the Origins of the New Conservatism, and the Transformation of American Politics.* New York: Simon & Schuster, 1995.

Choate, Pat. *Agents of Influence.* New York: Alfred A. Knopf, 1990.

Christian Coalition. *Contract with the American Family.* Nashville, Tenn.: Moorings/Ballantine/Random House, 1995.

Cohn, Norman. *The Pursuit of the Millennium: Revolutionary Millenarians and Mystical Anarchists of the Middle Ages.* New York: Oxford University Press, 1957.

Cose, Ellis. *Rage of a Privileged Class.* New York: HarperCollins, 1993.

Craig, Stephen C. *The Malevolent Leaders: Popular Discontent in America.* Boulder: Westview Press, 1993.

Crosby, Faye, and Susan D. Clayton. *Justice, Gender, and Affirmative Action.* Ann Arbor: University of Michigan Press, 1992.

Dees, Morris, and Steve Fiffer. *Hate on Trial.* New York: Villard Books, 1993.

Dionne, E. J. *Why Americans Hate Politics.* New York: Simon & Schuster, 1991.

_____. *They Only Look Dead: Why Progressives Will Dominate the Next Era.* New York: Simon & Schuster, 1996.

Dyer, Joel. *Harvest of Rage: Why Oklahoma City Is Only the Beginning.* Boulder: Westview Press, 1997.

Edelman, Murray. *The Symbolic Uses of Politics.* Urbana: University of Illinois Press, 1967.

_____. *Politics as Symbolic Action: Mass Arousal and Quiescence.* Chicago: Markham, 1971.

Edsall, Thomas Byrne. *The New Politics of Inequality.* New York: W. W. Norton, 1984.

Edsall, Thomas Byrne, with Mary D. Edsall. *Chain Reaction.* New York: W. W. Norton, 1991.

Ehrenhalt, Alan. *The Lost City.* New York: Basic Books, 1995.

Ehrenreich, Barbara. *The Snarling Citizen: Essays.* New York: Farrar, Straus and Giroux, 1995.

Ellison, Ralph. *Invisible Man.* New York: Modern Library, 1952.

Etzioni, Amitai, ed. *New Communitarian Thinking: Persons, Virtues, Institutions and Communities.* Charlottesville: University of Virginia Press, 1995.

Fallows, James. *Breaking the News: How the Media Undermine American Democracy.* New York: Pantheon Books, 1996.

Finlay, David J., Ole R. Holsti, and Richard B. Fagen. *Enemies in Politics.* Chicago: Rand, McNally, 1967.

Fischel, William A. *Regulatory Takings: Law, Economics, and Politics.* Cambridge: Harvard University Press, 1995.

Frank, Robert H., and Philip J. Cook. *The Winner-Take-All Society: How More and More Americans Compete for Ever Fewer and Bigger Prizes, Encouraging Economic Waste, Income Inequality, and an Impoverished Cultural Life.* New York: Martin Kessler/Free Press, 1995.

Freeman, Richard, ed. *Working Under Different Rules.* New York: Russell Sage, 1993.

Freud, Sigmund. *Civilization and Its Discontents.* New York: W. W. Norton, 1961.

Gay, Peter. *The Cultivation of Hatred,* vol. 3. New York: W. W. Norton, 1993.

Gaylin, Willard. *The Rage Within: Anger in Modern Life.* New York: Simon & Schuster, 1984.

Glass, James M. *Psychosis and Power: Threats to Democracy in the Self and the Group.* Ithaca, N.Y.: Cornell University Press, 1995.

Goleman, Daniel. *Emotional Intelligence.* New York: Bantam, 1995.

Goodsell, Charles. *The Case for Bureaucracy.* Chatham, N.J.: Chatham House Publishers, 1994.

Gottschalk, Peter, and Sheldon Danziger, eds. *Uneven Tides: Rising Inequality in America.* New York: Russell Sage Foundation, 1993.

Greenberg, Stanley. *Middle Class Dreams.* New York: Times Books/Random House, 1995.

Gurr, Ted Robert. *Why Men Rebel.* Princeton: Princeton University Press, 1970.

_____. *Rogues, Rebels, and Reformers.* Beverly Hills: Sage, 1976.

Gurr, Ted Robert, with contributions from Barbara Harff, Monty G. Marshall, and James R. Scaritt. *Minorities at Risk: A Global View of Ethnopolitical Conflict.* Washington, D.C.: U.S. Institute of Peace Press, 1993.

Gurr, Ted Robert, Ivo K. Feierabend, and Rosalind L. Feierabend, eds. *Anger, Violence, and Politics: Theories and Research.* Englewood Cliffs, N.J.: Prentice-Hall, 1972.

Hibbing, John R., and Elizabeth Theiss-Morse. *Congress as Public Enemy: Public Attitudes Toward American Political Institutions.* Cambridge and New York: Cambridge University Press, 1995.

Hobsbawm, Eric. *The Age of Extremes: A History of the World, 1914–1991.* New York: Pantheon Books, 1994.

Hoffer, Eric. *The True Believer.* New York: Harper & Row, 1951.

Hofstadter, Richard. *The Age of Reform.* New York: Alfred A. Knopf, 1956.

_____. *The Paranoid Style in American Politics: And Other Essays.* New York: Vintage Books, 1967.

Howard, Philip K. *The Death of Common Sense: How Law Is Suffocating America.* New York: Random House, 1995.

Johnson, Haynes. *Divided We Fall: Gambling with History in the Nineties.* New York: W. W. Norton, 1994.

Jones, Charles O. *The Presidency in a Separated System.* Washington, D.C.: Brookings Institution, 1994.

Kamber, Victor. *Giving Up on Democracy: Why Term Limits Are Bad for America.* Washington, D.C.: Regnery, 1995.

Karl, Jonathan. *The Right to Bear Arms: The Rise of America's New Militias.* New York: HarperPaperbacks, 1995.

Kazin, Michael. *The Populist Persuasion: An American History.* New York: Basic Books, 1995.

Kerbel, Matthew Robert. *Remote and Controlled: Media Politics in a Cynical Age.* Boulder: Westview Press, 1995.

Kurtz, Howard. *Media Circus: The Trouble with America's Newspapers.* New York: Times Books/Random House, 1993.

_____. *Hot Air: All Talk, All the Time.* New York: Times Books/Random House, 1996.

Kusnet, David. *Speaking American: How the Democrats Can Win in the 1990s.* New York: Thunder's Mouth Press, 1992.

Kuttner, Robert. *The End of Laissez-Faire.* New York: Alfred A. Knopf, 1991.

Lerner, Harriet. *The Dance of Anger.* New York: Perennial Library, 1985.

Lifton, Robert J. *The Protean Self: Human Resilience in an Age of Fragmentation.* New York: Basic Books, 1993.

Lipset, Seymour Martin, and William Schneider. *The Confidence Gap: Business, Labor and Government in the Public Mind.* Baltimore, Md.: Johns Hopkins University Press, 1987.

Lind, Michael. *The Next American Nation: The New Nationalism and the Fourth American Revolution.* New York: Free Press, 1995.

Lorenz, Konrad. *On Aggression.* New York: Harcourt, Brace, 1966.

Lowi, Theodore. *The End of Liberalism: Ideology, Policy and the Crisis of Public Authority.* New York: W. W. Norton, 1969.

MacKenzie, G. Calvin, and Saranna Thornton. *Bucking the Deficit: Economic Policymaking in America.* Boulder: Westview Press, 1996.

Madow, Leo. *Anger.* New York: Scribners, 1972.

Madrick, Jeffrey. *The End of Affluence: The Causes and Consequences of America's Economic Dilemma.* New York: Random House, 1995.

Maney, Patrick J. *The Roosevelt Presence: A Biography of Franklin Delano Roosevelt.* New York: Twayne, 1992.

McClain, Paula D., and Joseph Stewart Jr. *Can We All Get Along? Racial and Ethnic Minorities in American Politics, Second Edition.* Boulder: Westview Press, 1998.

McNamara, Robert. *In Retrospect.* New York: Times Books/Random House, 1995.

Mencken, H. L. *A Mencken Chrestomathy.* New York: Vintage Books, 1982.

Miller, Arthur. *After the Fall, a Play.* New York: Viking Press, 1964.

Nevins, Allan, and Henry Steele Commager. *A Short History of the United States.* New York: Random House, 1945.

New York Times. *The Downsizing of America.* New York: Times Books, 1996.

Nye, Joseph S. Jr., Philip D. Zelikow, and David C. King. *Why People Don't Trust Government.* Cambridge: Harvard University Press, 1996.

Penny, Timothy J., and Steven E. Schier. *Payment Due: A Nation in Debt, a Generation in Trouble.* Boulder: Westview Press, 1996.

Phillips, Kevin. *Boiling Point.* New York: Random House, 1993.

Piore, Michael J. *Beyond Individualism.* Cambridge: Harvard University Press, 1995.

Pomper, Gerald. *Passions and Interests: Political Party Concepts of American Democracy.* Lawrence: University Press of Kansas, 1992.

Popkin, Samuel L. *The Reasoning Voter: Communication and Persuasion in Presidential Campaigns.* Chicago: University of Chicago Press, 1991.

Powell, Colin, with Joseph Persico. *My American Journey.* New York: Random House, 1995.

Putnam, Robert, with Robert Leonardi and Raffaella Y. Nanetti. *Making Democracy Work: Civic Tradition and Modern Italy.* Princeton: Princeton University Press, 1993.

Roberts, Sam. *Who We Are: A Portrait of America Based on the Latest U.S. Census.* New York: Times Books/Random House, 1995.

Rohde, David W. *Parties and Leaders in the Post-Reform House.* Chicago: University of Chicago Press, 1991.

Rozell, Mark J., and Clyde Wilcox. *Second Coming: The New Christian Right in Virginia Politics.* Baltimore: Johns Hopkins University Press, 1996.

Sabato, Larry J. *Feeding Frenzy: How Attack Journalism Has Transformed American Politics.* New York: Free Press, 1991.

Samuelson, Robert J. *The Good Life and Its Discontents: The American Dream in the Age of Entitlement, 1945–1995.* New York: Times Books, 1996.

Saul, Leon J. *The Hostile Mind: The Source and Consequences of Rage and Hate.* New York: Random House, 1956.

Scheler, Max. *Ressentiment.* New York: Free Press of Glencoe, 1961.

Schimmel, Solomon. *The Seven Deadly Sins.* New York: Free Press, 1992.

Shklar, Judith. *Ordinary Vices.* Cambridge: Belknap Press of Harvard University, 1984.

Stearns, Harriet Zisowitz, and Peter Stearns. *Anger: The Struggle for Emotional Control in America's History.* Chicago: University of Chicago Press, 1986.

Stein, Maurice R., Arthur J. Vidich, and David Manning White, eds. *Identity and Anxiety.* Glencoe, Ill.: Free Press, 1960.

Tabor, James D., and Eugene V. Gallagher. *Why Waco? Cults and the Battle for Religious Freedom in America.* Berkeley: University of California Press, 1995.

Tavris, Carol. *Anger: The Misunderstood Emotion.* New York: Touchstone, 1982.

Teixeira, Ruy. *Why Americans Don't Vote: Turnout Decline in the United States 1960–1984.* New York: Greenwood Press, 1987.

———. *The Disappearing Voter.* Washington, D.C.: Brookings Institution, 1992.

Tolchin, Martin, and Susan Tolchin. *To the Victor: Political Patronage from the Clubhouse to the White House.* New York: Random House, 1971.

———. *Buying into America: How Foreign Money Is Changing the Face of Our Nation.* New York: Times Books/Random House, 1988.

_____. *Selling Our Security: The Erosion of America's Assets.* New York: Alfred A. Knopf, 1992.

Tolchin, Susan, and Martin Tolchin. *Clout: Womanpower and Politics.* New York: Coward, McCann & Geoghegan, 1974.

_____. *Dismantling America: The Rush to Deregulate.* Boston: Houghton Mifflin, 1983.

von der Mehden, Fred R. *Comparative Political Violence.* Englewood Cliffs, N.J.: Prentice-Hall, 1973.

Wells, H. G. *The Invisible Man and War of the Worlds.* New York: Washington Square Press, 1962. (*The Invisible Man* was originally published in 1897.)

Wilcox, Clyde. *Onward Christian Soldiers? The Religious Right in American Politics.* Boulder: Westview Press, 1996.

Wildavsky, Aaron, and Jeffrey L. Pressman. *Implementation.* Berkeley: University of California Press, 1973.

Williams, Redford, and Virginia Williams. *Anger Kills: Seventeen Strategies for Controlling the Hostility that Can Harm Your Health.* New York: HarperCollins, 1994.

Wills, Garry. *Under God: Religion and American Politics.* New York: Simon & Schuster, 1990.

Wilson, Carol Green. *Herbert Hoover: A Challenge for Today.* New York: Evans, 1968.

Wolfe, Alan. *One Nation After All.* New York: Viking Penguin, 1998.

Yandle, Bruce, ed. *Land Rights: The 1990s Property Rights Rebellion.* Lanham, Md.: Rowman & Littlefield, 1995.

# Index

WITHDRAWN